Crisis and Contempo

Crisis and Contemporary Poetry

Edited by

Anne Karhio, Seán Crosson and Charles I. Armstrong

palgrave
macmillan

First published 2011 by
PALGRAVE MACMILLAN

Palgrave Macmillan in the UK is an imprint of Macmillan Publishers Limited, registered in England, company number 785998, of Houndmills, Basingstoke, Hampshire RG21 6XS.

Palgrave Macmillan in the US is a division of St Martin's Press LLC, 175 Fifth Avenue, New York, NY 10010.

Palgrave Macmillan is the global academic imprint of the above companies and has companies and representatives throughout the world.

Palgrave® and Macmillan® are registered trademarks in the United States, the United Kingdom, Europe and other countries.

ISBN 978-1-349-31981-7 ISBN 978-0-230-30609-7 (eBook)
DOI 10.1057/9780230306097

This book is printed on paper suitable for recycling and made from fully managed and sustained forest sources. Logging, pulping and manufacturing processes are expected to conform to the environmental regulations of the country of origin.

A catalogue record for this book is available from the British Library.

Library of Congress Cataloging-in-Publication Data

Crisis and contemporary poetry / edited by Anne Karhio, Seán Crosson, Charles I. Armstrong.
p. cm.

1. English poetry—20th century—History and criticism. 2. English poetry—21st century—History and criticism. 3. Crises in literature. 4. Politics and literature—Great Britain—History—20th century. 5. Politics and literature—Great Britain—History—21st century. 6. Literature and history—Great Britain—History—20th century. 7. Literature and history—Great Britain—History—21st century. I. Karhio, Anne, 1975– II. Crosson, Seán. III. Armstrong, Charles I., 1969–
PR605.C77C75 2010
821'.92093581—dc22 2010027525

This publication was grant-aided by the Publications Fund of National University of Ireland, Galway

10 9 8 7 6 5 4 3 2 1
20 19 18 17 16 15 14 13 12 11

Contents

Acknowledgements

A book such as this would not have been possible without the support of various people and institutions along the way. In the first instance, we are grateful to all our contributors whose hard work and patience more than anything else has made this volume possible. This book began from a series of papers presented at the Nordic English Studies Conference in Bergen, Norway, in 2007 and we would also like to thank all those involved in the organization of that event for their support both during the event itself and subsequently as we endeavoured to bring this collection to publication. During the conference, a recurring theme across the papers became apparent that has provided us with the title and central rationale for this book. Subsequent to the conference, other contributors also engaged with the theme came on board and we are grateful for their contributions to this topic.

Neither could this volume exist without the work of the many poets considered, all of whom have in their own way made important interventions regarding the theme. We are grateful both to them and to their various publishers for the permissions given to reprint extracts from poems considered below. We thank Michael Longley and the Emory University's Manuscript, Archives, and Rare Book Library (MARBL) for the permission to quote from the poet's archive materials, Peter Fallon of Gallery Press, Wake Forest University Press for the rights to quote from Michael Longley and Ciaran Carson in the US, Gearoid Mac Lochlainn for the excerpts from 'The Lagan Blackbird', and SuAndi and Lemn Sissay for the excerpts from their writing.

We are grateful to our publishers, Palgrave Macmillan, for their belief in this project and support throughout its development, in particular to Paula Kennedy and Benjamin Doyle. We would also like to thank our institutions, both National University of Ireland, Galway (in particular its Publications Fund), and the Department of Foreign Languages at the University of Bergen for their financial as well as institutional support for this project. Equally important has been the support of all our families, and colleagues, who, as always, provided invaluable support (and sometimes welcome critical input) during the process.

We would also like to make the following acknowledgements:

Excerpts from 'Metro' by George Szirtes, from *New & Collected Poems*. By permission of Bloodaxe Books, 2008. Excerpts from *These Days* by

Leontia Flynn, published by Jonathan Cape. Reprinted by permission of The Random House Group Ltd. Excerpts from *Collected Poems* by Michael Longley, published by Jonathan Cape. Reprinted by permission of The Random House Group Ltd. Excerpts from 'September 1, 1939', copyright 1940 & renewed 1968 by W.H. Auden, *Collected Poems of W.H. Auden* by W.H. Auden. Used by permission of Random House, Inc. and The Wylie Agency. Excerpts from *Jizzen* (1999) and *The Tree House* (2005). Copyright © Kathleen Jamie. Used by permission of Picador/Pan Macmillan. Excerpts from poems included in the anthology *Harrowing of the Heart: The Poetry of Bloody Sunday* © 'Anonymous'/ The Museum of Free Derry ('Bloody Sunday Revisited'), Julieann Campbell ('Reluctant Role Model'), Seamus Deane ('After Derry, 30 January, 1972'), 'Gerry Dorrity ('One Sunday'), John Dunne ('Tribute to Lord Fenner-Brockway'), Hugh Gallagher ('Bloody Sunday'), Seamus Heaney ('The Road to Derry'), Emmylou Large ('Let the Stones Speak'), Paul Laughlin ('Remembering Bloody Sunday'), Declan McLaughlin ('Running Uphill'), Sharon Meenan and Killian Mullan ('I Remember'), Joe Mulheron ('Bloody Sunday'), Kathleen Patton ('Derry's Thirteen'), Scott MX Julieann Campbell and Tom Herron, and Guildhall Press. 'Counting the Dead on the Radio, 1972' is originally taken from *The Non-Aligned Storyteller* by Thomas McCarthy, published by Anvil Press Poetry in 1984. Excerpt from *The Hoop* by John Burnside. Copyright © 1988 by John Burnside. Reprinted by permission of Carcanet Press. Excerpt from *Butcher's Dozen: A Lesson For The Octave Of Widgery*. Copyright © 1972 by Thomas Kinsella. Reprinted by permission of the poet and Carcanet Press. Excerpts from *Gift Songs* (2007) and *Hunt in the Forest* (2009). Copyright © John Burnside. Reprinted by permission of Rogers Coleridge & White. Excerpt from *Averno* by Louise Glück. Copyright © 2006 by Louise Glück. Reprinted by permission of Farrar, Straus and Giroux, LLC. Excerpts from *Opened Ground: Selected Poems 1966–1996* by Seamus Heaney. Copyright © 1998 by Seamus Heaney. Reprinted by permission of Faber and Faber Ltd, and Farrar, Straus and Giroux, LLC. Excerpt from *District and Circle* by Seamus Heaney. Copyright © 2006 by Seamus Heaney. Reprinted by permission of Faber and Faber Ltd, and Farrar, Straus and Giroux, LLC. Excerpt from *Electric Light* by Seamus Heaney. Copyright © 2001 by Seamus Heaney. Reprinted by permission of Faber and Faber Ltd, and Farrar, Straus and Giroux, LLC. Excerpt from *Field Work* by Seamus Heaney. Copyright © 1979 by Seamus Heaney. Reprinted by permission of Faber and Faber Ltd, and Farrar, Straus and Giroux LLC. Excerpts from *New Weather* by Paul Muldoon. Copyright © 1973 Paul Muldoon. Reprinted by permission of Faber and Faber

Ltd. Excerpts from *Quoof* by Paul Muldoon. Copyright © 1983 Paul Muldoon. Reprinted by permission of Faber and Faber Ltd. Excerpts from *Meeting the British* (1987). Copyright © Paul Muldoon. Reprinted by permission of Faber and Faber Ltd, and Farrar, Straus & Giroux LLC. Excerpts from *Poems 1968–1998* by Paul Muldoon. Copyright © 2001 by Paul Muldoon. Reprinted by permission of Faber and Faber Ltd, and Farrar, Straus and Giroux, LLC. Excerpts from *Horse Latitudes* by Paul Muldoon. Copyright © 2006 by Paul Muldoon. Reprinted by permission of Faber and Faber Ltd, and Farrar, Straus and Giroux, LLC. Excerpts from *The Thing in the Gapstone Stile* (1996), *Dart* (2002) *Woods, etc* (2005). Copyright © Alice Oswald. Reprinted by permission of Faber and Faber Ltd, and Graywolf Press. Excerpt from *Three Books: Remains of Elmet, Cave Birds, River*. Copyright © 1993 by Ted Hughes. Reprinted by permission of Faber and Faber Ltd. Excerpt from *Wavelengths* by Michael Longley. Copyright © 2009 by Michael Longley. Reprinted by permission of Enitharmon Press. In all cases all efforts have been made to secure rights for material used, and full publication details for all quoted texts appear in the list of texts cited after each chapter. Should there be any material used here which is not credited appropriately, please contact the editors through the publisher. Every effort has also been made to keep quotations within the fair dealing guidelines as they apply within the UK.

Notes on Contributors

Charles I. Armstrong is a Professor of British Literature at the University of Bergen. He is the author of *Figures of Memory: Poetry, Space, and the Past* (2009) and *Romantic Organicism: From Idealist Origins to Ambivalent Afterlife* (2003), both published by Palgrave Macmillan. He is also the co-editor of *Postcolonial Dislocations: Travel, History and the Ironies of Narrative* (2006). His published work includes readings of contemporary poets such as Eavan Boland, Ellen Einan, Seamus Heaney, Geoffrey Hill, Paul Muldoon, Alice Oswald and J.H. Prynne.

Mary Kate Azcuy is an Assistant Professor at Monmouth University in New Jersey, USA. Her current scholarship focuses on contemporary American literature by women, specifically the poetry of Louise Glück and Mary Oliver, as well as the fiction of Leslie Marmon Silko and Annie Proulx. Additionally, Azcuy has recently published poetry in *Exquisite Corpse, Crossroads: A Southern Cultural Annual* and *Proteus*.

Guinn Batten, Associate Professor of English at Washington University in St Louis, is the author of *The Orphaned Imagination: Melancholy and Commodity Culture in English Romanticism* (1998). She has published a dozen essays on contemporary Irish poetry.

Scott Brewster is Director of English at the University of Salford. He is the author of *Lyric* (2009), and co-edited, with Michael Parker, *Irish Literature since 1990: Diverse Voices* (2009). Previous publications include *Inhuman Reflections: Thinking the Limits of the Human* (2000) and *Ireland in Proximity: History, Gender, Space* (1999). He has written widely on Irish writing, the Gothic and psychoanalysis, and is currently writing a book on Freud and commemoration.

Lucy Collins is a Lecturer in English Literature at University College Dublin. Educated at Trinity College Dublin and at Harvard University, where she spent a year as a Fulbright Scholar, she teaches and researches in the area of twentieth-century poetry and poetics. She has published widely on contemporary Irish and American poetry, including essays on Thomas Kinsella, Eileán Ní Chuilleanáin and Louise Glück. She is currently completing a monograph on Irish women poets, and an anthology, *Poetry by Women in Ireland 1870–1970*. A co-edited collection, *Aberration in Modern and Contemporary Poetry*, is due out in 2010.

Brendan Corcoran is an Associate Professor of English at Indiana State University, where he works on twentieth-century Irish and British poetry and edits the creative writing journal *Grasslands Review*. Recent publications include essays on Seamus Heaney, Derek Mahon, Michael Longley and Ciaran Carson. His essay on John Keats won the Keats-Shelley Association of America Prize for 2009. He has also published an interview with the Northern Irish poet Michael Longley. Current projects include a book on Seamus Heaney's elegiac poetics.

Seán Crosson has published widely on Irish poetry and literature and is author of *'The Given Note' Traditional Music and Modern Irish Poetry* (2008) and co-editor of the collection *Anáil an Bhéil Bheo: Orality and Modern Irish Culture* (2009). His research interests include Irish cinema, sport and film, and the relationship between poetry and music, and he has taught courses on this topic with the Centre for Irish Studies and the Discipline of English at National University of Ireland, Galway. He is currently Programme Director of the MA in Film Studies at the Huston School of Film & Digital Media at the National University of Ireland, Galway.

Janne Stigen Drangsholt is Associate Professor at the Department of Culture and Language Studies, University of Stavanger. Her latest article, 'Living Myth', was included in a collection entitled *Ted Hughes and the Classics* (2008). Her research interests include gender studies, television studies, Heidegger and the theories of radical orthodoxy.

Anne Karhio is Lady Gregory Fellow of the College of Arts, Social Sciences and Celtic Studies at the National University of Ireland, Galway. Her doctoral thesis is provisionally titled *A Slight Return: Poetic Discourse and the Formation of Place in the Poetry of Paul Muldoon*. She teaches contemporary Irish poetry and has published several critical essays on the work of Irish poets, including Paul Muldoon, Derek Mahon and Paula Meehan.

Ruben Moi is Assistant Professor and Research Fellow in English and Comparative Literature at the University of Tromsø, Norway. At present he is working on a large project entitled 'From the Frontiers of Writing: Ekphrasis and Transgressionality in Contemporary Northern Irish Poetics' and a monograph on Paul Muldoon. His most recent articles are '"The cure by poetry that cannot be coerced": Text, Canon and Context in Seamus Heaney's *Electric Light*' in Crowder and Hall's *Seamus Heaney. Poet, Critic, Translator* (2007) and 'Transtextual Conceptualisations of Northern Ireland: Paul Muldoon vs Seamus Heaney' in Rønning and

Johannessen's *Readings of the Particular* (2007). He has also published articles, essays and reviews on, amongst others, Martin McDonagh, Samuel Beckett, Harold Pinter and T.S. Eliot.

Eva Mueller-Zettelmann is an Associate Professor of English Literature and Cultural Theory at Vienna University, Austria. She studied in Graz and Oxford and has published on narratology, cultural memory, post-structuralism, genre theory, the theory and history of poetry and metapoetry, eighteenth-century women playwrights and children's literature.

Deirdre Osborne was born in Australia and has lived in London for over 20 years. She is a Senior Lecturer in Drama at Goldsmiths University of London. While her doctoral research investigated Victorian women writers, maternity and colonial ideology, her current research focuses on black British writing upon which she has published various essays. She edited a collection of plays and critical essays *Hidden Gems* (2008) and she is now writing *Critically Black: Black British Dramatists and Theatre in the New Millennium* (forthcoming).

Stephen Regan is Professor of English at the University of Durham. His publications include *Irish Writing 1789–1939: An Anthology of Irish Literature in English* (2004), *The Nineteenth-Century Novel: A Critical Reader* (2001), *The Eagleton Reader* (1998), *Philip Larkin: The New Casebook* (Macmillan, 1997), and *The Politics of Pleasure: Aesthetics and Cultural Theory* (1992). He has also written numerous articles on the work of modern Irish writers, including W.B. Yeats and Seamus Heaney. He is the founding editor of *The Year's Work in Critical and Cultural Theory*. His most recent book (co-edited with Richard Allen) is *Irelands of the Mind: Memory and Identity in Modern Irish Culture* (2008).

John Sears is Senior Lecturer in English Literature at Manchester Metropolitan University. He is the author of *Reading George Szirtes* (2008), and has published and presented widely on Szirtes's work and on other contemporary writers. He is currently completing *Stephen King's Gothic* (forthcoming).

Introduction

Anne Karhio, Seán Crosson and Charles I. Armstrong

Occasionally, major collective turning points find means of poetic expression that are not only apposite or equivalent to their own heft, but actually end up transcending the given circumstances, becoming exemplary utterances capable of capturing the underlying emotion of other events of a similar cast. W.H. Auden's 'September 1, 1939' is a classic example of this kind of crisis poem, as it not only reacts with alacrity to the news of the German invasion of Poland, but also has become an iconic reference point drawn upon in the aftermath of 9/11 and the recent financial crisis. It expresses a generalized sense of vulnerability: 'Defenceless under the night / Our world in stupor lies'. It shows how that sense is something shared in a globalized world: 'Waves of anger and fear / Circulate over the bright / And darkened lands of the earth'. Furthermore, it also highlights the fact that the poetic response must try to find its own place and measure amid a Babelian chaos of voices and rumours: the poet must seek to establish 'a voice / To unfold the folded lie' (Auden, 1977, pp. 246–7).

Although 'September 1, 1939' responds incisively to a particular moment, its underlying sense of alarm and quandary did not come completely out of the blue. A few months earlier, in April 1939, Auden had written a poem simply titled 'Crisis' (later renamed 'They') that was less convincing in its attempt to capture the essence of the moment. Nevertheless, the later poem has a compelling sense of particularity about it – a specificity of both time and space: not only do the opening lines situate the speaker in 'one of the dives / On Fifty-Second Street', but the poem also returns later to the New York setting. What might have seemed a distant and abstract political crisis is actually inscribed in the very place where we meet the poet: 'Where blind skyscrapers use / Their full height to proclaim / The strength of collective Man'. Seeking to find an individual – yet not isolated or narcissistic – response to the collective disaster of the moment, Auden's poem also pays witness to a crossroads of identity. Having recently left England behind, the poet must negotiate humanist responsibility with personal desire, balancing 'universal love' with the importunate desire 'to be loved alone'. For Auden, the personal crisis cannot be completely isolated from a sense of challenge to his very vocation. If 'In Memory of W.B. Yeats' had proclaimed that 'poetry makes nothing happen', it had of course also granted that the poet could – through indirect means – 'Teach the free man how to praise'. In 'September 1, 1939', the power of poetry is channelled towards a tacit or possible reply to an anguished question: 'Who can release them now, / Who can reach the deaf, / Who can speak for the dumb?' (ibid., 245–7).

Crises of politics, place, person and poetry will be addressed in this volume, which seeks to articulate fresh vantage points on how the poetry of the present responds to situations of turmoil and tension. How far back, beyond the precedent of someone like Auden, can we trace the issues that poetry is tackling today? From what underlying disaster or intrinsic fault does poetry's need to reach the deaf and speak for the dumb stem? There may not be easy answers to such questions; it is often in the nature of a crisis that a large part of its challenge will lie in the calibration and fine-tuning of questions, rather than in the arrival at pat formulations or solutions. Poetry's efficacy may be that it helps us approach or frame a problem, rather than providing the sort of technological or political solutions one seeks for elsewhere. It is possible to see crisis as endemic to modernity in general, as the desire to rationalize and control humanity tends to provoke recurring, large-scale disaster – as indicated in Adorno and Horkheimer's *Dialectic of Enlightenment* (2002). According to Adorno, lyric poetry's formalism is an indirect response that 'implies a protest against a social situation that every individual experiences as hostile, alien, cold, oppressive' (Adorno, 1991, p. 38). Ironically, the more radical forms of such formalism tend to alienate poetry from its potential audience, exacerbating or creating an inverse mirror image of the very crisis to which they respond. But if such an argument seems too abstract and isolated from concrete historical facts, more specific narratives are forthcoming. David Harvey has interpreted the aesthetic modes of modernism and postmodernism as responses to a changing experience of time and space in bourgeois Western society, resulting in a 'crisis of representation' (Harvey, 1990, p. 260).[1] For Harvey, the origins of these responses in Britain are to be found in the depression of the late 1840s, which 'shook the confidence of the bourgeoisie and challenged its sense of history and geography in profound ways' (ibid.) In Ireland, the same period saw a crisis of a very different kind, though one of no less profound an impact on the cultural and artistic life of the nation up until today. Apart from the tragedy of the millions who died of hunger, the famine also resulted in large-scale migration and a loss of language, both of which effects continue to play a crucial part in a perceived crisis of identity.[2] If neither place nor language can provide a fixed point from which to examine one's relation to the world, what does it mean to call oneself Irish, or, for that matter, British, Scottish or African-American? What, if anything, should poetry's function be in this situation? Simultaneously, however, wider issues concerning modernism and postmodernism as responses to social and historical developments, and the question of what is to follow them, continue to concern critics and poets alike.

If Harvey considers the crisis of the mid-nineteenth century to lie at the root of the emergence of first modernist and then postmodernist responses to the changing experience of space and time, the germs of poetry's relationship to crisis reach further back. Romanticism, notes Kate Rigby, 'has long been one of those points of eternal return for literary criticism, a touchstone on which successive generations of critics have tried out favored theories and approaches' (Rigby, 2004, p. 1). Certainly the experience of time–space compression can be linked to the industrial revolution, which also generated an aesthetic response in the form of the emergence of Romantic poetry. The revolution and its aftermath in France, as well as the responses to it on the northern side of the English Channel impacted in crucial ways on the society, and the literature, of late eighteenth and early nineteenth-century Britain. Recent debates on poetry's societal function and its (possible) autonomy as an aesthetic practice in many ways echo the situation of this earlier period. In Northern Ireland, questions of poetic responsibility or political disengagement have in recent decades been the object of intense critical disputes. The tension between an approach focusing on societal formations and more aesthetic or formalist understandings of poetry echoes the situation in America; the civil rights movements on both sides of the Atlantic have in many ways changed the ways in which poetry is read today. However, P.M.S. Dawson's outline of the situation in Britain two hundred years ago shows that the battlefield is in no way unprecedented:

> As upper- and middle-class intellectuals all the Romantic poets found themselves carried along on the movements of social change with

> whose consequences they were in various ways forced to quarrel. These movements were in the last analysis economic, comprising what have become known as the Agricultural Revolution and the Industrial Revolution, with their accompanying changes in attitude. (Dawson, 1993, p. 66)

For Dawson, the idealism of poets such as Shelley was based on values and ideas that ended up promoting those forces of capitalist economy to which the poets themselves would hardly have consciously subscribed; their faith in the medium became an unwilling accomplice to the underlying forces of emerging capitalism. Similarly, Hardt and Negri have tried to show the underlying common ground between avant-garde postmodernism and a global form of capitalism, which 'crisis is immanent to and indistinguishable from' (Hardt and Negri, 2000, p. 386). Literature's role as an oppositional practice and its relationship to the political has thus continuously been both highlighted and contested.

In a talk given late in 2008, the Galway-based poet Moya Cannon noted that 'nobody starts to write poetry because they are a very balanced person. They write because they're conflicted' (Cannon, 2008). Cannon's words exemplify how strong the belief in an underlying conflict or crisis continues to be in contemporary views on poetry. They also show how little this belief has changed during the past centuries: the British liberal spokesman Thomas Babington Macaulay noted in the early nineteenth century, albeit in a much more unappreciative tone when it came to the poetic minds of his time, that 'Perhaps no person can be a poet, or can even enjoy poetry, without a certain unsoundness of mind' (quoted in Dawson, 1993, p. 66). Both Cannon and Dawson also link this inner conflict to the workings of the surrounding society at large. For Cannon, the internal and internalized conflicts of poetry find their parallels in the wider contexts of cultural dialogue: 'as cultural tectonic plates rub against each other, that's when poetry happens' (Cannon, 2008). For Macaulay, it is society's turmoil that gives rise to poetic idealism: 'In a rude state of society men are children with a greater variety of ideas. It is therefore in such a state of society that we may expect to find the poetical temperament in its highest perfection' (Dawson, 1993, p. 66). Macaulay's words may have been far from praising, but it is noteworthy that two figures so far removed in historical and cultural context – as well as in their respective views on the value of poetry – so firmly believe in personal and social conflict as a prerequisite for the emergence of poetry.

Indeed, the fate of poetry, inasmuch as it has evolved throughout the past couple of centuries, is in various ways tied to the crises of society from which it arises, as well as their pressures on the poetic medium itself. In Paul Muldoon's poem on the Auden circle in the USA, '7 Middagh Street', this link is at one stage given an ironic overstatement: just arrived in New York, his Auden proclaims that 'history's a twisted root / with art its small, translucent fruit // and never the other way round' (Muldoon, 2000, p. 178). Though one should avoid simplification – as Muldoon does later on in the poem by contrasting this position with the more committed stance of Louis MacNeice – poetry might nevertheless be said to draw its energy from the various points and phases of societal transformation, which also repeatedly call its own existence and efficacy into question. It is here that the crisis of poetry should be seen more in the sense of the Greek *krinein*, as turning point, separation and judgement; only through the constant repositioning of itself in relation to the forces that surround it can poetry continue to justify its own existence. While twentieth-century poetry has in many ways sought to challenge the hegemony of the conflicted subject as a basis for poetic expression,[3] few would deny that a certain presupposition of a conflict, resistance or rebellion, often against the established notions of poetry's form and/or function, continues to be one of the driving forces of poetry as we understand it: the struggle of poetry with both tradition and innovation is what keeps it alive. For Stéphane Mallarmé, in his famous *Crise de Vers*, (French) poetry in turns flourished and stagnated as it sought either to conform to prevailing conventions or to rise above them:

> It sparkles for a while, dies down, then waits; it disappears altogether or perhaps wears away to the naked thread; there is repetition. Yet now [...] the poetic urge continues with renewed, through different, sparkle, responding to new circumstances.
>
> (Mallarmé [1895] 1980, p. 3)

Without an element of crisis, the grounds for poetry's own survival can be questioned. According to Paul de Man's iconoclastic argument in 'Criticism and Crisis' (which links closely to Mallarmé's article) such difficult moments are necessary in order to attain a crystallization of poetry's own singularity: 'We can speak of crisis when a "separation" takes place, by self-reflection, between what, in literature, is in conformity with the original intent and what has irrevocably fallen away from this source' (de Man, 1983, p. 8). Yet other voices would claim that the ascetic and innovation-hungry nature of the poetic modernism that followed in the wake of Mallarmé and other French Symbolists is more aptly diagnosed as a cause for crisis than as a fruitful response.[4] Certainly, if poetry is to be an alternative to, rather than a simple abettor of, the news media's sensationalism, then it must scrupulously question its own medium and *ethos*.

The poet Geoffrey Hill has called attention to the pervasiveness of what he calls the 'Entertainment overkill' (Hill, 1998, p. 27), acknowledging the Romantic William Wordsworth as a precedent for his own sceptical, sidelong glance on how poetry must find its own voice at a distance to that of the news media. According to this view, poetry can aspire to a more meditative and less self-serving vantage point on the issues that plunge the world into collective turmoil. The chapters in this collection attempt to do something similar on behalf of literary criticism – rearticulating the position of poetry in light of some of the central crises of recent decades, while also keeping an eye on certain elements of continuity with poetry written in the last couple of hundred years. In some ways these crises are new and specific to our age, in others they resemble questions that are much less so. If the Romantics responded to what they perceived as a crisis of artistic expression, the human community and the rural landscape at the rise of industrial capitalism, poets in the new millennium are faced with the challenges of the global marketplace where humans, both as members of communities and as individuals, are constantly subjected to the impersonal forces of the market economy. Similarly, if the perceived threats of 'the smoking chimneys and noisy factories' to nature and the countryside concerned the Romantics (Dawson, 1993, p. 67), the escalating ecological crisis of our days has in recent years been attracting an increasing number of responses from poets. And if the 'age of revolution' was concerned with the 'universal human values of freedom and equality', the rise of minority groups and their claim for a voice in an increasingly multicultural society has led to a continuation of struggles with questions of identity, difference and social justice.

The focus of this volume is on those events and dilemmas that both society and poetry have faced in the past sixty years or so, in other words during the period experienced first hand by the generations forming our contemporary society. The poetry discussed in this collection addresses crises from the Holocaust to the fall of the Twin Towers, from the marginalization of ethnic minorities and the destruction of the environment to the 'war on terror'. At the same time, these events have influenced various ways of questioning the role of poetic discourse and reception. The organization of this volume is thus based upon an understanding that crisis, in contemporary poetry, is not a simple or easily-defined phenomenon, but rather a condition that moves through the entire communicative chain. This can be illustrated via the schematics of Roman Jakobson's landmark essay 'Linguistics and Poetics' (Jakobson, 1987).[5] Famously, Jakobson suggested that evaluation of linguistic and poetic discourse requires an awareness not only of the 'message' of the poem or other verbal utterance, but also of the speaker (addresser) and the listener/reader (addressee) – as well as the functions of context, contact and code. Context makes the message 'graspable by the addressee' (and may be either 'verbal or capable of being verbalized'), a common code makes it possible for the addresser to encode and the addressee to decode the message, and contact signifies 'the physical channel and physiological connection between the addresser and the addressee' (ibid., p. 66).

Thus, the chapters by John Sears, Mary Kate Azcuy and Scott Brewster in Part I of this book focus on the addresser: on poetic responses to, and encodings of, events of crisis. Analysing poetry from the Holocaust to the fall of the Twin Towers, they confront the understanding of poetry as a lyric phenomenon that, in Jakobson's terms, aims for 'a direct expression of the speaker's attitude toward what he [or she] is talking about' (ibid.) They relate to late twentieth-century debates on expressive subjectivity in poetry by demonstrating the ways in which material and historical turmoil force the poetry to highlight and question its own devices (in line with Jakobson's 'poetic function'). Part II, which is centred on Northern Irish poetry (with essays by Ruben Moi, Seán Crosson, Stephen Regan and Charles I. Armstrong) scrutinizes the factor of 'context' in Jakobson's model inasmuch as it focuses on the various attempts by poets to communicate to an audience one specific experience of historical crisis in the twentieth century, one particularly intensely approached through poetry, namely the Northern Irish Troubles. Jakobson notes that even though 'an orientation toward the context – briefly, the so-called REFERENTIAL, "denotative", "cognitive" function – is the leading task of numerous messages, the accessory participation of the other functions in such messages must be taken into account' (ibid., p. 66). Thus the questioning of the linguistic and poetic medium's capacity to grasp the particular events to which they respond has been a constant preoccupation for poets from Northern Ireland, and is also examined in the chapters here. Part III, on place and landscape, emphasizes the factor of contact, and the function of the phatic in Jakobson's terms: in the essays by Brendan Corcoran, Lucy

Collins, Janne Stigen Drangsholt and Anne Karhio, emphasis is on the materiality of place and the materiality of language, and the possibility of establishing a channel of communication. Finally, the essays by Guinn Batten, Eva Mueller-Zettelmann and Deirdre Osborne in Part IV examine poetry from the point of view of its audience's expectations and/or reactions, in other words from the point of view of the function of the addressee, be he or she representative of the critic (Batten), the literary community (Mueller-Zettelmann) or the culturally determined expectations of the audience (Osborne). In Jakobson's terms, such approaches stress what he calls the 'conative' factor, placing emphasis on the implied recipient, and, at the same time, respondent.

The collection opens with a section devoted to the ways in which poetry's dealings with crisis raise difficult questions concerning personal and poetic identity, as poetry's lyric expressiveness is pushed to an uneasy limit. The Second World War looms large in this section, as it provokes poets to trace the effects of large-scale historical trauma on the individual. First of all, there is John Sears's essay 'Form, Historical Crisis and Poetry's Hope in George Szirtes's "Metro"', in which Sears finds Szirtes's poem centrally engaged with the challenges of representing crisis and trauma, in particular in regard to aspects of the Holocaust. For Sears it is the 'crisis of the relationship between the ethical and the aesthetic' that Szirtes's work represents, a crisis the poet attempts to resolve by deferring to other writings in a work that addresses the life of Szirtes's mother – a survivor of a German concentration camp. Also considered here is the relationship between form and crisis within poetry and the failure of words to perform the challenge presented to them in times of crisis. Sears draws on Andrew Benjamin's interpretation of 'hope', by which hope is 'displaced into a future that exceeds the present', to account for how Szirtes in 'Metro' comes to terms with crisis by asserting continuity.

Similar existential concerns are evident in Mary Kate Azcuy's examination of Louise Glück's post 9/11 poem 'October', a poem engaging with a world in crisis through an analysis of personal history and mythology, in particular 'a double persona' depicted in the figure of Persephone. Azcuy explores the way in which Glück draws on her own traumatic childhood experiences, including fighting with anorexia, to uncover 'current trauma', while returning to the myth of Persephone and Demeter to engage with a collapse of order in the contemporary world. For Glück, Azcuy suggests, the risk of repeating trauma while narrating one's story may also lead to silence at the heart of poetic expression. Furthermore, Glück, as Azcuy contends, finds redemption in the natural world and looks to the 'beauty of nature that has survived human atrocities' for hope.

After two chapters considering how, and how far, poetry can accommodate historically inflicted trauma, the subsequent contribution addresses how lyric poetry can turn away from expression altogether. In Scott Brewster's chapter, '*Hern*: The Catastrophe of Lyric in John Burnside', Burnside's poetry is examined through Derrida's image of *le hérisson*, the hedgehog, which is able to turn in on itself for protection but simultaneously exposes itself to the risk of obliteration. Brewster's reading of Burnside focuses on questions of lyric subjectivity, and how this subjectivity in poetry is constantly poised between absolute privacy and secrecy on the one hand, and, on the other, 'the customary, the familiar and the shared'. The interplay of withdrawal and encounter with the other, the essay suggests, is apparent in Burnside's poetry, which is 'shadowed by a sense of threat and vulnerability that underlies this lyric moment'.

Part II, 'A Special Case', turns to poetry's response to a particular and recent instance of political crisis. The chapters in this section look at literature's negotiations with its context – especially through a focus on how poetry from Northern Ireland approaches the articulation of an understanding of key events and stages of the Northern Irish Troubles. The section opens with Ruben Moi's essay, '"In a ghostly pool of blood / a crumpled phantom hugged the mud": Spectropoetic Presentations of Bloody Sunday and the Crisis of Northern Ireland', which draws on Derrida's concept of *hauntology,* or responsibility 'beyond all living present'. Through this concept, Moi examines the crisis of Northern Ireland and in particular poetic representations of Bloody Sunday. Moi reflects on the centrality of this event to the Troubles, as the point at which 'the crisis of Northern Ireland culminated', and gives special attention to works, such as Thomas Kinsella's *Butcher's Dozen,* that made up for their frequent lack of nuance and subtlety with the fire and passion of their direct engagement with the actions of that day and the subsequent whitewash of the Widgery Tribunal. For Moi, the questioning of responsibility in a violent society has been central to Northern Irish poetry in the final decades of the twentieth century, and this questioning he finds most apparent in the various engagements of poets with the events of Bloody Sunday. In each instance, poets are challenged by calls to respond directly – to speak out, to represent, and to challenge injustice. Yet as Moi's study suggests, such a challenge is far from straightforward and, apart from the threats to life that may exist in such contested spaces, it is the challenge to poets who wish to maintain their own artistic integrity – what Seamus Heaney has called 'the central preoccupying questions' (Heaney, 1980, p. 13) – that can be most difficult to resolve.

Seán Crosson's chapter examines the place of traditional music in the poetry of Seamus Heaney in a time of crisis. Heaney's attempts to come to terms with his own identity and poetic inheritance during the Troubles in Northern Ireland has been criticized for rehashing Romantic tropes of nineteenth-century Irish nationalism, while failing to engage sufficiently critically with the contemporary realities around him. Crosson argues that these criticisms are also relevant to Heaney's engagement with traditional music and song: the tradition Heaney draws from is largely that of Romantic and modernist aesthetics of poetry, where the function of art is seen in a highly individualized context. Much as the landscape has provided for Heaney a point of tradition, continuity and stability, traditional music has served a similar purpose in his poetry, connecting his work to an Irish tradition but without always acknowledging the communities from which this music has emerged or its political and social complexities, particularly in times of communal upheaval.

If Bloody Sunday marked perhaps the most profound moment of crisis in the early years of the Troubles, Stephen Regan's chapter, '"Crisis first-hand": Seamus Heaney before and after the Ceasefire', chooses as its historical focal point the end of the period marked by civil unrest in Ireland's North. Regan considers the creative challenges that face poets after an external crisis has subsided, in this case Northern Irish poetry after the ceasefire. As one commentator remarked 'What are you going to write about now?' The answer would seem to Regan to include 'a distinctive preoccupation with memory, forgiveness and reconciliation' as well as 'sustained intertextual experimentation'. Regan focuses in particular here on the work of Seamus Heaney and begins by considering Heaney's earlier engagement with the crisis of the Troubles, an engagement found wanting by other scholars but which Regan argues did include, when the occasion required it, speaking out 'forcefully against the British media, the British government and the British army'. In the aftermath of the 1994 ceasefire, however, Regan recognizes a movement in Heaney's poetry from 'emblems of adversity' (apparent, for example, in the Bog poem sequence of the 1970s), to 'emblems of reconciliation and renewal' in the post-ceasefire era.

One possible approach to poetic replies to the question addressed in Regan's essay – of what poets are going to write about now – is by focusing on the dimension of the quotidian in Northern Irish poetry and its relationship to crises, both personal and political, which is the central concern of Charles I. Armstrong's chapter. For Armstrong, the work of poets such as Seamus Heaney, Paul Muldoon, Ciaran Carson and Leontia Flynn, reveals a recurring engagement with aspects of the everyday, though often for quite different purposes, varying from the transcendental to the transgressive. Armstrong argues that 'everyday epiphanies' have an important role to play for these poets in assisting them in finding points of reference in a crisis concerning our perceptual access to the world. However, he is careful to emphasize that such engagements are not immune to the 'ideological underpinnings of the everyday'.

Not only poetry's political contexts, but also the very setting and topographical frame in which poetry unfolds is now in a state of crisis. Although it has long been unfashionable to see nature as an issue even partially independent of political concerns,[6] the recent ecological crisis has forced many to rethink these concepts. Reflecting such tendencies, the chapters in Part III consider, from different geographical and critical perspectives, questions of ecology, place and landscape.

The opening chapter of this section bridges the preceding chapters on lyric subjectivity and the Northern Irish conflict and concerns with place and landscape. In '"The memorial to all of them": Landscape and the Holocaust in the Poetry of Michael Longley', Brendan Corcoran reads Longley's poetry through its intertwining of poetic responsibility to remember with the ecological awareness of nature and landscape and with human destructiveness. The singularity of any act of atrocity, in particular the Holocaust, is brought into tension with the more universally human capabilities of destructive behaviour on the one hand, and, on the other, memory and grief. For Corcoran, Longley's engagement with the Holocaust 'suspends together the human voice of poetry with the vastness of atrocious death, not to redress such death but to imbricate human presence with its absence'. Simultaneously, however, Longley positions his own engagement with the historical events he did not personally witness in his reading of the landscape of Carrigskeewaun in county Mayo, and the burial sites that mark its graves, 'the literal place of the dead within the landscape'.

Ecological crisis and the potential of human destructiveness towards the natural world are the central concern of Lucy Collins's chapter, '"Toward a Brink": The Poetry of Kathleen Jamie and Environmental Crisis', which focuses on the work of the Scottish poet whose work reveals, Collins argues, 'the interwoven aspect of ecological concern' and 'its connections to social structures and personal events' as well as to debates in the wider world. Collins reflects on the role of poetry as a potential agent for change, particularly with regard to a concern for nature, an important 'form of political engagement' so long as issues of power are inseparable from the relationship of humans to the natural world. She examines Jamie's exploration of the interaction of the human and the natural world in her 2004 collection *The Tree House*, where poems such as 'The Wishing Tree' emphasize 'the need to engage with nature as equal not as master'. As Collins argues, Jamie's collection is 'shaped by the idea that human understanding can be fundamentally altered by renewed attentiveness to what already surrounds us – a core prerequisite of environmental reform'.

Janne Stigen Drangsholt notes the increasingly problematic identification between 'subject and landscape' that has developed with the rise of the postmodern idiom and its resulting in 'a kind of "crisis poetry", where the poetic subject is unable to place itself in any kind of "scape"'. Yet for Stigen Drangsholt, British poetry remains characterized by 'the thematization of landscape' as poets attempt to counter the sense of crisis through 'attempts at articulating a landscape or a sense of place', a place that is often constructed in quite different ways. She is particularly interested in how this process develops within Alice Oswald's poetry, 'frequently structured in terms of movement'. Stigen Drangsholt's analysis – which draws on readings of Romantic poetry by Harold Bloom and Martin Heidegger – foregrounds Oswald's focus on the natural environment while acknowledging Oswald's own contestation of her description as a 'nature poet'. In her readings of poems from Oswald's collections *Dart* (2002) and *Woods etc.* (2006), she finds a crucial connection between an understanding of place and an understanding of self, while the importance of opening 'oneself up to the difference of the other' is central to the title poem of the 2006 collection.

The interrelationship between materiality of place and language provides the focus of the last chapter in Part III: Anne Karhio's interpretation of the relationship between place and narrative in Muldoon's long poems. This chapter is framed by the responsibilities and relationship of poets to politics in Northern Ireland, and its affinity with such debates in the United States. Karhio focuses principally on the narrative elements in three of Muldoon's long poems, each taken from a separate point in his career – 'The More a Man Has, the More a Man Wants', 'Yarrow' and the title poem of the 2006 collection *Horse Latitudes* – and 'how they operate in portraying crisis and place' or 'crisis in place'. Within this analysis, she also outlines the development of form in poetry from the Romantics to the modernists, and the relationship of this legacy to more recent postmodern poetics. Karhio calls for the need to 'address both crisis of the narrative as well as narratives of crisis in poetry' and emphasizes the importance of considering the formal elements of Muldoon's poems as meaningful in relation to their more social and political concerns.

The chapters in Part IV, the final section of the book, address the interpretative frameworks of contemporary poetry: who reads and makes critical judgements on this poetry, and on what basis are these hermeneutical gestures made? Poetry's addressees are brought to the forefront here, reflecting a sense of crisis concerning poetry's audience that arguably has been a recurring feature since the first onslaught of modernism on Britain and Ireland. The work of Paul Muldoon is again the topic of the first chapter of the section, 'Paul Muldoon: Critical Judgement, the Crisis Poem, and the Ethics of Voice', in which Guinn Batten provides a discussion of the politics of the crisis poem and the frequent intersection of foreign and personal affairs. The essay highlights the function of judgement, not only on the part of the poet but also on that of the critic. Taking as her starting point what she considers critical misreadings of Paul Muldoon's poetic sequences 'Madoc' and 'Horse Latitudes', Batten argues that 'the idea that references not only are inevitably missed but, indeed, sometimes should be missed, is central to Muldoon's ethics of poetic voice in a time of crisis'. While relating the Special Powers Act enacted in Northern Ireland during the Troubles with the Homeland Security Act of the post-9/11 United States, Batten suggests, employing the ideas of Walter Benjamin, that 'crisis may become [...] the everyday condition of rule of law that creates what Muldoon would call "the doldrums" of our time'.

Eva Mueller-Zettelmann's essay 'Displacing the Crisis: New British Poetry, Cultural Memory and the Role of the Intellectual' addresses the existence of competing views of poetry's position in the contemporary British culture of poetry. Mueller-Zettelmann begins by remarking on the huge number of articles, editorials and public lectures devoted to the topic of a perceived crisis in British poetry, the result of its allegedly increasingly marginalized position in society. Her analysis explores the contending voices of what Michael Schmidt has called the 'gamekeepers' of contemporary poetry, thereby attempting to unearth the underlying issues in this sense of crisis, and is framed by the respective addresses to the St Andrews Poetry Festival (StAnza) of Neil Astley and Michael Schmidt. Mueller-Zettelmann charts a dialectic in British poetry that is apparent in these two presentations, from a concern with giving readers what they want (Astley) to those who believe editors and publishers are failing to alert readers to 'precisely those characteristics that make poetry special' (Schmidt). However, despite rumours to the contrary, Mueller-Zettelmann finds British poetry to be in a relatively healthy state. Thus, the perception of crisis in British poetry has more to do with social than with literary factors – particularly as the notion of Britishness itself comes under increasing pressure and poets seek to 'bring forth an elevating self-image for a nation in crisis'.

The final chapter of the book, Deirdre Osborne's 'The Body of Text Meets the Body as Text: Staging (I)dentity in the work of SuAndi and Lemn Sissay', is a study of two indigenous black British poets, SuAndi and Lemn Sissay, and is concerned with the various crises that can face minority ethnicities in their attempts to articulate themselves against 'canonical traditions of literary poetry'. If Mueller-Zettelmann's essay proposes that the suggested crisis of British poetry is really a crisis of the national ideals of poetry, Osborne examines the dilemmas facing those marginalized by such ideals. She looks at the two writers' efforts to assert distinctive voices from the margins, voices that reflect, and are shaped by, societal crises of repression, marginalization and racism within a white majority culture. In the process, SuAndi and Sissay are attempting to reshape the expectations of their audience. Osborne's examination is cognizant of both the implied and explicit implications of context – from literary legacies to poetic traditions and socio-cultural factors – and 'its effect upon meaning'. She focuses in particular on two self-performed monodramas, *Something Dark* (Sissay) and *The Story of M* (SuAndi), work which foregrounds the personal voice to stage the poets own '(I)dentity assertions'.

As this overview of the contributions to this collection indicates, the chapters below obviously cover no more than a small part of all the possible ways in which poetry can be said to address the notion of crisis, no matter which function of Jakobson's communicative scheme they can be seen to emphasize (or deem problematic). Neither can they claim culturally or geographically to cover the contemporary human and literary experience in any exhaustive way: the focus of this volume is narrowed down to poetry in English, with an emphasis on poetry from Britain, Ireland and North America. The volume includes chapters concerned with the work of established poets such as Seamus Heaney, Paul Muldoon and Louise Glück, but also includes fresh and, arguably, more marginalized voices, like those discussed by Deirdre Osborne. Despite its limitations, this collection aims to frame the kinds of challenges that poetry is facing in the new millennium. If, as Auden intimates, the effects of crisis will probably not leave us for long – 'We must suffer them all again', as he writes in 'September 1, 1939' – then both poetry and the interpretation of poetry might make us better qualified to rise to the occasion once they return.

Notes

1. According to Harvey, 'The depression that swept out of Britain in 1846–1847 and which quickly engulfed the whole of what was then the capitalist world, can justly be regarded as the first unambiguous crisis of capitalist overaccumulation. [...] the crisis of 1847–8 created a crisis of representation, and that this latter crisis itself derived from a radical readjustment in the sense of time and space in economic, political and cultural life' (Harvey, 1990, p. 260).
2. Indeed, Moynagh Sullivan has drawn attention to how a sense of ongoing crisis has been seminal to the critical discourses around Ireland, its culture and literature; see Sullivan (2005, p. 451).
3. Marjorie Perloff, for example, has shown how in the works of several contemporary American poets, the personal 'is not necessarily equivalent to the inward-looking gaze of the psychologically complex subject' (Perloff, 1996, p. 183).
4. For such a view on modernism, see for instance Eavan Boland: 'The Wrong Way' (Boland, 2000, pp. 215–18).
5. Jakobson's essay is based on a lecture in 1958 at a conference held in Indiana University, and was subsequently revised and first published in Thomas Sebeok (ed.) *Style in Language*. This introduction refers to the version published in *Language in Literature*, edited by Krystyna Pomorska and Stephen Rudy (1987).
6. Jonathan Bate has noted how the emergence of the 'polis' (the Greek root for 'political') may by definition be seen to mark a fall from nature as a phenomenologically experienced domain (Bate, 2000, p. 266).

References

Adorno, Theodor W. (1991) *Notes to Literature*, Vol. 1, trans. Shierry Weber Nicholsen (New York: Columbia University Press).

Adorno, Theodor W. and Max Horkheimer (2002) *Dialectic of Enlightenment*, trans. Edmund Jephcott (Stanford: Stanford University Press).

Auden, W.H. (1977) 'September 1, 1939', in *The English Auden: Poems, Essays and Dramatic Writings 1927–1939* (London: Faber and Faber).

Bate, Jonathan (2000) *A Song of the Earth* (London: Picador).

Boland, Eavan (2000) 'The Wrong Way', in W.N. Herbert and Matthew Hollis (eds) *Strong Words: Modern Poets on Modern Poetry* (Tarset: Bloodaxe).

Dawson, P.M.S. (1993) 'Poetry in an Age of Revolution', in Stuart Curran (ed.) *The Cambridge Companion to British Romanticism* (Cambridge: Cambridge University Press).

De Man, Paul (1983) *Blindness and Insight: Essays in the Rhetoric of Contemporary Criticism*, revised edition (London: Routledge).

Cannon, Moya (2008) 'Where Poetry is Supposed to Happen: A Personal Encounter with the Country and the City in Twentieth Century Irish Poetry',

Plenary lecture, DUCIS conference 'Rural and Urban Landscapes', University of Dalarna, Falun, 6 November 2008.
Hardt, Michael and Antonio Negri (2000) *Empire* (Cambridge, MA: Harvard University Press).
Harvey, David (1990) *The Condition of Postmodernity* (Cambridge, MA and Oxford: Blackwell Publishing).
Heaney, Seamus (1980) *Preoccupations* (London: Faber and Faber).
Hill, Geoffrey (1998) *The Triumph of Love* (Boston and New York: Houghton Mifflin).
Jakobson, Roman (1987) 'Linguistics and Poetics', in Krystyna Pomorska and Stephen Rudy (eds) *Language in Literature* (Cambridge, MA and London: Belknap Press of Harvard University Press).
Mallarmé, Stéphane ([1895]1980) 'Crisis in Verse', in Thomas G. West (ed.) *Symbolism, an Anthology* (New York: Methuen).
Muldoon, Paul (2001) *Poems 1968–1998* (London: Faber and Faber).
Perloff, Marjorie (1996) *Wittgenstein's Ladder: Poetic Language and the Strangeness of the Ordinary* (Chicago: University of Chicago Press).
Rigby, Kate (2004) *Topographies of the Sacred: The Poetics of Place in European Romanticism* (Charlottesville and London: University of Virginia Press).
Sullivan, Moynagh (2005) 'The Treachery of Wetness: Irish Studies, Seamus Heaney and the Politics of Parturition', *Irish Studies Review*, 13(4): 451–68.

Part I
The Limits of Expression: Representation and Identity

1

Form, Historical Crisis and Poetry's Hope in George Szirtes's 'Metro'

John Sears

George Szirtes's poetry constitutes an increasingly significant body of work addressing the historical crises experienced in mid-twentieth-century and post-war European histories and migrations. Szirtes was born in Budapest in 1948 to parents who had survived the Holocaust. Szirtes's family travelled, via Austria, to England in December 1956 as refugees from the communist invasion of Hungary. Written in English and published since the early 1970s (and recently collected by Bloodaxe as *New & Collected Poems* [Szirtes, 2008]), his poetry is influenced by English and Irish modernism and formalism and also, increasingly, by literary traditions made available by Szirtes's own extensive translating of Hungarian poetry into English. Szirtes's poetry is deeply concerned with exploring family encounters with history as offering provisional and incomplete coordinates for locating the self and its memories within wider historical contexts. Michael Murphy writes of the 'witness' that 'his poetry bears to events that engulfed Central Europe in the middle years of the 20th century' (Murphy, 2004, p. 143). 'Bearing witness' is indeed a key element in the processes of remembrance, reconstruction and retrieval that characterize much of Szirtes's work, which 'bears witness' in challenging and sometimes disturbing ways to moments of profound historical crisis that it seeks to comprehend and, perhaps, to alleviate.

'Metro' is the title poem of Szirtes's fifth collection, published in 1988. It responds to his return to Budapest after an absence of nearly 30 years, a return that is both geographical and historical. Return and absence are crucial elements of the poem; its engagement with crisis opens onto a double mourning, of the experience of loss as absence and of the impossibility of return as recuperation. The poem's expansive formalism centres on a symbolic refusal to enter a specific historical territory, that of the concentration camp. This refusal ('I stop dead at the gate'[1]) is both ethically correct and aesthetically critical, an expression of the poem's perception of the failure of art, a crisis of the relationship between the ethical and the aesthetic. 'Metro' negotiates this double consequence of its refusal to attempt to represent the unrepresentable by deferring intertextually to other writings. Deferral and refusal – the displacement of the poem onto the tradition on which it draws, and the poem's narrative arresting of its logical movement into and within a history on which it also draws – are structural expressions of the poem's analysis of (its) failure. This analysis seeks recompense in the enactment of a collision of English and European poetic traditions. At its simplest, this collision is found in wordplay – so the name of the Polish writer Nelly Toll evokes in Part 8 of 'Metro' (a critical section, as we shall see) an allusion to Keats's 'Nightingale' ode ('She tolls me back to the bleak scene before / The entrance' [p. 167]). This allusion relocates the poem in the history it seeks to reconstruct, and re-enacts (in its 'tolling' the self back from the brink of an imagined identification) the poem's moment of refusal at the 'entrance'. In a more complex way 'Metro' enacts, in its existence within the traditions to which it alludes, the possibility of continuity beyond this moment of refusal. This possibility – signified by the existence of the poem – is that of a hope that transcends the moment of historical crisis. Allusion thus both confronts and evades refusal. This chapter will read the rhetorical and intertextual strategies in 'Metro' for opening the space of tradition within which the poem inserts itself, in order partially to alleviate its historical refusal and affording, in the process, the possibility of hope.

'Metro' represents Budapest and its metro system as a series of metaphors, excavating and exploring personal memories, family narratives and national histories within a poetic space that is itself mobile, constantly shifting from one time frame to another as it maps memory and history. Its specific focus is on the partially recoverable histories of Szirtes's parents, and particularly that of his mother ('metro' is a near-anagram of 'mother'), immediately before, during, and after the Second World War. These histories are refracted through childhood memories and family narratives. The poem seeks a way of thinking and imagining them as constituted in an underground space, 'the cavity / Beneath the streets' (p. 153). This space (that of the Budapest metro and, metaphorically, of 'Metro') is constructed in-between discursive categories: part myth, part history and part memory, but wholly fitting into none of these, becoming the mobile space of family anecdote and inherited reminiscence. Punctuated by moments of allegorical diversion and symbolic complexity, biography becomes within this space simultaneously historical and conjectural. As such, it is expressive of the poem's desired recuperation of a destroyed past and hope for reconciliation with the ghosts of history, and offers the first level of its allusive density. Allegorically 'Metro' enacts a descent into hell, the hell of a history experienced at remove and in the movement of its removal, yet tangible in its emotional and physical traces. The poem is both intensely personal and strangely distant from its subject-matter, its modernist devices of montage and disjunction mobilizing a series of necessary defences to displace and, therefore, to try to comprehend the events and experiences to which it responds. It is a poem of profound post-war crisis, articulating through a problematically European (specifically Hungarian) experience a version of history centring on what Jacques Derrida has called 'the anniversary and repetition of the unrepeatable' (Derrida, 2003, p. 308), which intrudes into the forms and language of English poetry.

One aspect of this intrusion is evident in the poem's (unacknowledged) citation, in the second stanza of section 8, of the first two lines of Paul Celan's poem 'Ich bin allein' (published in *Mohn und Gedächtnis*, 1952, p. 166). This citation, repeated in abbreviated form two stanzas later (p. 167) alongside a phrase from another Celan poem ('Todesfuge' [Celan, 2009]) and connected to English translations of lines taken from the Holocaust writings of Nelly Toll, locates 'Metro' momentarily in relation to European traditions of post-Holocaust poetry. It constitutes a site within 'Metro' that opens the poem to another order of reading, moving it beyond personal and familial crises into an intertextual space, indicating the poem's reliance on previous poetic responses to the Holocaust in order to frame its own. The presence of Celan's German lines in Szirtes's poem (transforming the linguistic politics of the presence, earlier in the poem, of Hungarian place and street-names) redefines 'Metro' as a site of intense political significance. These lines effect a disruption of the poem's Englishness that unsettles and problematizes its response to history and brings into expression another covert crisis, one concerning the efficacy of the language and forms available to English poetry (specifically the forms implicit in the poem's frequent Shakespearean and Keatsian allusions and its mobilization through these of traditions of English pastoral) in the face of recent European history. More broadly still, it experiences this crisis as one pertaining to the efficacy of poetry itself.

'Metro' is a major post-memorial poem, occupying a critical position in Szirtes's now extensive oeuvre. It is the central poem in a trilogy of long works – the other poems are 'The Photographer in Winter' (1986) and 'Transylvana' (1994) – addressing the life of the poet's mother, who survived incarceration in the women's concentration camps at Ravensbrück (published versions of 'Metro' omit the umlaut) and Penig. Described inaccurately by one reviewer as an 'unrhymed sonnet sequence' (Beake, 1991, p. 53), the poem comprises a 780-line sequence of sixty curtailed 13-line sonnets divided into ten sections. The specific problems presented by a long poem – tensions between lyric and narrative modes, sustaining themes and symbolic patternings, establishing coherent relations between parts and whole – are important in considering the poem's exploration of relations between form and crisis. Repetition, in the sense of formal consistency, structures the poem, but is resisted by the irregular rhyme and metre of the poem's stanzas, holding only loose forms that Szirtes deploys to imply organization. Variation of repetition, in terms of formal incompleteness and generic fragmentation, mimics the impossibility of full knowledge – 'Even now I know little about my mother' (p. 156), the poem laments, echoing itself later: 'Even now I don't know what the truth is' (p. 160). Sean O'Brien remarks that 'Metro' is 'pre-occupied with dissolution' (O'Brien, 1988, p. 56), a formal consequence of the failure of words and poetic structures to perform the functions demanded of them. Repetition thus complements variation, incompleteness and 'dissolution' as a feature of form and language that characterizes and distinguishes the poem. Incomplete repetition, in the form of citation of and allusion to other texts, constitutes here a significant instance of this, one that marks 'Metro' in terms of a relation to tradition. This relation, in turn, is indicated by the poem's movement between autobiographical, biographical and speculative modes of representation, its offering – as if they were history – of 'Escapades, / Adventures, tragedies' (p. 161), in order to fulfil a desire 'To find a history which feels like truth' (p. 154).

The pivotal position of 'Metro' in its author's trilogy of poems emphasizes its concern with Szirtes's 'in-between' (that is, neither fully Hungarian nor fully English) cultural identity. The poem is characteristic of Szirtes's work in that it enacts a writing of this 'in-between' status in its own structural indeterminacy. It offers a narrative that tries to account for a series of historical events construed as accidents ('Adventures, tragedies') of identity and location. It refers to these as 'The accident of being who one is' and 'The accident of being in a place / At one time not another' (p. 158). The poem's effort to account for these 'accidents of being' is conditioned by its awareness of the inadequacy of the resources available to it. These resources comprise memory, history, family narratives, documents, photographs and allusions to other poems. The poem's work is performed with and on these materials, which act as traces of content. Their inadequacy in relation to their desired function is expressed in the poem's recognition of the restricted capacity of words and poetic structures to recapture a past 'which remains forever another place' (p. 158). Nevertheless these resources are deployed, in the poem's complex meditation, in relation to a project that expresses 'hope'; the 'hope' that is named elsewhere in Szirtes's poetry, at the conclusion of the later meditation on his friendship with W.G. Sebald, 'Meeting Austerlitz'. This later poem ends in 'the Esperia Hotel in Athens', a name that, in the poem's last line, 'as you know, means hope' (Szirtes, 2004, p. 26).

One element of crisis in 'Metro' resides in the contrast between the potential reassurance offered by the shared knowledge of such concluding hope, and the impossibility of conceiving hope out of, or perceiving it amid, the history to which it responds. This is the place in 'Metro' where poetry's efficacy as an expression of hope comes into question. 'The dead have no use for art' (p. 166), the poem asserts. 'Use' here implies function and value, countering the functionless and valueless world of a past summarized in a single word: 'Ravensbruck' (p. 166). Nevertheless, the poem exists as an attempt or essaying: 'I float on my own craft, / And try to write the half dead a live song' (p. 166). This is the crisis addressed throughout 'Metro', a question that links the poem to familiar aesthetic debates 'after Auschwitz': what is the use or value of art in relation to the uselessness of posterity consequent on such historical trauma? What redress (in Seamus Heaney's terms) can poetry offer (Heaney, 1995)? 'Metro' answers this question through involvement of the representation of what it refers to as 'Brief episodes / of dire intensity' (p. 161), moments of intense historical crisis re-experienced in their reliving in words. These words follow such a moment of 'dire intensity', describing how 'The waters / Close about my grandfather and fold / Over him in Auschwitz' (p. 161). Such horrific conjunctions of the personal and the historical mark the poem's engagement with historical trauma and its 'episodes' of 'intensity'.

'Intensity' here names also the time of poetry described by Andrew Benjamin. Benjamin's analysis of 'Present Hope' in poems by Paul Celan and Edmond Jabès (Benjamin, 1997, pp. 119–53) affords ways of thinking about the functions and forms of 'hope' in Szirtes's poem. Hope, for Benjamin, offers an excess to that which is hoped for. It is a form of awaiting, an expectation, that exceeds the present of the act of hoping: 'with hope, something else is enacted, something other than what is being hoped for' (ibid., p. 119). The place of hope, its siting in the future present of hoping, is also its time, displaced into a future that exceeds the present. Hope thus expresses the possibility of continuing, of living on, and of survival: 'Something endures' (ibid., p. 122) despite and because of the deepest 'loss'. Benjamin describes 'this complex site' (ibid., p. 119) in relation to poetry, a mode of writing where 'time inheres in openings, in the complex presence and relation of words, in repetition, and, therefore, in versification as well' (ibid., pp. 119–20). Poetry's verbal and formal complexity affords its particular relation to the complexity of hope. In particular, poetry's deployment of repetition (understood here as a basic element of form) works on the time of the poem in specific ways: it 'will work to delimit the present, turning it into a site of intensity' (ibid., p. 120). This 'intensity', and its experience in the 'brief episodes' that punctuate the narratives and times of 'Metro', will take on specific resonances in this discussion.

It should be noted that 'Metro' never directly confronts or names its essaying of hope. Instead the poem offers a variety of distorting tropes, repetitions or rhetorical displacements that redirect its efforts at narrative reconstructions towards a general concern with the ineffectiveness of verbal reconstructions of the past. These include references (in the poem's final sonnet) to escape and marriage (see p. 171) as post-traumatic signifiers of living on, and the poem's reliance on a synaesthetic rendering of experience which recodes other sense experiences as visual ('I see a voice' [p. 153], 'Their voices are not heard but seen' [p. 155]). These elements of 'Metro' offer movement and displacement as forms of evasion, enabling the poem's performance of a kind of escape from history, an 'evasion' or escape that is reworked rhetorically as 'escapades' (p. 161). Its major 'evasion' is the reconstitution of 'hope' as 'desire' (initiated by the poem's epigraph from Derek Mahon, repeated as the title of section 7: 'What should they do there but desire?' [Mahon, 1993, pp. 62–4]). 'Metro' calls desire, a physical and aching longing, 'the undersong' (p. 155) to its surface narrative; desire is also 'the thread' (p. 155) dependent upon a series of metonymic shifts that redefine the poem's narrative. 'Undersongs' is also the title of part 2 of 'Metro', in which, after a horrific image of a 'brother' who 'disappears', 'dropped [...] in the ditch / Among the rest' (p. 155), the poem shifts rhetorical gear:

> The ditch becomes a pit,
> The pit a symbol, the symbol a desire,
> And this desire's the thread.
>
> (p. 155)

The 'thread' binds the metonymic movement 'ditch – pit – symbol – desire', an expression of narrative as a kind of 'becoming' (and a shift of historical proximity deictically marked in 'this') that displaces one of the poem's sites of intensity from horror to its assimilation and encoding in an ancient trope, the 'thread' offering the 'clue' to follow into the poem's 'tunnels' (p. 155) until one reaches the poem's critical refusal to follow any further. Any hope here is sublimated as 'desire', unsatisfiable, an 'undersong' the poem seeks but fails fully to detect or represent. The crisis in the intensity of 'hope' is defused by the deferral implicit in 'desire'.

The poem's 'episodes of dire intensity' are expressed in part through the resonances accruing to the word 'betrayal'. 'Metro' insists on 'betrayal' as an action resulting in an emotional condition, a loss of trust that extends to symbolize other losses. 'Betrayals' is the title of section 5 of 'Metro', echoing the last word of section 4 ('And only she remains to be betrayed' [p. 159]). The word insists at the opening of section 5:

> Betrayed? She thought and felt she was. But who
> Betrayed her (if it was betrayal) and how?
> Betrayal by omission was the way,
> Betrayal by those she trusted.
>
> (p. 160)

The intensity expressed here through repetition functions doubly to indicate both a historical betrayal (that which led to the mother's capture by the Hungarian Nazis in Budapest) and, more covertly, an anxiety in relation to a contemporary betrayal – the betrayal implicit in the poem's failure ('by omission') adequately to represent its subject-matter. Repetition of the word 'betrayal' locates the action centrally within the poem and defines it as a historical event which can only insist on its occurrence and its significance within the poem. Nevertheless within the poem's scale of ontological reliability 'betrayals' constitute not 'facts' (p. 159) but 'conjecture[s]' (p. 159). Its insistent repetition is undercut by qualifying clauses: 'She thought and felt she was [betrayed]' locates the experience within an imagined subjectivity, while the bracketed clause 'if it was betrayal' overtly questions the 'conjecture'. The problematic moment of betrayal embodies, in these uncertainties, the poem's location of moments of ethical crisis within its 'episodes of dire intensity'.

Just as the poem examines 'betrayal' as a condition of historical suffering, the language it must use is treacherous, threateningly uncontrollable: 'the words / Are muddy, full of unintended puns / And nervy humour' (p. 154). The poem's repetitive, Hamletesque rhetorical dismissals – 'The rest is data', 'Facts, bare bones, the rest / Are silences'

(p. 159) – reverberate most powerfully in the broken spaces that 'Metro' constructs and the shattered bodies ('bare bones', 'the skeleton' [p. 159]) over which it moves. The poem mobilizes a will-to-knowledge encoded as a despair of ever knowing enough, a despair that, in appealing for value, asserts the devaluation of all logic and form: 'How much is all this information worth?' (p. 160). This questioning of value recurs throughout 'Metro'. Section 7 asks 'Is this really a valuable darkness?' (p. 164). Photography, the mother's profession and trade, is offered in section 4 as 'this security, this collateral' (p. 158). Such concerns with value – the value of representations in relation to reality, or of symbolic experiences in relation to real ones – are versions of the poem's questioning of its own value as poem, a questioning wherein resides the poem's deepest crisis. When, in the final section, the poem seems to afford some notional peace in the possibility that 'we tell old jokes / And pay our debt to history with rhymes' (p. 170), the weight of the preceding sections forces us to infer that this 'debt' is actually unpayable, that 'rhymes' constitute no form of currency adequate to the value of the 'debt' owed to 'history'. 'Value', in relation to the poem's sense of its own efficacy, thus implies 'worthlessness', and contains an implicit uncertainty, in such a rhetorically complex poem, about the value of rhetorical movements, displacements and comparisons (metaphors of desire, forms of narrative, recurrent tropes) as forms of representation.

Lexical repetitions like that of 'betrayal' mirror the formal patterns and economies that structure 'Metro'. Form, repetitively incomplete, enacts the poem's content. The curtailed sonnets' incompleteness enacts the poem's response to – its attempt to represent – the incompleteness of the history it struggles to recuperate or redress, and the incompleteness of the biographies it seeks to reconstruct. This struggle is one expression of the crises addressed in 'Metro', crises which are condensed in the poem's relentless counterpointing of its barely sustained formal constraint with the evident yet unrepresentable horror of its subject-matter. The 'dissolution' consequent on formal incompleteness is a signifier of the 'awkward poetics' Antony Rowland has associated with much Holocaust writing, its tendency to exploit forms which distance or alienate the reader in order to disrupt conventions of comfort, familiarity, assurance (Rowland, 2005, pp. 1–27). 'Awkwardness' of form is manifest in many ways, from fragmented or incomplete formal structures to repetitive or insistent formal tics. It alerts the reader to a series of provisional and unsustainable ethical and ideological positions 'necessary' to respond adequately to the specific and unthinkable demands of Holocaust writing.

Lists exemplify one extreme of the awkwardness of the post-memorial poetics of 'Metro'. As a form of poetic expression, the list enacts a condition of poetic exhaustion which is also necessarily an expression of the continuance of poetry. The poetic exhaustion signified by the list is evident throughout the poem in unanswered or rhetorical questions: 'How many / Perished here: the artists, writers, / Musicians, plumbers, brothers?' (p. 161). 'It's lists and rosters, jigsaws piece by piece' (p. 161), this sonnet concludes. And yet the poem continues in its listing, in its enumeration of everyday realities:

> Straight ahead of you
> A lift-cage dressed in iron broderie,
> A smell of coffee brewing, an envelope
> Slit like a wound, the darker recesses
> Of sitting rooms, momentarily opened.
> (p. 164)

The everyday world listed here signifies the banality and the necessity of continuity, indicating at the same time the potential exhaustion of poetic language in the face of historical trauma. Any intensity here is displaced onto the rote mechanism of the list as sheer accumulation of detail, an accumulation that redefines the poetic in terms of recording, and simultaneously separates this poetic 'recording function' from the world described so that what is recorded is inevitably also lost.

Andrew Benjamin, examining Celan's use of the word *auseinandergeschrieben* or 'writing-asunder', describes writing after the Shoah as subject to 'a twofold determination':

> On the one hand, it is what brings language and whatever sense of propriety language will have into play. On the other hand, in the context of [Celan's poem], writing stages an act of recovery, as long as this is understood as claiming, first that language can never recover what is lost, and second, that language will have had to have recovered from what has been lost. Part of what will be involved in its capacity to recover from, will be the recognition that it cannot recover what was lost.
>
> (Benjamin, 1997, p. 123)

Writing's 'act of recovery' thus involves a double recognition, that writing cannot recuperate that which has been lost, and then that writing itself can only recover itself or be recovered out of that initial recognition.

'Metro' articulates this double recognition in its deployment, through the rhetorical functions of lists, of a poetics of exhaustion that is also and simultaneously a poetics of continuity. This possibility, Benjamin notes, resides in language's necessary difference from 'what it occasions' (Benjamin, 1997, p. 123). This, Benjamin argues, is the founding 'writing-asunder': language is at no point commensurate with what it represents but its possibility signifies instead a non-original 'in-betweenness', a separation of word and thing in which word is not thing and thing is not word. The alertness of 'Metro' to this divided condition, within which resides the word's potential redemption from the condition of loss encountered in the thing, is evident in its embedding and encoding of its author's divided experience and in its recognition that its own words are 'written-asunder'. It offers, in re-enacting historical experience by impersonating the mother's voice, 'My words for what she meant, in a general sense' (p. 158). The poem's words thus substitute not for the mother's words (writing replacing direct speech) but for 'what she meant', a poetic rendition of indirect speech, further displaced by the adjunct 'in a general sense'. This system of exchange implies a value-equivalence that the poem's implicit irony undercuts; 'in a general sense', lacking the specificity of the list, nevertheless conveys the generality that the list's rhetorical function suggests.

This generality locates the question of authenticity in 'Metro', and specifically the question of the poem's relation to the putative 'authenticity' of poetic language. As we have seen, the poem's formal and linguistic characteristics counter conventional structures, inviting instead a consideration of 'Metro' in terms of 'awkward' poetics. 'Authenticity' is questioned in its repeated allusions to Shakespeare (specifically Hamlet's last words, 'The rest is silence' [*Hamlet* V ii], but also *Romeo and Juliet* [II. i.42–3]: 'The things that might smell sweet by any other / Name we give ...' [p. 158]). These allusions situate the poem in relation to an English tradition of tragedy ('Escapades, / Adventures, tragedies ...' [p. 161]) which offers, if not an ethical framework for the consideration of its subject-matter, at least a literary embedding of the poem's distancing from its history, its location in a language (that is, English) different from the European experiences it reconstructs. These experiences return, however, in other intertextual allusions and borrowings, specifically the quotation in section 8 of Celan's 'Ich bin allein' and of a phrase adapted from his 'Todesfuge'. Celan's poems afford 'Metro' a negative affirmation of its own place in the post-Holocaust poetic tradition that also affirms a hope in poetry. This affirmation of hope is nonetheless simultaneously an expression of a crisis in poetry's efficacy. 'Metro's enactment of its own crisis, a tension between formal constraint and the insistent horror of the poem's subject matter, is implicit within this negative affirmation of hope. Celan's poems appear in 'Metro' as fragments, elements in a list (of allusions and quotations) deployed to indicate allegiance to and dependence upon a tradition. The citation and repetition of Celan's lines offers quotation as 'site of intensity', opening a space within the poem for a specific and awkward kind of literary resonance extended in further citations from Polish writer Nelly Toll's *Behind the Secret Window*, her account of surviving the Nazi occupation of Lvov (Toll, 2003). The sonnets in which these citations occur are complex and require careful exposition in order to account for this resonance.

Section 8 of 'Metro', entitled 'Stopping Train', arrives initially in the traumatic past evoked, as noted earlier, by the single word of the place-name: 'Here's Ravensbruck' (p. 166). Death's presence is immediately asserted, but reclaimed from its historical distance in the presence of the narrating voice: 'I stop dead at the gate' (p. 166). This 'presenting' of death is magnified by the failure of communication that concerns this sonnet. The poem refuses entry into the camp, eschewing the burden of an impossible enterprise in an extended disavowal of the efficacy of poetry adequately to represent this past: 'No wreath of words arranged across blank pages' (p. 166). It is here that 'Metro' asserts through the act of refusal its own uselessness ('The dead have no use for art') and, in doing so, asserts simultaneously its renewal. It offers 'Writing white' in 'white ink' as counterpoint to 'black paper' (p. 166), a conventional signifier of mourning. The poem's concentration on 'writing', 'ink' and 'paper' reduces it to a material object, repudiating aesthetic claims in the moment of arrival at the site of historical trauma. This is counterpointed by allusions to Schubert and D.H. Lawrence ('Their coming through' [p. 166] echoes the title of Lawrence's 1917 collection *Look! We Have Come Through*) which effect further intertextual displacements.

The next sonnet addresses the poem's compulsion to address this history, accounting for it in terms of the benefit of retrospective knowledge: 'And if I bring you here and push you in / It's only because I know you once came out' (p. 166). This double movement, of poetic action (repetition) and (fore-)knowledge of escape, again seeks exoneration for the poem's desire to represent. 'If' and 'only' offer rhetorical pleas for forgiveness, which lead us towards the poem's first crucial citation of Celan. We approach it, along with the poem's addressee: 'You cross the black bridge thus' (p. 166). But this approach is not simple, however simply it is expressed. 'The black bridge' implies a crossing that is also a mourning, a crossing into an underworld (different from but implicit in the 'underworlds' of the poem) that is also an intertextual and inter-linguistic movement. It is after this act of crossing that the poem presents its first citation from Celan: '*Ich bin allein, / Ich stell die Aschenblume ins Glas voll / reifer Schwärze*' (p. 166) ('I am alone, I put the ash flower in the glass full of ripe blackness'[2]). The siting of this citation is crucial to its comprehension in relation to the rest of 'Metro'. The crossing of the 'black bridge' asserts a movement into negation, into the solitude of 'ripe blackness' that Celan's poem invokes. This solitude is the solitude of writing, the poem's recognition of its own failed, ethically refused reconstruction of the past it represents, and thus of the absence of that past and of those who populate it. 'Metro' asserts in its citation of Celan the negation of its recuperative project, its abandonment into intertextual allusion and citation, and the recognition of poetry's failure as the ground of its survival. The siting of the citation echoes the content of Celan's lines, the 'placing' imitating the 'putting' of the flower in (its) place, 'in the glass full of ripe blackness'. Siting and citation thus double the process of placing in the poem, its insistent deictic location and relocation: '*Here*'s Ravensbruck [...] I bring you *here*' (p. 166). Within these sitings, a deixis of proximity – the proximity of horror and its ethical demand, and of unrepresentability and its aesthetic demand – indicates the import of the crisis to which 'Metro' is responding. Celan's lines serve to displace Szirtes's poem into a proximity to its specific historical trauma that is unattainable in its use of 'my words for what she said'. This proximity is desired and resisted in 'Metro', and is figured in the counterpointing of the poem's critical refusal to 'enter' the history of the Holocaust with the invitation implicit in its insistent allusions to Celan.

'Desire' returns after this citation in a further self-exoneration, offered to 'replace what was voluptuous / In bodies full of warmth' (p. 166). The interplay here of '*Aschenblume*', 'bodies' and 'warmth' indicates the poem's 'undersong' at this point, which is the point at which the second allusion to Celan appears: '*das aschenes Haar* [sic] / Which is also mine' (p. 166), a phrase adapted from 'Todesfuge':

> Dein aschenes Haar Sulamith wir schaufeln ein Grab in den Lüften da liegt man nicht eng [...]
>
> ('Your ashen hair Shulamith we shovel a grave in the air there you won't lie too cramped'[3])

The '*aschenes Haar*', echoing the '*Aschenblume*', relocates the horror in human bodies. The narrator immediately claims this horror – 'Which is also mine' – an appropriation which is also an assertion of identity that inserts the lyric subject into the history narrated, identifying narrational consciousness with the poem itself: 'I wait outside your school / Of hard correction' (p. 166). It is here, in the act of 'mouthing words' in 'a feminine tongue', that the poem's narratorial identification with the mother is, momentarily, complete. Its problematic and awkward act of historical ventriloquism (section 6, presenting the narrative of the mother, is entitled '*In Her Voice*') enables an evasion of its own movement into history and allows, instead, a dramatization of historical trauma that is both an enactment and a refusal.

'Metro' subsequently turns to a conceptualization of tradition in relation to family. The succeeding stanzas, which invoke Nelly Toll and reiterate the lines from Celan, address history as 'this bequest' (p. 166) which, it suggests, posterity should assume. In its attention (via Nelly Toll's observations of daily minutiae) to metonymic historical details the poem addresses the 'superfluous' (p. 166), that is, moments and perceptions of a significance in excess of the moment of refusal. 'Superfluity' figures the burden of living on in a history beyond the end of history; if 'Metro' affords 'love' in its pun on Nelly Toll's home town of Lwow, that 'love' is an expression of hope, figured as paradisical belief ('God is Lwow' [p. 167]), an illumination afforded by, among other things, art: 'Paper of deep black / Is lightened by her painting' (p. 167). The 'lightening', here, is both illumination and the relief of the burden of historical refusal. What 'Metro' discloses in the 'undersongs' it maps is the possibility of an aesthetic redemption that exists in tension with aesthetic failure, a dialectic of refusal and acceptance that the poem's very existence expresses, and which it encodes, at the beginning of section 10, as 'beauty and terror' (p. 168).

The analysis of crisis in 'Metro' is thus enacted in a tension between refusal and desire. 'Hope', the possibility of moving beyond the moment of historical refusal, is found in 'love' and 'Lwow', the poem's word-play on the real and ethical geographies of the Holocaust. Nelly Toll and Paul Celan counterpoint Keats and Shakespeare in constructing a tradition and a range of intertextual references that establish 'Metro' within that tradition. The poem's constant returning to moments in history and then back to its own figurings and narrations of them implies a recursive movement that resists the arrest of refusal and enacts, again, a form of redemption in repetition. Ultimately 'Metro' negotiates crisis by asserting, as responses to the possibility of arrest, the continuity dependent upon different kinds of movement. Mobile memories and histories, rhetorical listings of displacement and accumulation, and intertextual displacements all effect the poem's response to the crisis of historical trauma as a double 'act of recovery' both of poetry itself and of the possibility (or necessity) of living on beyond the moment of crisis, an insistence that within poetry's failure resides its possibility.

Notes

1. George Szirtes, *Metro* (Szirtes, 1988); reprinted in Szirtes (2008, pp. 151–71, here p. 166). Subsequent quotations will be from this edition .
2. Translated by Vivian Smith (Smith, 2009).
3. Translated by John Felstiner (Celan, 2009).

References

Beake, Fred (1991) 'Generations of Recent Poetry', *Stand*, 32(2) (Spring 1991): 49–56.

Benjamin, Andrew (1997) 'Continuing with Poetry: Celan and Jabès', in *Present Hope: Philosophy, Architecture, Judaism* (London: Routledge).

Celan, Paul (1952) *Mohn und Gedächtnis* (Deutsche Verlags-Anstalt: Stuttgart).

—— (2009) 'Deathfugue', trans. John Felstiner, http://www.poetryfoundation.org/archive/poem.html?id=179933 (date accessed 18 August 2009).

Derrida, Jacques (2003) 'Shibboleth', in Neil Levi and Michael Rothberg (eds) *The Holocaust: Theoretical Writings* (Edinburgh: Edinburgh University Press).

Heaney, Seamus (1995) *The Redress of Poetry* (London: Faber and Faber).

Mahon, Derek (1993) *Selected Poems* (London: Penguin).

Murphy, Michael (2004) *Poetry in Exile: A Study of the Poetry of W.H. Auden, Joseph Brodsky and George Szirtes* (London: Greenwich Exchange Press).

O'Brien, Sean (1988) 'Big Questions', *Poetry Review*, 78(3) (Autumn).

Rowland, Antony (2005) *Holocaust Poetry: Awkward Poetics in the Work of Sylvia Plath, Geoffrey Hill, Tony Harrison and Ted Hughes* (Manchester: Manchester University Press).

Smith, Vivian (2009) 'Poems after Paul Celan', Poetry International Web, http://australia.poetryinternationalweb.org/piw_cms/cms/cms_module/index.php?obj_id=851 (date accessed 18 August 2009).

Szirtes, George (1988) *Metro* (Oxford: Oxford University Press).

—— (2004) *Reel* (Tarset: Bloodaxe Books).

—— (2008) *New & Collected Poems* (Tarset: Bloodaxe Books).

Toll, Nelly (2003) *Behind the Secret Window* (New York: Puffin Books).

2

Persona, Trauma and Survival in Louise Glück's Postmodern, Mythic, Twenty-First-Century 'October'

Mary Kate Azcuy

The six-part poem 'October' (2002)[1] – from Louise Glück's (2006) collection *Averno* – begins in autumn, the inception of the dying season. The poem's speaker traverses between the hybrid persona of Glück and the mythic goddesses Persephone and Demeter and the voices of the individual women. These women exist in a liminal landscape after the violence and destruction of the twenty-first-century's reality of terrorism and war. In the poem's central argument, Glück questions – via an aporetic dialogue[2] – whether or not to continue existence as the existential-humanist writer,[3] pondering the consequences of living or dying in the postmodern-classical[4] wasteland, either a place to end in the apocalypse or a place to recreate 'everything that was taken away –' (Glück, 2006, p. 7).[5] She uses mythology, persona,[6] prosopopeia, and silence to explore past and present trauma in the postmodern void. This void is such as Jean Baudrillard observed and prophesied – a place where America has 'come to the end' (Baudrillard, 1988, p. 98), and where Glück questions her role in recreating the myth and representing the historical. She tells us, 'This is the present, an allegory of waste' (p. 11).

The allegorical 'October' references an implied story of immense suffering that cannot be remembered, forgotten, or fully represented within history. As Jean-François Lyotard (1990, p. 3) warns, 'The Forgotten is not to be remembered for what it has been and what it is because it has not been anything and is nothing, but must be remembered as something that never ceased to be forgotten.' In 'October', notably a post-9/11 poem, the event is unnamed, the horror too catastrophic, the poem too small a measure for immeasurable horror. Instead of writing about 9/11 directly in the narrative, Glück relates the after effects of cataclysmic trauma. In the world of secrecy, where the unspeakable exists, the story is fragmented like the poetic line, and 'the story of the traumatic event surfaces not as a verbal narrative but as a symptom' (Herman, 1992, p. 1).

In *Averno* and 'October' the subject's story implies both mythical and historical incidents. Firstly, the mythic involves the unspeakable horror of Persephone's death and thus Demeter's loss of her child. Glück's *Averno* reflects the *Homeric* 'Hymn to Demeter', where Demeter's young daughter, Korê, plays in a summertime field – at Averno, the Romans' mythic Avernus,[7] the opening to the underworld – when her uncle, Hades, kidnaps her, takes her to the underworld, rapes and kills her, making her his death-bride, Persephone. Demeter's sorrow and anger lead to the death of all earthly life. Eventually Zeus, Korê's father, intervenes and instigates Hades' release of Persephone to her mother, Demeter. Before returning, Persephone eats three pomegranate seeds; consequently, she must return to the underworld for a season (here winter), when her mother is retraumatized and again causes all earthly life to cease.

Demeter and Persephone suffer an endless cycle of repeated traumas, and the women's stories represent a condition that might be interpreted in terms of post-traumatic stress disorder (PTSD), according to the definition given by the renowned trauma scholar and literary theorist, Cathy Caruth:

> [In PTSD] there is a response [...] to an overwhelming event or events, which takes the form of repeated [...] thoughts or behaviors stemming from the event, along with numbing that may have begun during or after the experience, and possibly also increased arousal to [...] stimuli recalling the event
>
> (Caruth, 1995, p. 1)

These mythic figures join Glück and find world events and current retraumatizing stimuli in the postmodern, twenty-first-century's October. In the myth, this is the month when Demeter anticipates her daughter's departure while Persephone anticipates death and return to the underworld. The women's initial sorrow is marked in autumnal death. The ancient, mythic event transforms into an endless cycle of PTSD, as these women find themselves still suffering at the cusp of the new millennium, at the edge of Hell, Averno, retraumatized by their own circumstances.

The second incident implied in the subject's story is historical: October 2001 denotes the date when American forces invaded Afghanistan and when workers were continuing to look in the rubble at Ground Zero in New York City for the dead after 9/11 in a place that represents 'pure absence' (DiPrete, 2006, p. 2). This place – the pit of death – serves as the stage for these traumatized women, who 'carry an impossible history within them, [as] they become themselves the symptom of a history' (Caruth, 1995, p. 5). Glück uses ancient myths to reflect suffering and catastrophic loss in an event never seen before; thus, she relates these traumas in ancient, epic, mythic and Aeneidian terms.

In her poetry, Glück intertextualizes, responds to and integrates many ancient myths by poets – including Virgil, Hesiod, Homer and Ovid – and *Averno* implies such a mimetic structure. Glück joins her voice to the mythic suffering of Demeter and Persephone and moves between the ages and the women's stories. Daniel Morris – in *The Poetry of Louise Glück: A Thematic Introduction* – discusses Glück's use of myth:

> Glück compels many readers to become fascinated with the mythic personae she has created, and destroyed, by connecting her biography to classical and biblical sources via her commentary. She does so, however, with extreme diffidence, as a hovering figure, a 'voice without a body', as she says in 'Circe's Grief'.
>
> (Morris, 2006, p. 45)

In 'October' the persona states her disassociation from a body – 'you can't touch my body now' (p. 7) – and draws forward the voice that looms in the poem. This spectral body serves as a Greek daimon/spirit in the liminal space between life and death. Plato, in the *Symposium*, uses Diotima to describe the daimon:

> a great spirit (daimon), and like all spirits he is intermediate between the divine and the mortal [...] between gods and men [...] he is the mediator who spans the chasm which divides them, and therefore in him all is bound together, and through him the arts of the prophet [...] all prophecy and incantation, find their way.
>
> (Plato, 2008, p. 31)

The daimon/persona of Glück/Persephone/Demeter connects these women in a conversation with the world yet provides spectral disassociation – a safety net – a space for Glück to mediate personal traumas via another character, another body, a place between existence and non-existence. In developing what he termed *hauntology*, Jacques Derrida provided a means of approaching this companion spirit, advising interaction with the daimon:

> to live by learning how not to make conversation with the ghost but [learn] how to talk with him, with her, [learn] how to let them speak or how to give them back speech, even if it is in oneself, in the other,

> in the other in oneself: they are always *there*, specters, even if they do not exist, even if they are no longer, even if they are not yet.
>
> (Derrida, 1994, p. 176)

Glück discusses – in her essay 'Education of the Poet' – such a Derridean hauntology and reciprocity as 'liberat[ing] a human voice; [that] you release into the world again [as] a companion spirit' (Glück, 1994, p. 128). This spirit lives in Glück via Demeter and Persephone as a mimetic structure (Cahn, 1984, p. 33). Using their stories of survival after crisis, Glück tries to understand life after loss, as the companion spirit inside the writer finds freedom. In an interview with Flavio S. Campos, Glück confirmed the link between this spectral-poetic being in her work and herself, 'a spirit disguised in a human body' (Campos, 2006).

As the daimon, Glück's persona traverses the chasm as the intermediary through time and place in a liminal *inbetweenness*, a place Cathy Caruth terms a 'traumatic void' (Caruth, 1995, p. 7). For Glück that void is Averno – here attributed to Virgil's *Aeneid* – the mythical space that is the opening to the underworld where all of the women suffer. Virgil describes 'the foul-smelling gorge of Avernus' (Virgil, 2006, 6.237) that is 'shielded well by a dusky lake and shadowed grove. / Over it no bird on earth could make its way unscathed, / such poisonous vapors steamed up from its dark throat / to cloud the arching sky' (ibid., 6.277–80). In *Madness Unchained: A Reading of Virgil's Aeneid,* Lee Fratantuono locates a space between Averno and Persephone's Aeneidian underworld (Book VI) – 'a place where Virgil's audience [finds] more time to ponder questions he has raised in his narrative. He will provide answers now, among the dead. Virgil's classroom is hell and his teachers are ghosts' (Fratantuono, 2007, p. 158).

In this death space, the women face Virgil's charge from the *Aeneid* (6.743) – that 'Each one of us suffers our family ghosts' (cited in Fratantuono, 2007, p. 188). The women question their ghosts, their pasts, their difficult lives, and remember the parts their family members have played in their suffering. The traumatized women are the spectral ghosts of their own lives, numb as a result of PTSD; the women exist in a 'blankness – the space of unconsciousness' (Caruth, 1995, p. 8). The women interpret this blankness, this traumatic void, as equivalent to death. They connect death and their difficult lives: 'death cannot harm me / more than you have harmed me, / my beloved life' (p. 10). Each woman now questions the architect of her destruction.

Continuing a mimesis of Virgil, Glück uses Averno – 'the realm of shadows' (Virgil, 2006, 6.447) and Persephone's underworld – as a backdrop, in order to pose questions and search the dead world for answers via an aporetic dialogue. Persephone questions her family ghosts and what her family has done, the harm inflicted on her life. Her father condoned her abduction and death; her uncle raped and murdered her and keeps her imprisoned in the underworld. The adult Persephone is a living shade, the victim of incest and parricide and, although she is queen of the dead, she is powerless to reclaim or control her life of her own free will. For her 'survival itself [is] a crisis' (Caruth, 1995, p. 21). Even her beloved mother insists that Persephone suffer an eternal death and rebirth cycle. In her adult act of self-preservation and rebellion, she turns from the commanding voices of father, husband and mother that demand, '*Come to me,* said the world' (p. 9). Her reply is: 'Very simple. But there was no voice there' (ibid.) Persephone answers the commands of trauma by finding silence.

Similarly, Demeter questions familial betrayal, as she suffers the continuous loss of her child due to her husband/brother Zeus who condoned the abduction and betrothal of Persephone, ignored the women's cries for help, and allows the situation to continue in perpetuity. Demeter proclaims that 'the earth is bitter' (p. 15). She is so angry that she ignores the reciprocal pleas of the gods and humans to return life – '*Come to me,* said the world' (p. 9) – and in her depression loses confidence. Assigned the role of goddess of agriculture (law and order), Demeter now finds herself 'not competent to restore it [life]' (p. 13). Thus Demeter, too, responds in silence.

Now the silenced, destroyed life force becomes the obsessed mother who waits by the entrance to Averno, listening for her child: 'I can't hear your voice' (p. 5). The mother acts as a *matrona,* who watches over the space of death for her child, a place where she suffers horrific loss until her daughter returns – in rebirth – each spring. Caruth associates such an obsession with child-loss as a 'negative relation [that] becomes more radical [and is used] for the forgetting or displacing of this trauma [the child's death]' (Caruth, 2009, p. 34).

Demeter waits by the space of Averno, the path to Persephone's dominion and death space, a place Aeneas describes as 'shadowed paths, / consuming the space between, and approach[ing] the doors' (Virgil, 2006, 6.735–6). In 'October' (p. 13) this space between is described:

> The bland
>
> misery of the world
> bound us on either side, an alley
>
> lined with trees; we are

companions here, not speaking
each with his own thoughts;

behind the trees, iron
gates of the private houses,
the shuttered rooms

Demeter's separation from her job, life and motherhood, is symbolized by the gates to Persephone's underworld. Each separates mother from vocation and daughter from life. Mother and daughter are 'not speaking', trapped in sorrow behind the iron gates, imposed boundaries, separated from the potential and positive life space on earth. Persephone and Demeter are assigned to these imprisoning, gated spaces, as they suffer eternally repeated traumas, connoted by 'deserted, abandoned' rooms that are equated with death and depression. The 'alley / lined with trees' blocks mother from daughter and creates a barrier to the integration of the traumatic event, which is depicted in the splintering of self displayed via the rooms and the multi-voiced persona.

The third person in the persona is a representation of the author, Glück. She, too, suffered from many traumas, including mother loss and her own subsequent anorexia. She could not connect to her mother, who suffered her own trauma, the death of an earlier child. Daniel Morris agrees that Glück's traumas warrant examination: 'Trauma theory illuminates Glück's writings about the hard facts of mortal life and the conflicted experiences of family life' (Morris, 2006, p. 134). Glück uses the Demeter and Persephone story as a vehicle in order to retell her suffering that is 'buried in the unconscious' and too difficult to address directly (Alexander, 2003, pp. 6–7). Glück relates to Persephone, who finds her mother compliant as an accomplice in her suffering. Daniel Morris relates Margaret Ann Gordon's insight that 'Persephone [...] and the anorexic teenager [Glück] all return from the edge of personal destruction, even if their new identities are marred by traumatic memory' (Morris, 2006, p. 101). Glück, too, uses silence. As a child she knew her mother found 'speech was the [...] consoling human sound'; Louise's 'response was silence' (Glück, 1994, p. 5). Later, silence turned into a place of contemplation and power for Glück: 'I have had to get through extended silences. By silences I mean periods [...] during which I have written nothing' (ibid., p. 16).

Glück uses the stalled, silent women – in contemplation – and warns the instigators of trauma: 'you can't touch my body now' (p. 7). In trauma, all of the women disassociate from their bodies. Glück disassociated from her body because of the trauma of mother-loss and subsequent anorexia. Persephone disassociates from her body because she suffered rape and murder and is a living shade. Demeter disassociates from her body/earth because of the death of her child and subsequent obsession and depression. These three women sit, in silence, on the edge of oblivion, and try to survive.

The women wait at the closed space of abduction – at Averno – the scarred earth and place of wounding trauma. The word *trauma* comes from the Greek word *titrosko* – which means wound, bodily injury. The wounded women question: 'wasn't my body / rescued, wasn't it safe // didn't the scar form, invisible / above the injury' (p. 5). A parallel can be drawn between this image of the scarred, injured earth and PTSD, with each new injury or scar equalling the repetition of traumatic memory. The disassociated persona hovers as a spectral voice that no longer wants to be connected to earthly suffering or the possibility of being re-traumatized. The scarred body is protected by disassociation, numb from PTSD, and can no longer feel: '[My body] has changed once, it has hardened, / don't ask it to respond again' (p. 7).

The persona looks to past injuries, adjusts, and uses the voice of spectral disassociation in a metamorphic transformation; her body hardens, and she isolates herself within her mind. The image of the hardened body connotes a statue, the past goddess, the female power immortalized in stone, and the spectral dead – all of whom understand return and retraumatization and must disassociate in order to survive: 'My body has grown cold like the stripped fields; / now there is only my mind, cautious and wary, / with the sense it is being tested' (p. 7). The aforementioned 'cold body' represents the traumatized, disassociated women, as well as the dead from the historical event, whereas 'the stripped fields' (p. 7) are the obliterated spaces, Ground Zero and Averno, conjoined via the unifying mask and persona.

Glück uses disassociation and the hybrid story of the persona to circumvent a direct addressing of personal and communal trauma resulting from 9/11 at Ground Zero. In *Testimony: Crisis of Witnessing in Literature, Psychoanalysis, and History*, Shoshana Felman and Doris Laub find such action 'designates not simply a metaphorically substitutive event, but an event that is historically impossible: an event without referent' (Felman and Laub, 1992, p. 102). Glück uses the fictive Persephone myth and Averno in such a substitution and as a *prosopopoeia* (from the Greek *prosopon* meaning death mask). In literature the *prosopon* is used to give voice to the voiceless, the dead and particular places: Persephone at Averno and the murdered of 9/11 at Ground Zero (Wofford, 1992,

p. 179). In *Institutio Oratoria* (1.xii.31), Quintilian states that 'With the help of this form of language, it is permitted to bring the gods down from the skies, and to evoke (or bring forth) the dead. Cities, even, and peoples, receive the gift of voice' (cited in Wofford, 1992, p. 179). Glück's poem joins persona/daimon and prosopopoeia, and together these relate as 'tropes used here – of the landscape echoing and so taking on a voice, of personification [...] they tell the story of the land speaking the language of violence' (ibid., p. 194).

In 'October' Glück observes the world and remembers violence in late summer, relating the rape and death of Korê to the destruction of 11 September 2001:

> Summer after summer has ended,
> balm after violence:
> it does me no good
> to be good now;
> violence has changed me.
>
> . . . . . .
>
> A day like a day in summer.
> Exceptionally still [...]
> [...] Night like a night in summer
> ...
> Once more, the sun rises as it rose in summer;
> bounty, balm after violence.
>
> (p. 7)

The return of summer – one year after 9/11 and an eternity of returns for the mythic Persephone – shows the repetition of life in endless cycles, the seasons. With this, the women wait by the precipice, look to history, and find that life's survival appears to be an eternal continuation of epic violence, horror, death and war.

The aforementioned intertextual elements join the women to the cultural contexts of communal suffering via the mythic event as well as the historical incident associative of 9/11 (Graham, 2000, 41–3).[8] In 'October' the first person 'I' returns and remembers being the child, Korê in the field, then Glück, as a child in New York City, joining those lost in the pit, all defenceless:

> I was young here. Riding
> the subway with my small book
> as though to defend myself against

this same world:

you are not alone,
the poem said,
in the dark tunnel.
(p. 14)

Glück hesitates to author the story, yet as she remembers the past, the artifact, the book, she brings life back via the story. Pierre Janet has determined that 'memory is an action: essentially, it is the action of telling a story' (Janet, 1984, 2, p. 272). This use of memory in re-membering the splintered, traumatized women involves the women and their stories. The unification of these stories relates to the hybrid, one-voiced persona as well as the connection to the communal. This unification is tantamount to a movement toward integration, wholeness and recovery. Daniel Morris comments that Glück casts 'the lives of her speakers as damaged texts that require commentary if they are to become legible [and] that occurs at the end of a traumatic episode' (Morris, 2006, p. 101). After contemplating such episodes, the women are united in, and joined by, each other; 'you are not alone'. They establish a community 'in the dark tunnel' (ibid.) of the aftermath and look to the initiating stressor, 9/11.

The main, underlying story needing voice in 'October' is 9/11, the referent traumatizing episode. Deborah M. Horvitz observes the way in which female American authors 'recreate the event [of trauma and] assume responsibility for "witnessing" and testifying to traumatic events that are pervasively cultural and, at the same time, experienced and interpreted as personal' (Horvitz, 2000, p. 1). Glück uses the 'I' to draw these multiple (communal, personal, mythic) traumatic stories forward into the current space, the postmodern void. The void is a place of absence and obliteration, causing the 'wind's cries, whistling over the bare ground' (p. 5). It constitutes a type of nothingness envisioned by Michel Foucault in the following terms: 'Death's annihilation is no longer anything because it was already everything [...] the nothingness of [...] it is experienced from within as the continuous and constant form of existence' (Foucault, 1988, p. 16).

Glück questions where to continue in a Beckettian wasteland – in nothingness, in silence – from the place of suffering:

in anticipation of silence.
The ear gets used to them.
The eye gets used to disappearances.
(p. 11)

> ...
> A wind has come and gone, taking apart the mind;
> it has left in its wake a strange lucidity.
>
> How privileged you are, to be still passionately
> clinging to what you love;
> the forfeit of hope has not destroyed you.
>
> (p. 12)

In destruction the *matrona* clings to hope and the annual return of her beloved child; the child, too, hopes for return, and the poet clings to what she knows, poetry, yet she sees the destroyed world, the world the women destroy as inverted creators, goddesses of death, creating only 'pure silence'. In a traumatized dislocation and inversion, the women listen for silence.

Glück, the author, tries to find the message, the sound, from the muse, a divinity, or self. She questions a Hesiodic theological and prophetic moment where the Muses 'breathed a voice into me, / and power to sing the story of things / of the future, and things past' (Hesiod, 1991a, 2.33–5). Glück knows that history repeats itself, so she ponders how to arrest the present and not move forward: 'Tell me this is the future, / I won't believe you. / Tell me I'm living, / I won't believe you' (p. 8). This is the world Catherine Gallagher and Stephen Greenblatt, in *Practicing New Historicism*, find a 'Nightmarish counter-history, in which everything is present [...] Everything is in shreds [...]' (Gallagher and Greenblatt, 2001, p. 72). Glück sits as judge and jury for the world lost in the violence of the twentieth and twenty-first centuries, a new Iron Age. Here, in a Foucauldian collapse of order, humans have created chaos – world wars, atomic annihilation, genocide, the Holocaust, terrorism, 9/11 and the subsequent wars – where 'The songs have changed; the unspeakable / has entered them' (p. 11). As the poet who recants the power of the story, Glück suffers in a way not that different from Hesiod before her: 'And I wish that I were not any part / of the fifth generation / [...] For here now is the age of iron' (Hesiod, 1991b, pp. 169, 170, 173).

Glück, Persephone and Demeter all suffer as creators in a double bind. For Persephone, her regal power only exists in her death, as she has the power to recreate life as the gift of rebirth to the honourable dead. In order to have her dead daughter, Persephone, returned to her, Demeter – the keeper of earthly life – must kill life to unleash her power, forcing the male gods to respond to her demands: 'mythology of the past is used here to convey psychological truths of the present, describing a society in which chaos is symbolically represented in the deadly mother [...] the destruction equals an existential act of defiance' (McDonald, 1990, p. 65). Reflecting Demeter's existential act, Glück is confined by the restrictions of a double bind: in writing the story she releases trauma, yet in the telling she continues the story's existence; therefore, the existential-writer gives the story life. The question becomes how to arrest horror and continue as a writer/creator?

In 'Education of the Poet', Glück discusses this bind for the writer, relative to bearing witness:

> Even for the writer whose creative work arises out of the act of bearing witness – even for such a writer, a subject, a focus must present itself, or be found. The artist who bears witness begins with a judgment, though it is moral, not aesthetic [...]. When the aim of the work is spiritual [...]. A metaphor for such work is the *oracle*, which needed to be fed questions. In practical terms, this means that the writer who means to outlive the useful rages and despairs must somehow learn to endure the desert.
>
> (Glück, 1994, pp. 15–16; emphasis added)

The 'desert' in question here is equivalent to the deserted space at Averno, the postmodern void, at the advent of the twenty-first century – the American desert that Baudrillard related to as the America already annihilated (Baudrillard, 1988, p. 98). Glück connects the oracular metaphor to her silence as the existential-author-creator: 'You hear this voice? This is my mind's voice; / [...] don't ask it to respond again' (p. 7).

This oracular, meditative position relates to the Aeneidian Sibyl, as 'the prophetess fell silent' (Virgil, 2006, 6.66) Apollo begins his puppetry of the Sibyl:

> But the Sibyl, still not broken in by Apollo, storms / with a wild fury through her cave [...]. / [...] exhausts her raving lips, overwhelming her untamed heart / [...] re-echoing [...]. Sibyl chants her riddling visions filled with dread [...] as she shrouds the truth in darkness'.
>
> (Ibid., 6.93, 94, 96, 118–20)

Glück, the poet, searches the desert for answers via her aporetic dialogue; she does not submit to puppetry or the mimicry of words created by the ancient systems (patriarchal systems) that continue horror in the twenty-first century.

As the prophetic poet, Glück challenges the idea of a presiding prime mover, the absent voice, sees the future, and denies it. She searches the desert, the landscape, and finds, ironically, the silence she has orchestrated in her anti-creation, her refusal to acknowledge fictive systems that subjugate women and cause destruction:

> I can't hear your voice
> ....
> I no longer care
> what sound it makes
>
> when was I silenced, when did it first seem
> pointless to describe that sound
>
> what it sounds like can't change what it is.
> (p. 5)

Glück searches the abyss for understanding – for words, songs, poetry, a voice, life itself – and finds only silence and death. She has no answers, only internalized questions, her mind's voice. This is an existential-nihilistic moment for Glück where she identifies her own power and the writer's voice. She is the sage who must continue the story, the existential creator waiting to move beyond human violence.

If the story looks back or moves forward she risks re-injury; whereas, in silence, the possibility of her own sane, existential power stalling the horror of history seems ideal, silence ending her culpability seems feasible. This disruption cannot, however, erase history. Umberto Eco explains the postmodern silent-response, in the 'Postscript' to *The Name of the Rose*:

> The past conditions us, harries us, blackmails us. [...] The postmodern reply to the modern consists of recognizing that the past, since it cannot really be destroyed, because its destruction leads to silence, must be revisited [...].
>
> (Eco, 1984, p. 530)

Therefore, silence is not the correction needed to save the new century or to continue to save Glück. Glück knows salvation from trauma and her protection exist in poetry. In order to move suffering into form, for her own sense of understanding, she must find the voice, sound.

As noted earlier, Glück has, oftentimes, used silence as a mechanism of control that later translated into a space of contemplation before the creation of poetry. In an interview with the *Harvard Advocate*'s Brian Phillips she explained the space of silence in relation to her writing process:

> My compositional process almost always begins in a kind of despondency, or hopelessness, or desolation, usually born of a conviction that I will never write again [...] long hiatuses of silence and periods of despondency, like in the desert, that have come to seem to me the norm of my aesthetic life [...] which isn't to say those passages are not brutal. So that each of my books really begins with a prayer, you know: Appear to me again. Let me be suffused with the wish to, and ability to, make meaning out of language.
>
> (Phillips, 1999)

In 'October', silence moves Glück toward dialectic and dialogue. She slowly allows sounds to return in an invocation, ironically, with words she mistrusts: 'the word itself / false, a device to refute / perception – At the intersection, // ornamental lights of the season' (p. 13). These words come slowly, as a distant sound, a memory of the past, and an act of restoration: 'I was young here' (p. 14). The sounds will return to the world in a prayer for self and community: *'you are not alone'* (ibid.) She must learn to address this declaration as her own potential and power in her re-unification and not as a threat to stay within the limits of patriarchal control. Rather than as a threatening voice of male domination, she must approach it as her own empowered voice in recreation. This voice joins individual and persona to the communal lament that will allow for trauma to move into catharsis in order for the women to return to creating.

The voice, the sound, the solution is the story, the lyric poem that acts as a communal lament for the dead, a Kaddish, a mourner's prayer, where the poet or sage recreates the world from the voice of ancient suffering. These songs relate the death dirges where 'Greek women [...] voice their grief for the dead in [...] [poetic laments] orally composed songs' (Blok, 2001, p. 104). In 'October' Glück understands the purpose of the songs: 'The songs have changed, but really they are still quite beautiful. / They have been concentrated in a smaller space, the space of the mind. / They are dark, now, with desolation and anguish' (p. 11).

In this solitude Glück delicately returns to the lyric, music and poetry. The lament is ancient, a song of ages of death and suffering where 'the notes recur. They hover oddly' (p. 11). Glück has warned that in the creation of the poem, she is haunted by notes that hover: 'To perceive it at all is to be haunted by it; some sound, some tone becomes a torment – the poem embodying that sound seems to exist somewhere already finished' (Glück, 1994, p. 16). In section four of 'October', the language in which to express this lament is still forming; she calls forth the song, the majesty of sorrow that must embrace the personal and the communal, *Maestoso, doloroso* (p. 12). Yet an orchestration does not appear on the scene, as a funerary world still exists.

Glück recalls that with the arrival of music comes the season of death, which is reflective of the fourth of Virgil's *Georgics*, where autumn relates the Orphic dirge. In the process of reformation and return, Glück finds frailty and understands the Orphic curse: 'The light has changed; / middle C is tuned darker now. / And the songs of morning sound over-rehearsed. // This is the light of autumn, not the light of spring. / The light of autumn: *you will not be spared*' (p. 11). The songs are filled – as is life – with 'desolation and anguish' (ibid.) that occurs and recurs in 'the light of autumn' (ibid.) and not in the spring of rebirth, reincarnation, 'not the light that says / *I am reborn*' (ibid.) The women must come to terms with the reality of life, which is death. Here, Glück – like Virgil – finds that 'winter joins late autumn (autumn in its first chill) as an evocation of death' (Fratantuono, 2007, p. 175). Glück allows sound and song to return, in order to mourn the dead, yet she remains silent: 'I am / at work, though I am silent' (p. 13).

For Glück, this silence constitutes a place to contemplate and reconcile the women's roles. She is the creator of the poem and her own view of reality, and she can reflect on the past in art; Persephone is queen of the dead in the underworld, who restores life to those she deems worthy, and visits her mother on earth; Demeter is the earth goddess, the regulator of seasons and law who restores life after death, and she is also a mother. The women's roles remain the same, yet their perceptions shift from a place of absence to one of empowerment. They have decided on life after trauma, healed, and now create instead of destroy. Glück hesitates to spell this out because in accepting, addressing, and recreating the story, she gives power to false hope:

> as though it were the artist's
> duty to create
> hope, but out of what? what?
>
> the word itself
> false, a device to refute
> perception [...]
>
> (p. 13)

Glück finds her responsibility as the creator unbearable.

In defence of such acts of writing and creation, Hélène Cixous claims in 'The Laugh of the Medusa' that *écriture feminine* embraces a political voice, a place of resistance where a woman 'must put herself into the text – as into the world and into history – by her own movement' (Cixous, 2001, p. 2039). Cixous implies that such 'writing is precisely the very possibility of change' (ibid., p. 2043). Similarly, Kelly Oliver relates that Kristeva connects this writing – as a unification of social, cultural and female – with a shift in power from the displaced to the included:

> [Otherwise] the individual cannot have meaningful experiences, but only traumatic ones, because meaningful experience requires some assimilation into the social order. Kristeva defines trauma as what is unrepresentable as a result of the inability to assimilate the meaning of the traumatic experience into the social.
>
> (Oliver and Edwin, 2002, p. 57)

For Glück, using language becomes the act of *résistance*: the attempt at unification of female and male, communal and personal, trauma and recovery. Glück traverses the millennia as Virgil and Aeneas, Demeter and Persephone, the poet and the survivor, in order to relate the aftermath and impact of tragedy. She uses persona to unify ancient suffering, depicted in the Demeter and Persephone myth, as well as her own struggles, in order to reflect trauma in a post-apocalyptic, twenty-first-century space that encompasses not only Ground Zero of her native New York, but also the ancient Averno. The way towards resolution of chaos and horror in the post-traumatic void lies in allowing the story to be told, the ancient story, the current story, the literal and the metaphoric, as words quietly return to the destroyed world as a lament for the dead. Glück, the procreator, calls forth existence in the lyrical incantation: *Maestoso, doloroso* (p. 12).

Notes

1. Former United States Poet Laureate, current Yale Professor of Creative Writing, and native New Yorker Louise Glück's six-part poem 'October' first appeared in *The New Yorker* magazine (28 October 2002). The poem was later published as a chapbook (2004), and it is the first poem in her collection *Averno* (2006). Glück first uses the Persephone persona – which is central to 'October' – in the 'Pomegranate' in 1975.
2. Plato's *Theaetetus* poses aporetic questions; see Derrida (1993, p. 78) and Plato (2006, p. 33). Also, Plutarch's *Aporia* embodies powerlessness.

3. See Sartre (2001, p. 45).
4. See Jencks (1973, p. 385).
5. All subsequent quotations are from 'October' (Glück, 2006) and are given in the text.
6. See Dodd (1992, p. 155). Dodd uses the term 'classical persona'.
7. Avernus (Lago d'Averno) is a lake in southern Italy. In religion and mythology, the Romans considered it an opening to the underworld. In Virgil's *Aeneid*, it is where Aeneas enters the cave to the underworld.
8. In *Intertexuality: A New Critical Idiom* (2000) Allen Graham discusses such an intertextual recognition and connection relative to that envisioned by Julia Kristeva – in 'Word, Dialogue and Novel' (1980, p. 65) – where she sees poetic language 'as an *intersection of textual surfaces* rather than a point (a fixed meaning), as a dialogue among several writings: that of the writer, the addressee (or the character), and the contemporary or earlier cultural context' (Graham, 2000, p. 38). Graham continues that Kristeva is in conversation with Bakhtin's dialogism where 'The dialogic word or utterance is double-voiced, heteroglot, and possesses a meaning (A) at the same moment that it possesses an alternative meaning or meanings (not-A)' (ibid., 43).

References

Alexander, Jeffery C. (2003) *The Meaning of Social Life: A Cultural Sociology* (Oxford: Oxford University Press).

Baudrillard, Jean (1988) *America*, trans. C. Turner (London: Verso).

Blok, J.H. (2001) 'Women's Speech in Classical Athens', in A. Lardinois and L. McClure (eds) *Virtual Voices: Making Silence Speak: Women's Voices in Greek Literature and Society* (Princeton, NJ: Princeton University Press).

Cahn, Michael (1984) 'Subersive Mimesis: T.W. Adorno and the Modern Impasse of Critique', in M. Spariosu (ed.) *Mimesis in Contemporary Theory* (Philadelphia, Pennsylvania: John Benjamins).

Campos, Flavio S. (2006) 'Pulitzer Poet Reads at Hillel', *The Harvard Crimson*, 6 April 2006, http://www.thecrimson.com/article.aspx?ref=51251 (date accessed 1 May 2008).

Caruth, Cathy (1995) 'Introduction', in *Trauma: Explorations of Memory* (Baltimore: Johns Hopkins University Press).

—— (2009) *Empirical Truths and Critical Fictions: Locke, Wordsworth, Kant, Freud* (Baltimore: Johns Hopkins University Press).

Cixous, Hélène (2001) 'The Laugh of the Medusa', in V.B. Leitch et al. (eds) *The Norton Anthology of Theory and Criticism* (New York: Norton).

Derrida, Jacques (1993) *Aporias*, trans. Thomas Dutoit (Palo Alto, CA: Stanford University Press).

—— (1994) *Specters of Marx: The State of the Debt, the Work of Mourning and the New International*, trans. Peggy Kawuf (New York: Routledge).

DiPrete, Laura (2006) 'Foreign Bodies', in *Trauma, Corporeality, and Textuality in Contemporary American Culture* (New York, London: Routledge).

Dodd, Elizabeth Caroline (1992) *The Veiled Mirror and the Woman Poet: H.D., Louise Bogan, Elizabeth Bishop, and Louise Glück* (Columbia, Missouri: University of Missouri Press).

Eco, Umberto (1984) 'Postscript', in *The Name of the Rose*, trans. W. Weaver (New York: Harcourt).
Felman, Shoshana and Doris Laub (1992) *Testimony: Crisis of Witnessing in Literature, Psychoanalysis, and History* (New York: Routledge).
Foucault, Michel (1988) *Madness and Civilization: A History of Insanity in the Age of Reason*, trans. Richard Howard (New York: Vintage).
Fratantuono, Lee (2007) *Madness Unchained: A Reading of Virgil's Aeneid* (Lanham, MD: Lexington Books).
Gallagher, Catherine and Stephen Greenblatt (2000) *Practicing New Historicism* (Chicago: University of Chicago Press).
Glück, Louise (1994) *Proofs and Theories: Essays of Poetry* (Hopewell: Ecco Press).
—— (2006) *Averno* (New York: Farrar, Straus and Giroux).
Graham, Allen (2000) *Intertexuality* (London: Routledge).
Hesiod (1991a) *Theogony*, trans. Richard Lattimore (Ann Arbor, MI: University of Michigan Press).
—— (1991b) *The Works and Days*, trans. Richard Lattimore (Ann Arbor, MI: University of Michigan Press).
Herman, Judith (1992) *Trauma and Recovery* (New York: Basic Books, Perseus).
Horvitz, Deborah M. (2000) *Literary Trauma: Sadism, Memory, and Sexual Violence in American Women's Fiction* (Albany: SUNY Press).
Janet, Pierre (1984) *Les medications psychologiques*, 3 vols (Paris: Société Pierre Janet).
Jencks, Charles L. (1973) *Modern Movements in Architecture* (New York: Anchor Press).
Kristeva, Julia (1980) 'Word, Dialogue and Novel', trans. Alice Jardine, Thomas Gora and Léon Roudiez, in L. Roudiez (ed.) *Desire in Language: A Semiotic Approach to Literature and Art* (New York: Columbia University Press; London: Basil Blackwell).
Lyotard, Jean-François (1990) *Heidegger and the 'Jews'* (Minneapolis, MN: University of Minnesota Press).
McDonald, Marianne (1990) 'Suzuki's "Clytemnestra": Social Crisis and a Son's Nightmare', in *Views of Clytemnestra, Ancient and Modern. Studies in Comparative Literature*, vol. 9 (Lewiston, NY and Queenston, Ontario: Edwin Mellen Press).
Morris, Daniel (2006) *The Poetry of Louise Glück: A Thematic Introduction* (Columbia, Missouri: University of Missouri Press).
Oliver, Kelly and Steven Edwin (2002) *Between the Psyche and the Social: Psychoanalytic Social Theory* (Lanham, MD: Rowman and Littlefield).
Phillips, Brian (1999) 'A Conversation with Louise Glück', *Harvard Advocate*, Summer 1999, http://www.hcs.harvard.edu/~advocate/ (date accessed 1 May 2008).
Plato (2006) *Plato's Meno*, intro. and trans. Dominic Scott (Cambridge: Cambridge University Press).
—— (2008) *Symposium*, trans. Benjamin Jowett, http://classics.mit.edu/Plato/symposium.html (date accessed 1 May 2008).
Sartre, Jean Paul (2001) 'Existential Humanism', in Stephen Priest (ed.) *Jean-Paul Sartre: Basic Writings* (New York: Routledge).
Virgil (2006) *Aeneid*, trans. Robert Fagles (New York: Penguin).
Wofford, Susan L. (1992) *The Choice of Achilles* (Palo Alto, CA: Stanford University Press).

3

Hern: The Catastrophe of Lyric in John Burnside

Scott Brewster

The lyric poem emerges *in* crisis; the lyric poem emerges *as* crisis. Prevailing critical assumptions over the last two centuries have tended to privilege certain features of lyric, such as its timelessness, emotional sincerity and self-sufficiency. Paul Celan, however, imagines a different kind of lyric passion, where the future-oriented poem yearns for, or is destined to, some unforeseen addressee:

> A poem, being an instance of language, hence essentially dialogue, may be a letter in a bottle thrown out to sea with the – surely not always strong – hope that it may somehow wash up somewhere, perhaps on a shoreline of the heart. In this way, too, poems are *en route*: they are headed toward.
>
> Toward what? Toward something open, inhabitable, an approachable you, perhaps, an approachable reality.
>
> (Celan, 1986, pp. 34–5)

We might therefore argue that it is the sense of suddenness, surprise and uncertain encounter occasioned by the poetic experience that marks out modern lyric. The lyric utterance longs for an intimacy that is self-sustaining, yet it seeks from the outset to find its way to another's heart. On a distant shoreline, the poem's appeal may become readable and reproducible, and it may find habitation; but both the journey and the arrival are matters of chance and danger, impossible to calculate in advance. The poetic experience envisaged by Celan is characterized by what Derek Attridge has termed the 'sense of strangeness, mystery, or unfathomability [...] involved in every encounter with the literary' (Attridge, 2004, p. 77). The other that emerges in the work of literature need not be disturbing or startling, since the other 'is a version of the familiar, strangely lit, refracted, self-distanced' (ibid., p. 76). In Celan's fable, the 'approachable you' to whom the poem is headed will cease to be other, at least momentarily, as the imagined encounter takes place. There can be no direct apprehension between these singular entities, only remote sensing: yet the event of their encounter would open both to contingency, the possibility of transformation and contamination. In its very emergence, the lyric stands at a critical crossing-point, poised between security and threat, spontaneity and reiteration, immediacy and posterity.

Jacques Derrida identifies precisely such a fate for the poem in his essay 'Che cos'è la poesia?' ('What is poetry?'). Derrida likens the poem to *le hérisson*, or the hedgehog, a creature able to turn in on itself for protection but in that act exposing itself to the risk of obliteration. Whilst the poem can retreat self-defensively, turning 'its pointed signs toward the outside', it is also obliged to scuttle precariously across the thoroughfares of language, where it exposes itself to chance, letting itself be 'torn to pieces by what bears down upon it' (Derrida, 1991, p. 235). This double movement, involving both withdrawal and an awkward engagement with the outside, characterizes that which Derrida terms the 'poematic' (ibid., p. 233). The poem is a 'learning-by-heart'; on the one hand, it yearns to retain 'an absolutely unique form' (ibid., p. 229), to name 'pure interiority, independent spontaneity' (ibid., p. 231), yet it also makes appeal to the laws of mnemotechnics, 'to the automobile that surprises your passion and bears down on you as if from an outside' (ibid., p. 231). Thus, in the movement of the poematic, the poem opens itself up to ceaseless repetition through the operation of memory and necessarily consigns the uniqueness of its address to the established codes of language, yet it simultaneously emerges from its defensive shell as a startling, singular event. The poematic marks both a retreat into 'pure' self-containment, and a countervailing exposure to distress and contamination; in its encounter with the other, the poem opens itself up to danger, but also to the possibility of the unprecedented. The poem must be understood as an event, something that happens *here* and *now*, at a moment of crisis: 'Just this contamination, and this crossroads, this accident here. This turn, the turning round of *this* catastrophe' (ibid., p. 235).

As Timothy Clark points out, Derrida's *hérisson* acknowledges Friedrich Schlegel's invocation of the hedgehog in one of his *Athenaeum Fragments* (1798). Schlegel characterizes the fragment, in relation to the dream of an absolute, transcendent poetic, as 'entirely isolated from the surrounding world and [...] complete in itself like a hedgehog' (Clark, 1997, p. 261). Schlegel conceives of the hedgehog-poem as perfectly self-enclosed, a fragment that encapsulates the whole. Its universality thus transcends its self-enclosure and its particularity, and this opening-out has epitomized dominant theories of the modern lyric. Yet, for Derrida, the poematic cannot merely retreat into pure self-containment and self-communion: it is, rather, an experience of interruption, wounding and remoteness. In its learning-by-heart, the poem issues a passionate call in the face of darkness and silence, appealing to the anonymous 'you' who stumbles upon it, and upon whom it stumbles, risking disaster. The poem is headed toward the other, 'obliged to address itself to someone, singularly to you but as if to the being lost in anonymity, between city and nature, an imparted secret, at once public and private, *absolutely* one and the other [...]' (Derrida, 1991, p. 223).

In 'Che cos'è', the identity of this vocative 'you' remains elusive. It is not reducible to a writer or reader, nor to a sender or a receiver in the conventional model of poetic communication, and there is no clear distinction between the poem directed towards another, and the poem addressed only to itself. Rather, as both Derrida and Paul Celan propose, the poetic constitutes 'an event in language considered as a matter of desire and beseeching' (Clark, 1997, p. 260). This appeal constitutes an interruption of language, but in the very same instance the poem entrusts itself to readability, contamination and effacement (ibid., p. 277). In its double movement away from and towards such vulnerability, the poetic experience at once evades and confronts the crisis of exposure. The poem is a gift, but its arrival or acceptance threatens its annihilation: in the 'emblematic story' of the poem, it says 'destroy me [...] do what must be done so that the provenance of the mark remains from now on unlocatable or unrecognizable' (Derrida, 1991, p. 227). The poem's appeal is both injunction and confrontational challenge: to risk, even invite, destruction as it enters language is also paradoxically a homecoming. The poem invites the disfigurement or obliteration of dissemination, but this threat of destruction is also a form of survival. In this way, the poem is always *en route*, and can never return safely.

Various forms of risk and danger shadow John Burnside's poetry, prose and journalism: the crisis of masculinity (Brewster, 2006) and the challenges of fatherhood; a growing ecological threat; the 'anticipation' and 'dread' that followed the destruction of the Twin Towers and its consequences for global security (Burnside, 2003); and the counterpointing of a fleeting sense of light and wonder with darkness and potential violence. Yet a central preoccupation of his poetry is the crisis associated with the lyric moment itself. The fleeting revelation of 'the beauty of the impossible' in Burnside's poetry is often shadowed by a sense of threat and vulnerability that inaugurates the lyric moment. Burnside remarks that 'the lyrical impulse begins at the point of self-forgetting'

(Burnside, 2000, p. 260), and both his poetry and prose have shown a deepening fascination with the ethics of retreat and (self-)obliteration, and how this might be reconciled with responsibilities to family, to others (human and non-human) and to the environment. The interplay of risk and responsibility, withdrawal and obligation in Burnside's work from the late 1980s can be read in relation to the poematic. Burnside's lyric longs for concealment, purity and withdrawal, but this retreat is compromised by the absolute obligation to open out, with all the attendant risks of adulteration. As such, Burnside's work stands as an exemplary instance of the way in which modern lyric courts the crisis of encounter and exposure, inviting whilst also attempting to relinquish, to forestall or anticipate, such an arrival or collision.

In Burnside's early collections, the call of the past – calling and responding to the past – is central. The learning-by-heart is a form of poetic remembering that displaces the distinctions between 'before' and 'after': memory is produced, rather than confirmed and, like the poetic, brings 'what it relates into being by force of its own event' (Clark, 1997, p. 275). The poem gathers echoes that appear familiar but those echoes are also obscured by the very act of calling. In this way, the poem resists the process of retrieval and thwarts access to its secrets. I have written elsewhere of the close association between the poematic and the poetic act of dating in Derrida's essay 'Shibboleth: for Paul Celan' (Brewster, 1998, pp. 57–9): like 'Che cos'è', it is concerned with the singularity of the poetic. Derrida conceives of the date as at once singular and unique, and also reiterable and open to the act of reinscription. In preserving the memory of a date, one breaks 'the silence of pure singularity', and to speak of the date is also to 'efface it, make it readable, audible, intelligible *beyond the pure singularity* of which it speaks' (Derrida, 1992, p. 382). Like the hedgehog, the date retreats defensively, harbouring its secrets, but it too is *en route*, relinquishing its singularity, risking the effacement that naming and commemoration will bring.

Two poems from Burnside's first collection, *The Hoop* (1988), perform these different aspects of poematic naming and commemoration: namely, the constitutive – and potentially destructive – nature of learning-by-heart, and the inability of poetic experience to lead back 'home'. Section four of the title poem delves and forages in a procedure reminiscent of the etymological explorations of Seamus Heaney's *North* (1975), and more particularly Geoffrey Hill's *Mercian Hymns* (1971):

> *Hern*. I only heard the word used once
> and yet it echoes down the tunneled years.
> I search in books for significance

books do not give, although the word appears
in lexicons: *Old English, secret place*
or corner, (rare, obscure).
Whenever darkness stains

my skin with history, or tracks my face
with freezing water, this word seems a key
and, breathless in the labyrinth, I trace

a thread between one wall that seems to me
extended randomly to hide the night,
and something else that almost fails to be

turning in upon itself and, knotted tight,
centres the hoop and makes a hern of light.
(Burnside, 1988, p. 40)

In Hill's poem, the Mercian hinterland holds out the promise of a linguistic treasure-trove to be explored, yet the text is haunted by the loss of such riches. The imagined landscape is littered with remains, residues and traces of vanished cultures, and the act of retrieval is amateur in the strictest sense, an act of passionate devotion. It is also a highly self-conscious, learned project, however; it invents, rather than restores, a cherished cultural archive. Mercia constitutes a *heimlich* space, a repository of hidden secrets and buried histories to be excavated and perused. Yet, however alluring, that past remains remote to the singular inhabitant, or author, of this uncanny 'kingdom'. The complex temporalities of this anamnesis – the addressee of this elliptical poem is invited to share in a privacy that cannot be shared, to identify with a strange child remembering a time that 'never was' – produces a 'fostered' strangeness that suggests the harbouring or nurturing of that which is not one's own (Hill, 1985, p. 110). In its custodianship of secret or lost knowledge, invocation of pagan and Christian spirituality, and instinct for withdrawal, *Mercian Hymns* clearly anticipates Burnside's poetics and, in one sense, proposes the type of intimate, inherited history that Burnside terms 'a paradise learned by heart' (Burnside, 1991, p. 54).

The rare or obscure word *hern* – heard only once by the 'I' but preserved in the memory as if learned by heart – is ineluctably bound up with questions of historicity and historical memory. Its definition – '*Old English, secret place / or corner, (rare, obscure)*' – is reminiscent of Freud's *unheimlich*, and *hern* acquires a similar uncanny force in the poem. To think history through its 'echoes down the tunneled years' is to stir poematic anamnesis. By recalling the obscurity of *hern*, the speaker is at once drawn into an intimate relation with history's secrets and estranged by that act of recovery. To search 'in books for a significance / books do not give' is to be frustrated by the enigmatic lure of a textuality that permits and refuses access to its secrets. As the text's organizing absence, *hern* exemplifies this strange call of memory. An archaic word for a secret place, *hern* is nonetheless the key to unlock the secrets of the text's 'labyrinth'. This mysterious word offers and withholds, reveals and conceals. Old and long familiar, it guides the speaker only to another hidden, self-enclosed space: the text's thread leads to an obscure corner, a place of light that fails to illuminate a passage through the text's tenebrous maze. As a cryptic, elusive password to the imparted secrets of language and the past, *hern* represents a repository of residues that are also dead-ends. A dark, concealed space, the centre of 'The Hoop' is a crypt, in Derrida's terms: the crypt is 'withdrawn, forever beyond the reach of any hermeneutic exhaustion [...] it does not conceal a single determinate secret, a semantic content waiting for the one who holds a key behind the door' (Derrida, 1992, pp. 404, 413). Although *hern* 'seems a key' when 'darkness stains / my skin with history', it encourages and thwarts the passion for meaning. The thread that the speaker traces locates only 'something else that almost fails to be / turned in upon itself'. This syntactical and semantic compression bears eloquent testimony to the self-contained, hedgehog-like nature of the poematic, and its soft-footed tread along these dark corridors. With *hern* at its heart, the poem is both receptive and spiky, tentatively opening out to interpretation and 'knotted tight' against intrusion, at once retreating from exposure and stepping uncertainly onto the routes of communication.

'Anamnesis' (Burnside, 1988, p. 62) reflects on the labyrinthine elusiveness of memory, and the catastrophic possibilities of poematic exposure. Memory is a smiling 'double agent' like 'Harry Lime', leading and being led 'through scalars and cosines' to 'the murmur of cuckoo clocks'. The spatial coordinates of trigonometry permit access to a fictive temporality. These cuckoo clocks measure inauthentic time: just as the cuckoo disturbs a nest, so stable or continuous time is unhoused, opened out to invasive otherness. The poem's allusion to *The Third Man* – someone ahead is splashing through a sewer into 'flashlights and guns', as Lime does at the climactic point of the film – grants an illusory, cinematic authenticity. In a conventional logic of retrieval, the obscurity of the labyrinth might be said to have been illuminated, but the flashlights and guns represent the threat of oblivion. The cinematic 'frame' evokes the laws of 'mnemotechnics' that for Derrida constitute, yet are resisted by, the poematic. The cinematics evoked here, an imbrication of spontaneity and reiteration, might be said to share certain constitutive features with the poematic: cinema stages a seamless present by projecting a sequence of frames, this technical repetition becoming the very image of a singular moment, a here and now. The intimate immediacy of the cinematic image projects an illusory presence and presentness that can be endlessly replayed. Harry Lime's demise can be relayed continuously, the shadowy character's destruction confirmed and yet deferred, still to happen in its first time. This fictive event can be grasped in its spontaneity only at the moment its uniqueness is open to repetition. Memory 'reels' here: the past is recorded for posterity, and yet the reproduction of a moving image each time produces a sense of shock, surprise, confusion. By using a cinematic trope, 'Anamnesis' suggests that remembering is less retrospective than projective, an act turned to the future as much as to the past. The reeling of memory possesses the power to efface the past yet render it readable, a poetics of survival that Derrida describes in 'Shibboleth: For Paul Celan' as 'the anniversary repetition of the unrepeatable' (Derrida, 1992, p. 371). This is an act of remembering without the hope of retrieval or restitution. Poematic remembering simultaneously invents, commemorates and risks obliterating the moment of encounter with the past, a moment that becomes the 'hurried figure' that is Harry Lime, forever resisting capture but endlessly drawn to the crisis of exposure.

A gradual change has taken place in Burnside's recent collections: the initial sense of withdrawal and homesickness, to which the poematic experience constitutes threat, has shifted to an acceptance of risk and exposure as constitutive of the poetic experience. The poems explicitly relinquish the sacral yet yearn for, and head toward, the transfiguring encounter. *Gift Songs* (2007) consistently explores the possibility of the 'nothing of the self / that is the here and now' (Burnside, 2007, p. 41). In the first section of 'Five Animals', an Arctic Fox, glimpsed by 'luck' as the speaker pulls off the road for a break, shows no surprise at this human intrusion. The animal is accustomed to

> the logic of the wilderness that says
> where nothing seems to happen
> all the time
> what happens is the chance
> that something might.
>
> (Ibid., p. 36)

While the fox steers clear of any collision, its remote environment resembles Celan's shoreline: inhabitable, approachable, and prepared for the accidental and unprecedented encounter.

This lonely, but open, road takes us to Burnside's most recent collection, *The Hunt in the Forest* (2009) which, like its predecessor, is concerned with what the poem gathers in, and how it simultaneously opens itself out to the unforeseen experience. 'Annunciation', the fourth section of 'In Memoriam', recalls 'stories they used to tell / for the soon-to-be-dead' that capture 'the perfect lull / between lost and found', a moment 'suspended, like a missed Annunciation' (Burnside, 2009, p. 9). This perhaps apocryphal sense of suspension is connected with a more 'personal' moment when 'you turned to the window, lightened with expectation, / and something was there, after all' (ibid.) The anticipated 'something' is *en route*, in the same instance seeking habitation from and constituting the 'you' who crosses its path:

> and out on the road
>
> a grey wind in from the sea to gather you home:
> no sign of the angel, no word, no Annunciation,
> only the cool of it, finding your lips and fingers
> and burrowing in, for the sweetness that darkens the
> bone.
>
> (Ibid., p. 10)

It is the lowly *hérisson*, a creature, that is 'angelic, perhaps'; no angel appears in Burnside's poem. The hedgehog-poem enters language as a breath, a movement, a barely discernible force, yet this uncertain entrance is also a decisive turn, a moment of catastrophe. The very opening to the call of the other which inaugurates the poem also means that it will become a matter of reiteration through the 'lips and fingers' it finds, hence inviting oblivion. This annunciation constitutes the experience of the poematic: an impending collision, a moment of crisis, where the hedgehog-poem, and the force that threatens its destruction (the uncertain 'you', the automobile, dissemination), arrive together.

As 'Le Croisic' in *Gift Songs* concludes, 'what matters is not the event, but the light-framed hem / of the moment's annunciation' (Burnside, 2007, p. 74). The lyric poem is the annunciation of an event: it offers no transfiguring closure, no declaration or proclamation, but rather it risks annihilation in its invocation of the other. In its emergence, the poem lets down its defences and casts itself onto the busy thoroughfares of language. This bearing-across into language is, for Derrida, 'a traversal *outside* yourself, away from *home*, venturing towards the language of the other in view of an impossible or denied translation, necessary but desired like a death [...]' (Derrida, 1991, p. 225). This annunciation is wounding, not only because the poetic interrupts and makes its mark on language, but also because it exposes itself to effacement through the 'force of its reception' by its addressee (Clark, 1997, p. 277). As Clark points out, the poem and its recipient are mutually constituted in the space opened by this interruption (ibid., p. 276). The poem can be understood as an event that exceeds definition, that is not a recognition of 'anything it does not itself institute, singularly, and for the first time' (ibid., p. 263). Thought of in this way, the poem cannot answer the question of *what it is*. This is the lyric moment: out on the road, heading home, but also an intrusion, a 'burrowing in' from the outside that lays bare a dark, private refuge. As Celan remarks, the poem 'is lonely and *en route*' and it is placed at its inception '*in the mystery of encounter*' (Celan, 1986, p. 49: translation modified). The poem begins in this encounter, but this mystery is also its destination.

References

Attridge, Derek (2004) *The Singularity of Literature* (London: Routledge).

Brewster, Scott (1998) 'A Residual Poetry: Heaney, Mahon and Hedgehog History', *Irish University Review*, 28(1) (Spring / Summer): 56–67.

—— (2006) 'Beating, Retreating: Violence and Withdrawal in Iain Banks and John Burnside', in James McGonigal and Kirsten Stirling (eds) *Ethically Speaking: Voice and Values in Modern Scottish Writing* (Amsterdam: Rodopi).

Burnside, John (1988) *The Hoop* (Manchester: Carcanet Press).

—— (1991) *Common Knowledge* (London: Secker and Warburg).

—— (2000) 'Strong Words', in W.N. Herbert and Matthew Hollis (eds) *Strong Words: Modern Poets on Modern Poetry* (Newcastle: Bloodaxe).

—— (2003) 'Poet Sees the Plight', interview with Lesley McDowell, *Sunday Herald*, 19 January 2003.

—— (2007) *Gift Songs* (London: Jonathan Cape).

—— (2009) *The Hunt in the Forest* (London: Jonathan Cape).

Celan, Paul (1986) *The Meridian*, Speech on the Occasion of Receiving the Georg Büchner Prize, Darmstadt, 22 October 1960, in *Collected Prose*, trans. Rosemarie Waldrop (Manchester: Carcanet Press).

Clark, Timothy (1997) *The Theory of Inspiration: Composition as a Crisis of Subjectivity in Romantic and Post-Romantic Writing* (Manchester: Manchester University Press).

Derrida, Jacques (1991) 'Che cos'è la poesia?' ('What is Poetry?'), in *A Derrida Reader: Between the Blinds*, trans. and ed. Peggy Kamuf (Hemel Hempstead: Harvester).

—— (1992) 'Shibboleth: For Paul Celan', trans. Joshua Wilner, in Derek Attridge (ed.) *Acts of Literature* (London and New York: Routledge).

Hill, Geoffrey (1985) *Collected Poems* (Harmondsworth: Penguin).

Part II

A Special Case: Crisis and Poetry in Northern Ireland

4

'In a ghostly pool of blood / a crumpled phantom hugged the mud': Spectropoetic Presentations of Bloody Sunday and the Crisis of Northern Ireland

Ruben Moi

Hauntology, Derrida terms his philosophical investigation of *'responsibility,* beyond all living present, within that which disjoins the living present, before the ghost of those who are not yet born or who are already dead, be they victims of wars, political or other kinds of violence, nationalist, racist, colonialist, sexist or other kinds of exterminations, victims of oppressions of capitalist imperialism or any form of totalitarianism' (Derrida, 1994, p. xix). Such a responsibility entails a quest for unfound justice irreducible to laws and legal documents, requires 'respect for justice concerning those who *are not there*' (ibid., p. xix), and continuously unsettles an unknown future: 'This question *arrives,* if it arrives, it questions with regard to what will come in the future-to-come' (ibid., p. xix). Such justice, according to Derrida, assumes the qualities of the spectre; it defies the finality of life and death, but is dependent upon both dimensions. Justice based upon the life of the living present enters the problems of relativity, whereas any metaphysical underpinning of justice transports the concept beyond its empirical and ontological actuality. Justice is not immediate consensus – if that were ever a possibility – nor arbitrary legal decision, nor does it possess an ontological solidity of Kantian proportions.[1] Justice is 'neither substance, nor essence, nor existence, *is never present as such*' (ibid., p. xviii). As the spectre appears as the manifestation of the spirit, the spirit of justice disappears whenever the ghost shows itself. Justice appears as spectral possibilities: untimely, uncertain and unsettling moments of responsibility that haunt the living present with a commitment to the dead of the past and the living of the future. Spectral moments arrive again and again to raise the problems of justice for the dead and the undead. 'To learn to live finally' (ibid., p. xv), for the individual human being under the onerous obligation of responsibility, becomes a question of empathy and death: 'To live, by definition, is not something one learns. Not from one self, it is not learned from life, taught by life. Only from the other and by death' (ibid., p. xviii).

As is well known, Derrida's analysis of judicial axiomatics and human responsibility in *Spectres of Marx* constitutes a double examination of the spirits of Shakespeare's *Hamlet* and Marx's radical theories in response to Fukuyama's triumphalist celebration of free market economics in the crisis of communism (Fukuyama, 1992). In Derrida's hauntology, the spirits of responsibility, radical critique and emancipatory promise in Marx's a-religious and internationalist communism eclipse the spectres of historical materialism, class struggle and revolution.[2] Consequently, Derrida's deconstructive reading of responsibility, justice, victims of violence[3] and the spectral legacies of Marx and Shakespearian tragedy appears pertinent to any place divided against itself at a disjointed time that has caused the questions of responsibility and justice to be raised repeatedly in a catalogue of aesthetic representations. As such, Derrida's hauntology is of great relevance to the aesthetics and the hermeneutic discourses of the Northern Ireland crisis in general, and the events of Bloody Sunday in particular.[4]

The latter part of the introductory statement by Derrida – 'political or other kinds of violence, nationalist, racist, colonialist, sexist or other kinds of exterminations, victims of oppressions of capitalist imperialism or any form of totalitarianism' (Derrida, 1994, p. xix) – accumulates a list of principal dehumanizing evils that appear foreclosed and disproportionate if applied to any specific geopolitical location, a list that would be severely contested in Northern Ireland as anywhere else. Nevertheless, the damnatory diatribe delivers accusations of relevance to a range of different positions in the complex conflict of Northern Ireland, just as the former part – '*responsibility*, beyond all living present, within that which disjoins the living present, before the ghost of those who are not yet born or who are already dead' (ibid.) – probes concerns of human dignity anywhere. The responsibilities of the living and the dead in a violent society predicated upon multiple discourses of law have impinged upon the artists of the place. In the poetics of Northern Ireland during the last three decades of the previous millennium, the questioning of responsibility has not been one focus out of many, rather it has been by far the dominant one.[5]

It comes as no surprise that so many poets reacted with alacrity to the disaster of Bloody Sunday and the crisis of Northern Ireland. What really comes as a great surprise is that hardly any critical attention has focused exclusively on the poetic presentations of Bloody Sunday, arguably one of the most critical moments in the recent history of Northern Ireland.[6]

Literary hermeneutics and cultural debate tend to assign analyses of Bloody Sunday to the disciplines of history, social sciences and psychology, while, frequently and derivatively, they, nevertheless, draw upon these very sciences to buttress their arguments. Another obvious tendency consists of collapsing specific moments of crisis into the general rubric of 'Troubles'. A third reason for the omission is the avoidance of specific examples and case studies in principled polemics. In the polarized positions of many critical discourses in Northern Ireland, Bloody Sunday is just another incident in the long history of imperial injustice, or just another tragic event in an almost endless list of heinous atrocities. Only recently has this deficiency of cross-disciplinary discussion of Bloody Sunday been somewhat mended by two books that overlap with this chapter: Tom Herron and John Lynch's *After Bloody Sunday: Representation, Ethics, Justice*, published by Cork University Press in 2007 and Julieann Campbell and Tom Herron's collection of the poetry of Bloody Sunday, *Harrowing of the Heart*, published by Guildhall Press in Derry in 2008.[7] The latter includes the majority of texts that will be discussed below.

Bloody Sunday caused a decisive shift in the history of the Troubles. The killing of thirteen civil rights marchers (and one who died later from injuries) and the widespread injury, damage and fear caused by the British Parachute Regiment in the Bogside district of Derry on 30 January 1972 – 'a microcosm, a symbol of what Britain does in Ireland' (Herron and Lynch, 2007, p. 2)[8] – haunts not only Derry and Northern Ireland but also Ireland, England and the wider world. The massacre of civilians involved an unusually high degree of state involvement. The event precipitated violence on a grand scale by state army and paramilitary groups and concomitant intercommunal violence in Northern Ireland. Bloody Sunday caused the discontinuation of local government at Stormont and the introduction of Direct Rule from Westminster. The suspect and partial Widgery Report on the tragedy traumatized large parts of the population north and south of the border by basically exonerating the Army and blaming the victims. As this volume was being completed (July 2010), the most comprehensive judicial inquiry in British history, the Lord Saville Inquiry established by Prime Minister Tony Blair in January 1998, had just delivered a new report on the events of the tragic day, declaring the victims of the attack innocent.[9] If the irresponsible and much vilified Widgery Report manifests a spectre of justice that reveals the absence of any judicial spirit, the Saville tribunal presents another spectral possibility where the ghosts might be laid to rest and the spirit of intergenerational and transjudicial responsibility might arrive.[10] Naturally, the tragedy, the official report of traducement by state authority and the Saville Inquiry instigated counter-hegemonic documentation and commemoration by the local community, as well as alternative aesthetic apprehensions by a variety of artists.

In the crisis of Bloody Sunday and the conflict of Northern Ireland, the Field Day Project, with its peripatetic theatre performances, pamphlet series, radio programmes and wide-ranging cultural activities and intellectual debate, answers the Marxist call for action over interpretation and the Derridean responsibility of 'committing oneself in performative fashion' (Derrida, 1994, p. 50).[11] Such performative responsibility and commitment unfold in 'a more or less secret fashion, and thus more or less public, there where this frontier between the public and the private is constantly being displaced, remaining less assured than ever, as the limit that would permit one to identify the political' (ibid., p. 50). Indubitably, Brian Friel's *The Freedom of the City* (1973) and the series of plays it inaugurated stage questions of justice in the voice of the victims returned from the grave and inspect the borders between the private, the public and the political. Richard Norton-Taylor's documentary drama *Bloody Sunday: Scenes from the Saville Inquiry* (2005) appears as another spectral manifestation of the Bloody Sunday hauntology. This stage tribunal offers a 'staging for the end of history' (Derrida, 1994, p. 10), a performative interpellation in legal procedures which activates an emancipatory promise, as it presents a selection of twelve witness examinations from the Saville hearing to public evaluation, before the public report has been released from the remits of the law. Similarly, two films, Jimmy McGovern's *Sunday* (2002) and Paul Greengrass's *Bloody Sunday* (2002) intervene in the private, the public and the political determinations of justice and conduct performative hermeneutics, 'an interpretation that transforms the very thing it interprets' (Derrida, 1994, p. 51). Their interpretation of Bloody Sunday is bound to bear upon the investigation into the events of the day.

If McGovern and Greengrass's films ghost the unresolved present, Thomas Kinsella's *Butcher's Dozen: A Lesson for the Octave of Widgery* (first published by Peppercanister Press in 1972, the poem was reprinted in *Harrowing of the Heart*, 2008) has done so for almost four decades. Kinsella's poetic clamour constitutes a spectroscopic poem, which combines cultural activism with Derridean hauntology. Derrida's reminder of Marx's current importance retains the famous political proverb: 'The philosophers have only *interpreted* the world in various ways, the point, however, is to *change* it' (Derrida, 1994, p. 51). Kinsella's publication career combines poetic imagination with political action. In 1972, partly as a direct consequence of Bloody Sunday, he took charge of the means of his own literary production for the more immediate involvement of his poetry with the social conditions of his own time by founding his own press, Peppercanister.[12] *Butcher's Dozen* was on the streets within a week of the Widgery Report.

In respect of Fukuyama's maniacal exorcism, Derrida asserts: 'As at the time of the *Manifesto*, a European alliance is formed which is haunted by what it excludes, combats or represses' (ibid., p. 61). In like manner, the judico-military corroboration of the Widgery Report proved a prototypical site of ghost production in its own omissions, agendas and denials of responsibility and justice.[13] In line with so many other deeply offended Derry civilians, Kinsella pinpoints the Widgery Report as the cradle of political corruption of the law. In his own commentary he declares:

> *Butcher's Dozen* was not written in response to the shooting of the thirteen dead in Derry. There are too many dead, on all sides, and it is no use pitting them hideously against one another. The poem was written in response to the Report of the Widgery tribunal. In Lord Widgery's cold putting aside of the truth, the *n*th in a historic series of expedient falsehoods – with Injustice literally wigged out as Justice – it was evident to me that we were suddenly very close to the operations of the evil real causes.
>
> (Kinsella, 1992, p. 21)

Kinsella's embittered, phantasmagorical and spectropoetic vision enlivens the fates of the victims and the misrulings of Widgery. In the haunted verses the persona conducts his own interrogation of justice with the ghosts of the thirteen dead:

> There in a ghostly pool of blood
> A crumpled phantom hugged the mud:
> 'Once there lived a hooligan.
> A pig came up, and away he ran.
> Here lies one in blood and bones,
> Who lost his life for throwing stones'[14]

Evidently, this ghost, as the other twelve, haunts the place, in almost Shakespearian fashion, as a revenant of rectification. The terrestrial embrace and the demotic tongue ('pig' for armoured vehicle) suggest inseparable local affinities, just as the marching tetrameter and the bombastic couplets ring with militant polemics. With great plangency, the elaborate assonance of o's (and u's) intones the lines with dolorous sonority, echoing the typical *ochone* of Irish mourning. A narrative hiatus between the two last couplets renders the murderous act unutterable and opens a space for infernal imagination. This supernatural séance places the question of justice in a relational position between the dead and the living and, as later lines reveal, beyond the inadequacies of 'rotten laws' (ibid., p. 28). With capital fury – 'I went with Anger at my feet' (ibid., p. 24) – the visitor to the ghastly site reports the condemnation of the Army's actions and the subsequent Widgery whitewash in the bitter ironies and vile accusations of the ghostly voices: 'Careful bullets in the back' (ibid., p. 25), 'Judged, condemned and shamed in one' (ibid., p. 25), 'A most imperial success' (ibid., p. 27), 'the news is Out. The troops were kind. / Impartial justice has to find / We'd be alive and well today / If we had let them have their way' (ibid., p. 26). Truth is immanent, justice transparent: 'Does it need recourse to law / to tell ten thousand what they saw?' (ibid., p. 26). Investigations and tribunals only obfuscate what is clear and evident, and incriminate the innocent. The stigma branded upon the victims by the Widgery Report prescribes the future generations of Colmcille's town with original sin: 'Good men every day inherit / Father's foulness with the spirit' (ibid., p. 30). The vital choir of communal condemnation enlists the persona, the observer who visits the ghostly site after the tragedy, into their punitive position of liminal limbo: 'I stood like a ghost' (ibid., p. 30). In its anger, unequivocality, accessible vocabulary and uneven prosody Kinsella's poem screams and rings with the voice and rhythms of anguished unsettlement. Clichés, stock allusions, and down-right doggerel ensure accessibility. In its ghosted demand for justice, Kinsella's poem is spectropoetic.

Kinsella's hauntological harangue makes no bones about truth, blame and consequences. Reprobative rhetoric aligns with communal sensibility without resistance. The revisitations of ghosts and phantomalization of identity stem from political evasion of responsibility and institutional misconstruction of justice, a report that engenders a miasma of spectral avouchment by deferring and displacing questions of responsibility and principles of human rights. However, this explicit act of monological patriotism posits a number of questions about artistic autonomy and communal commitment. The poem's unanimous refutation of the Widgery Report and its undifferentiated presentation of truth undoubtedly impugn the impartial idea of justice the poem seeks to address.

Partiality and fuzzy form also distort habitual ideas of poetic proprieties, whether these are aligned under the banners of modernist aesthetics from New Criticism to Adorno, or postmodernist tenets of indeterminacy, adlinguisiticity or contextuality. *Butcher's Dozen* does not present itself as a perfected artefact or formal experiment which separates the aesthetics from the ethics, or as a contemplative literary construction that strives to depart from local affinities in an embrace of international ecumenism. Neither does it adopt a meta-poetic stance in which a self-introverted and free-floating play on language bears no relation to the social situation from which it stems. In this perspective of hermeneutic paradigms, Kinsella's verses amount to an apparition of the emotional engagement, social situatedness, historical conditioning and political awareness that many dominant theories of literature combat, refuse or exclude. If New Criticism, as has been frequently disclosed,[15] continues conservative concepts and complies with the cultural values of the centre, and postmodernist theories dissolve distinct oppositions and complicate questions of identity, the form and function of Kinsella's poem resist appropriation by literary hegemonic templates and retain a confrontational position in a dialectic discourse.

Kinsella's convocation of assumedly exorcized imaginative spirits is a likely reason for the resulting critical censure and the poem's exclusion from anthologies.[16] Judged by the overruling affidavits of well-established literary models, the improprieties of *Butcher's Dozen* will be labelled propaganda rather than poetry, as Kinsella's deliberate and direct interference with the crisis opposes ideas of aesthetic autonomy and poetic decorum. Such judgement ignores, if it does not exclude, the Irish court of poetry which presides over Kinsella's act of defiance. Although his Dantean séance is ghosted by the fury and agitation of Shelley's 'England in 1819' and 'A Song. Men of England', its spectro-poetic remit reaches further than English Romanticism. Swift's sardonic satire sanctions the caustic invectives. Brian Merriman's *Midnight Court* suggests the primary spectral site in its phantasmagoric travesty of justice and parodic respiritualization of the *aisling*.[17] Arnold Bax's 'Dublin Ballad – 1916', which was banned by the English authorities for acrimonious accusations of imperial injustice, warrants demagogic defamation. At times when state authority and judicial institutions violate democratic responsibility, if not the law, poets and people seek to redress the balance by creative acts. Belligerent bathos and versified invectives in Kinsella's *Butcher's Dozen* reveal and respond to the stupefying exonerations and blatant communal stigmatization of the state-sponsored Widgery Report.[18]

Kinsella's unapproved spectropoetics presides over the collected poems in *Harrowing of the Heart*, of which many, arguably, pummel the reader with more pugilist polemics than poetic power. They are hauntological; they endeavour to articulate forms of heartfelt responsibility towards the dead of the past and the unborn of the future, who have so far been muted, marginalized, murdered by peremptory legalism. Most of the verses on Bloody Sunday testify to a personal sense of 'disjointed living' and miscarriages of justice. 'It's hard to build a future when you're haunted by the past', asseverates Declan McLaughlin's 'Running Uphill' (McLaughlin, 2008, p. 81), in plain diction, and the concluding lines declare the tangible absence of the dead among the living, and their mistrials, as the reasons for pain and suffering:

> For your justice never added up to the murder that we saw.
> And time don't make no difference
> To the people that still care.
> In thousands we march the streets
> Still knowing that you're there.
>
> It's like running uphill.
> It's like running uphill.
>
> (Ibid., p. 82)

The impingement of the dead upon the living, which preconfigures the life of the living, clamours with audible anguish and adopts suitable poetic forms. Of the people who repetitively 'retrace the steps of the dead', 'Their screams / Will not leave this place / While that offence remains', bewails, Hamlet-like, the communal voice of Paul Laughlin's 'Remembering Bloody Sunday' (Laughlin, 2008, p. 74). After a long litany of listless lamentations, 'I remember…', 'I remember…', 'I remember…', Sharon Meenan and Killian Mullan's poem unexpectedly concludes: 'And I wasn't even born' (Meenan and Mullan, 2008, p. 80). The final verse repeats the poem's title; thus, the speaker is confined by the list of indelible memories and a circular structure from which he or she cannot escape. Together with the conflation of two authors into a singular persona, the poem's formal configuration suggests an apprehensive power of spectres that places the individual in the grip of inescapable structures of the past. In their incarceration in memory and communal acts of resistance, these poems enact Derrida's statements that 'haunting belongs to the structure of every hegemony' and 'the dead can often be more powerful than the living' (Derrida, 1994, pp. 37, 48).

'One should never speak of the assassination of a man as a figure', Derrida (ibid., xv) argues against the obfuscation of murder by statistics, symbolism, rhetoric, martyrology, even deconstruction – the forces of numbers, logic, language, religion and well-established Derridean methodology that tend to delete or to align human singularity with a grand purpose: 'A man's life, as unique as his death, will always be more than a paradigm and something other than a symbol' (ibid., xv). Whether the victims of Bloody Sunday were murdered or not in terms of the letter of the law is part of the past and present Bloody Sunday dispute, but the lethal retribution of bullets and military machinery by professional soldiers for stones and slogans from civil rights activists tends to offend the spirit of justice; rendered laconically as 'A march for peace that ends in murder' in Martin Wray's 'The Fateful Day' (Wray, 2008, p. 87), and as 'the lethal ballistics of territory / sovereignty asserted by the injection of bullets' in the military jargon of the anonymous 'Bloody Sunday Revisited' (Anonymous, 2008, p. 72). In Thomas McCarthy's 'Counting the Dead on the Radio', a bewildered boy of a Republican family in Ireland exclaims: 'Mama, a whole regiment has been attacked / by a Catholic priest waving a blood-stained / handkerchief. That's what the radio says' (McCarthy, 2008, p. 56). This grim irony of inversion also records the horrifying spectralization of media themselves, how they assure and determine public discourse and opinion through a technology which is neither absent nor present, living nor dead, a mechanical configuration of individual, or in this case, collective fate.

Possibly, Derrida's caveat of never speaking of man as a figure can also be interpreted as an admonition to resist figuration, an appeal for direct and demotic expression to which many of the committed poets in *Harrowing of the Heart* respond avidly. 'British butchery – nothing new', states Kathleen Patton's 'Derry's Thirteen' (Patton, 2008, p. 17) and continues in the same condemnatory vein: 'For cunning, lies and propaganda / British troops are world renowned' (ibid., p. 18). In their invincible conviction of inhuman transgression of individual life, these curt and crude verses locate the quest for justice in a temporal scale and global perspective that surpass the letter of the law and the subjective moment of grievance: '*responsibility*, beyond all living present' (Derrida, 1994, p. xix). In the hauntology of Bloody Sunday poetry, several of the poets express in an ordinary idiom the visitations of judicial spectres. 'The real tribunals are the funerals' and 'The truth shot down will rise again' Scott MX Turner declaims in '1 Para' (Turner, 2008, pp. 101, 102). 'The Widgery mockery', 'there is no doubt / On England's proud history a crime added yet / How can we forgive them? How can we forget?'

asks the desperate voice at the end of Joe Mulheron's 'Bloody Sunday' (Mulheron, 2008, p. 35). An utterly resigned recrimination inverts the cliché of complaisant justice in Hugh Gallagher's 'Bloody Sunday': 'But Derry will never forget, nor forgive' (Gallagher, 2008, p. 54). In a technique of petrifaction in 'Let the Stones Speak', Emmylou Large sets up a speaking stone as the judicial correlative to reveal the imbalance of singular subjects of law and summary justice: 'Only a pawn in a battle between the law / And the innocent' (Large, 2008, p. 70). The deracinated voice parallels the ignoring of human specificity, and the incisive line-break cuts out the distance between accusatory institution and individual on trial.

'It is a proper characteristic of the spectre, if there is any, that no one can be sure if by returning it testifies to a living past or a living future', Derrida explains (Derrida, 1994, p. 99), and the prospect and process of the new Saville Inquiry place questions of justice in an uncertain temporal liminality. 'And to this day they have the nerve / To refuse us the justice we all deserve', Martin Wray's 'The Fateful Day' timely recounts (Wray, 2008, p. 88), a sturdy statement that contrasts with the more optimistic appeal of John Dunne's 'Tribute to Lord Fenner-Brockway': 'The wish of innocence – true, / Lord Saville – now – it's up to you' (Dunne, 2008, p. 86). In Gerry Dorrity's 'One Sunday', the annual commemoration of Bloody Sunday and the commencement of the Saville Inquiry cause the spectres of the past to stir again. A father recounts his story to his child, and this initiation juxtaposes generational shifts in mood and marks an undecided moment of past transgression or propitious possibility:

> We buried fourteen bodies, they buried the truth.
> But now there's this enquiry, if that is any use.
> I'll be interested to hear what they offer as an excuse.
>
> So on Monday I am going for a walk with my Daddy and
> his Dad.
> We'll walk beyond the Guildhall Square.
> I want to see what happens, I hope it turns out fair.
>
> (Dorrity, 2008, p. 99)

'One can never distinguish between the future-to-come and the coming back of a spectre' (Derrida, 1994, p. 38). If many of the Bloody Sunday poems proffer a direct and idiomatic counter-argumentation to the mandarin legalese of the Widgery Report, some of them also register in revocative circularity the hesitant moments of transition suggested by the Saville procedures.

The hauntology of Kinsella's *Butcher's Dozen* and most of the poems mentioned so far derive their horror and apprehension from the victims and irresponsibilities of an immediate time and a proximate place. Lexis and licence are authorized by communal commitment and Irish literary genres. Unappeasable spirits prevent Bloody Sunday from becoming a closed case. Proximal cause is legitimate in Derrida's philosophical excursion into the axiology of justice as mourning, 'in attempting to ontologize remains, to make them present, in the first place by *identifying* the bodily remains and by *localizing* the dead' (ibid., p. 9). But Derrida also highlights the '*international* character' and the '*geo-political*' (ibid., p. 38) legacy of Marx's communism and emphasizes the spectral qualities of responsibility. 'That which disjoins the living present' (ibid., p. xix) is not always already present to itself; rather it tends to 'exceed any presence as presence to itself' (ibid., xix). Responsibility and justice are entangled with temporal deferral and spatial distancing that distort simplistic self-identifications and decentre narcissistic necromancy. In this respect, Seamus Deane's 'After Derry, 30 January 1972' and Paul Muldoon's 'The Year of the Sloes, for Ishi' (1973) approach Bloody Sunday from the opposite end of the spectrum.

Where Kinsella's poem hugs the bloody mud of Derry streets and many poems register local specificities in topicality, idiom and time, Deane's cosmogony bears no trace of such affinities, apart from in its title. An offence against mankind affects the whole universe, from cosmic infinity to entomological survival in a post-human world.

> Only the insects
> Grovel for their life, their strange heads
> Twitching. No one kills them
> Anymore. This is the honeymoon
> of the cockroach, the small
> spiderless eternity of the fly.
> (Deane, 2008, pp. 32–3)

In Deane's grandiloquent apocalypse, not even signs of human spirit survive. Darwinian and destitute, Deane associates the murderous instinct of man, and by titular implication Bloody Sunday, with natural law.

Muldoon's commemorative elegy captures in original figuration and highly stylized stanzas a similar moment of civilization's extinction, but this narrative poem is haunted by human irresponsibility on a grand scale.

The dedicatee, Ishi, was the last surviving member of the Californian Yahi tribe, which had been discovered as late as 1910. Consequently, Ishi's fate represents the annihilation of a race by the human evils of conquest and colonialism. A cosmic scale and a circular calendric time mark Muldoon's commemorative elegy:

In the Moon
Of Frost in the Tepees,
There were two stars
That got free.
They yawned and stretched
To white hides,
One cutting a slit
In the wall of itself
And stepping out into the night.[19]

Two supernovae transform to skins in a descent from metaphysical and universal enlightenment to a corporeal embodiment and temporal condition that anticipate subsequent xenophobia and genocide. The lyrical phrase for a winter month eclipses the normal English vocabulary of the calendar and imbues the line with Amerindian sonority and inclement temperature. Furthermore, a remarkable self-celestial simile delineates a centripetal transition of the star back into a nocturnal dimension. Evident metaphors for the two Indian survivors, the lone stars are engulfed by tropes of light and darkness; they are extinguished at the dawn of colonial conquest:

In the Moon
Of the Leaves Falling,
[...]
Someone was asking for six troopers
Who had lain down
One after another
To drink a shrieking river.

In the Moon
Of the Trees Popping, two snails
Glittered over the dead Indian.
I realized that if his brothers
Could be persuaded to lie still,
One beside the other

Right across the Great Plains,
Then perhaps something of this original
Beauty would be retained.
(Ibid., 47)

The violent destruction of the Indian couple by colonial brutality which marks the annihilation of an entire population presents a case of human irresponsibility and legal injustice that still haunts the USA. But, as Muldoon informs us, the poem was written in response to Bloody Sunday.[20] This act of hauntology has little self-presence; it pits the 'attempting to ontologize the remains' and 'localizing the dead' (Derrida, 1994, p. 9) in the mourning of the dead in Derry against a geopolitical history, differentiation and disjuncture.

On the one hand, Muldoon's analogical approach to Bloody Sunday and the crisis of Northern Ireland supports Kinsella's dialectic confrontation and endorses the Republican view of the situation as a colonial crisis caused by British imperialism. In this respect, the poem represents the British as the archetypal violent aggressor and the Irish as the quintessential victim of jingoistic suprematism, a clear-cut presentation of the conflict that no doubt enflames the one party as much as it infuriates the other. Bloody Sunday and the guerrilla activity of outnumbered paramilitaries against the machinery and apparatus of a state army support such interpretation, but in this case its tone is subdued and subtle, not least in comparison to *Butcher's Dozen*. On the other hand, Muldoon's poem arises as a spectre to haunt the spirit of self-righteous schismogenesis inscribed in much of the combat poetics of the day. The displacement of colonial conflict to another time and a different continent resists the temporal immediacy, spatial proximity and simplistic self-identification that tended to confine the outlook at the time. Furthermore, the analogy that corroborates the standard story of expulsion of Irish people by British imperialism also extends this account of emigration history to questions of participation by Irish immigrants in the colonial conquest of America, an obvious impertinence to the prevailing moral alibi of early-1970s nationalism. These revocations of Amerindian persecution challenge the unchecked perpetuation of nationalist grievances almost thirty years before Liam Kennedy's revisionist acronym 'mope' – the most oppressed people ever – has become an acceptable term even in Republican strongholds.[21]

The Amerindian strategy of Muldoon's Bloody Sunday poem refracts the immediate with the infinite, the localized with the globalized, the self with the other. As an appropriate elegy of Bloody Sunday, the poem ambiguates the very conditions it commemorates. Muldoon's deconstructive poetics liberate in the insurrectionary imperative an internal critique of aspects that are potentially inimical to the emancipatory process. 'The Year of the Sloes, for Ishi' addresses questions of responsibility and justice in a hauntological manner in which the disjointed and disproportionate allow for new spectral instantiations.

Muldoon's spectralization of justice in Derry and refraction of a monologically committed communal stance in 'The Year of the Sloes, for Ishi' in 1973 anticipate the revisions Heaney conducts, at a later stage of his career, of his own prior complicity. While Heaney's ghost soliloquies in 'Station Island' (Heaney, 1984, pp. 61–97) revaluate much of his former affinities in the light of a Joycean liberation from the nets of nationality, family and religion, 'The Road to Derry' is part of the personal canon he revises.

> My heart besieged by anger, my mind a gap of danger,
> I walked among their old haunts, the home ground where they bled;
> And in the dirt lay justice like an acorn in the winter
> Till its oak would sprout in Derry where the thirteen men lay dead.
>
> (Heaney, 2008, p. 19)

'The Road to Derry' has never been included in any volume and was only published in the *Derry Journal* on the twenty-fifth commemoration of Bloody Sunday. 'I think it is in order to print this abbreviated version now, twenty-five years after the drive from Belfast to Derry on the day of the funerals' (ibid., pp. 141–2), he declares in the accompanying letter. Perhaps Heaney realized he added insult to injustice to the local community by his auspicious accolade in the end of the poem, but probably, he refrained from its direct involvement, an involvement which might have been even more direct in the early version which has since been edited. 'Casualty', his other poem on Bloody Sunday, confirms such suspicion. This poem annuls any easy access to the atrocity and presages the critical moment of re-invention in 'Station Island'. Heaney's triptych, one of the many elegies in *Field Work* (1979), asks critical questions of an IRA reprisal bombing in the aftermath of Bloody Sunday. Louis O'Neill, one of his friends, unnamed in the poem, was killed when he broke the IRA curfew and went drinking in a Protestant pub that was blown up. Bloody Sunday and sectarian strife inscribe this elegy in capital letters – 'PARAS THIRTEEN, the walls said, / BOGSIDE

NIL' (Heaney, 1979, p. 22) – still the poem mainly prolongs the life of the victim and inspects the indeterminable foundations of justice. One of the haunting features of the Derridean phantom is its liminality: 'One does not know if it is living or if it is dead' (Derrida, 1994, p. 6), exactly the limbo of uncertainty in the opening line: 'He would drink by himself' (Heaney, 1979, p. 21). The initial sentence places the subject of commemoration in a liminal position of temporality and mood, the habitual past includes hypothetical continuance: the dead one is very much present and alive to the speaker. Past life or present death, differences characterize their relations as much as communal identification: 'incomprehensible / to him, my other life' (ibid., p. 48). The survivor learns from the other and from death. 'To whom, finally, would an obligation of justice ever entail a commitment?' Derrida asks (Derrida, 1994, p. xx), and 'Casualty' meditates upon similar imputations: 'How culpable was he / that last night when he broke / our tribe's complicity?' (Heaney, 1979, p. 23). If the injustice of Bloody Sunday was buttressed by the law, alternative laws do not necessarily guarantee justice. Legislation of any kind needs to probe the responsibility under which it is enacted, beyond the relativity of national jurisprudence and communal imperatives. Heaney's poem constitutes a subpoena of the different ideological props of legislation in its questioning of the responsibility for the death of an individual. In its questioning of the military massacre of Bloody Sunday, the martial laws of the IRA, and individual responsibility, the poem searches inconclusively for a justice that hovers between metaphysical precedence and ontological difference: in the words of Derrida, 'at the internal border of the external border, it is a heterodidactics between life and death' (Derrida, 1994, p. xviii). In its posthumous communion with the living memory of companionship and in its scrutiny of state-sponsored massacre, auto-authorized acts of reprisal and the human rights of the individual being, 'Casualty' presents another spectral moment in the poetry of Bloody Sunday.

Derrida's poetic and philosophical hauntology of a responsibility to be learnt from death and the other and a type of justice beyond the law, intermittently apparent between the metaphysical speculation and ontological difference – 'the undeconstructibility of a certain idea of justice (dissociated here from law)' (ibid., 90) – hardly ever assumes moments of realization. However, gross violations of the spirit of justice – royal usurpation, elimination of Marxism, hegemonic exclusions, civil rights suppression, and a flawed legal system, as much as transgressions of law – regicide, massacre, murder – call the spectres to disturb indefinitely the foundations of law, the body politic, legal proceedings and individual conscience. In this respect, the plethora of spectropoetic manifestations in the literary representations of Bloody Sunday testifies to lack of responsibility and broken spirits of justice. While registering class differences and demands for reform at a specific historical juncture, these hauntological poetics conduct a radical critique of systematic injustice and retain an emancipatory promise of some redress for the dead and living subjects of British law in Northern Ireland. 'The pledge is given here and now, even before, perhaps, a decision confirms it. It thus responds without delay to the demand of justice' (ibid., 31). In Derry, Northern Ireland, and other places in this unjust world; already, now and again, poets, artists and ordinary civilians will take up the responsibility which haunts them and quest for poetic justice until, in the final words of Julieann Campbell's 'Reluctant Role Model', 'until our day comes' (Campbell, 2008, p. 123).

Notes

1. For two other essays by the same author which discuss the imperium of law, and its inextricable composition with literature, see Derrida (1992a, pp. 3–68 and 1992b, pp. 181–221).
2. If the questions of responsibility and justice in Derrida's hauntology offer an apposite angle onto the crisis of Bloody Sunday, the legacy of historical materialism, class struggle and revolution offers another (see McCann [1974] 2006).
3. *Spectres of Marx* (Derrida, 1994) is dedicated to Chris Hani, the leader of the South African Communist Party and a fierce opponent of Apartheid, who was assassinated on 10 April 1993, as an instance of naming the numerous victims of unjust history.
4. For other discussions of poetry and culture in Ireland and Northern Ireland that engage with the multifarious writing of the French intellectual, see for example Brewster (1998, pp. 56–67), Docherty (1997, pp. 147–55, 206–23), Graham (2001), Moi (2007a, pp. 172–89 and 2007b, pp. 217–29) and Wills (1993).
5. Frank Ormsby tends to capture accurately the entrapment of artists throughout the Troubles: 'It is arguable that *any* poem by a Northern Irish poet since 1968, on whatever subject, could be termed a Troubles poem, in that it may, consciously or unconsciously, reflect the context in which it was written' (1992, p. xviii). See also comments by a range of poets: Eavan Boland (1970, p. 12), Seamus Heaney (1980, p. 13), Michael Longley (1971, p. 9), Derek Mahon (2000, p. 154) and Paul Muldoon (1981, pp. 136–7). The Troubles also reigns as the main criteria of selection in Padraic Fiacc's anthology from 1974. For a selection of volumes in which the Troubles permeate the entire book, see John Montague (1972), Seamus Heaney (1975), Michael Longley (1979), Paul Muldoon (1983), and most collections by Ciaran Carson, particularly *The Irish for No* (1987) and *Belfast Confetti* (1989). Violence hermeneutics also predicate much of the critical discourse, see for example Edna Longley (1986 and 1994), Wills (1993), Donoghue (1986, pp. 182–97),

McDonald (1997, pp. 41–81) and Johnston (2003, pp. 113-133). For two recent books that examine the legacy of violence in drama and on a large scale, see Fitzpatrick (2010) and Farquharson and Farrell (2008).

6. Kirkland (1996) does not mention Bloody Sunday, neither does Deane (1985a), Edna Longley (1986 and 1994), McCormack (1986) or Paulin (1984). Even Deane's *Field Day Anthology* (1991), the ultimate manifestation of the ideology-driven culture project based in Derry, only contains intermittent references to Bloody Sunday.
7. Other recent books that bring new perspectives to bear on Bloody Sunday are Dawson (2007), Hayes and Campbell (2005), McCann (2006), Ó Dochartaigh (1997), O'Brien (2002), Pringle and Jacobson (2001) and Ziff (1998). Two informative websites are the Museum of Free Derry, http://www.museumoffreederry.org (accessed 13 October 2009) and the Bloody Sunday Trust, http://www.bloodysundaytrust.org (accessed 13 October 2009).
8. Bloody Sunday Initiative (1992), 'Programme of Events: Bloody Sunday 1972–1992': 1. Quoted in Herron and Lynch (2007, p. 2).
9. For recent evaluation of the Saville Inquiry, see Bew (2007, pp. 62–81). See also the official website: http://www.bloody-sunday-inquiry.org (accessed 6 July 2010).
10. The Saville Inquiry certainly annuls the Widgery Report, the only official truth until its publication. Had the ruling of Widgery been still valid, there would have been no reason for a new tribunal. The new report exonerated the victims of Bloody Sunday and found the British Army responsible, but it is not known whether any individual, officer or soldier, will be convicted.
11. In the preface to their first collection of pamphlet manifestos the directors say: 'Field Day could and should contribute to the solution of the present crisis by producing analysis of the established opinions, myths and stereotypes which had become both a symptom and a cause of the current situation' (Deane, 1985b, p. 7). The Field Day Project culminated in a comprehensive anthology edited by Deane in 1991. For critical evaluations of the project, see Graham (2001), Edna Longley (1994, pp. 22–44), Kirkland (1996, pp. 134–46), Pelletier (2006, pp. 66–78) and Richtarik (1994).
12. As a renewal of the pamphlet tradition, Peppercanister facilitated immediate publication and an alternative procedure to presses and periodicals. Peppercanister takes its name from St Stephen's Church in Dublin (locally known as the Peppercanister because of the steeple's visual resemblance to a peppershaker) and suggests, possibly, a new spiritual institution of dissent and unpalatable tracts.
13. Mullan (1997) and Walsh (2000) offer comprehensive correctives to the report. For the widespread reviling of the report, see Daly (2000, p. 211), Friel (1999, p. 57) and Deane (2000, p. 10).
14. All references to Kinsella's *Butcher's Dozen*, first published in 1968 and since in other pamphlets, are to the version included in the anthology by Campbell and Herron, *Harrowing of the Heart* (2008).
15. For a critical corrective of the implicit values of New Criticism in the context of Northern Ireland, see Kirkland (1996, pp. 53–85).
16. Although Kinsella is included in all of the following five anthologies, *Butcher's Dozen* is never selected: Fallon and Mahon (1990), Kennelly (1981), Kinsella (1986), Muldoon (1986) and Montague (1974). Poet and poem are

also omitted from Paulin's *The Faber Book of Political Verse* (1986). Despite intense reviewing at the time of its publication, the poem has faded from critical debate. Kinsella accounts in short hand for the congeries of political and stylistic disparagement in his republication of the poem for the twentieth commemoration (1992, pp. 21–2).

17. This typical Gaelic dream poem, which mainly evolved in the eighteenth century, laments the deplorable state of the Irish people after Cromwellian campaigns and Williamite coercion and envisages liberation and revival of fortune by the return of the Stuarts. For a selection of examples of this genre, see Kinsella and Ó Tuama (1981). Seamus Heaney reviews Kinsella and Ó Tuama's collection and discusses Merriman's *Midnight Court* in, respectively, 'The Poems of the Dispossessed Repossessed' (1988, pp. 30–6) and 'Orpheus in Ireland' (1995, pp. 38–62). See also Heaney's translation of Merriman's burlesque nightmare (and extracts from Ovid's *Metamorphoses*), *The Midnight Verdict* (2000). In Derek Mahon's 'Derry Morning', one of the few Bloody Sunday poems by established poets not collected in *Harrowing of the Heart*, the *spéirbhean*, the star woman of the *aisling*, awakens in the aftermath of an actual historical nightmare, which happens to be Bloody Sunday: 'An early crone, / muse of a fitful revolution / wasted by the fray, she sees her *aisling* falter in the breeze' (1999, p.108).
18. Prime Minister Heath reminded Widgery that 'we were in Northern Ireland fighting not only a military war but a propaganda war' (Mullan, 1997, p. 186).
19. References to 'The Year of the Sloes, for Ishi' point to Muldoon's original publication, since the version in *Harrowing of the Heart* has lost the final stanza.
20. See Kendall (1996, pp. 17, 41) and Wills (1998, p. 38).
21. See Kennedy (1996, p. 217).

References

Anonymous (2008) 'Bloody Sunday Revisited', in Julieann Campbell and Tom Herron (eds) *Harrowing of the Heart: The Poetry of Bloody Sunday*, p. 72.
Bew, Paul (2007) 'The Bloody Sunday Tribunal and the Role of the Historian', in Harriet Jones et al. (eds) *Contemporary History on Trial* (Manchester: Manchester University Press).
Boland, Eavan (1970) 'Creativity', *Irish Times*, 14 August, p. 12.
Brewster, Scott (1998) 'A Residual Poetry: Heaney, Mahon and Hedgehog History', *Irish University Review*, 28(1): 56–67.
Campbell, Julieann and Tom Herron (2008) *Harrowing of the Heart: The Poetry of Bloody Sunday* (Derry: Guildhall Press).
Carson, Ciaran (1987) *The Irish for No* (Oldcastle: Gallery Press).
—— (1989) *Belfast Confetti* (Oldcastle: Gallery Press).
Daly, Edward (2000) *Mister, Are You a Priest?* (Dublin: Four Courts Press).
Dawson, Graham (2007) *Making Peace with the Past? Memories, Traumas and the Irish Troubles* (Manchester: Manchester University Press).
Deane, Seamus (2000) 'Foreword', in Eamonn McCann, *Bloody Sunday in Derry* (Dingle: Brandon Press).

—— (1985a) *Celtic Revivals* (London: Faber and Faber).
—— (1985b) *Ireland's Field Day* (London: Hutchinson).
—— (1991) *Field Day Anthology of Irish Writing* (London: Faber and Faber).
—— (2008) 'After Derry, 30 January 1972', in Julieann Campbell and Tom Herron (eds) *Harrowing of the Heart: The Poetry of Bloody Sunday*, pp. 32–3.
Derrida, Jacques (1992a) 'Before the Law', in Derek Attridge (ed.) *Acts of Literature* (London: Routledge).
—— (1992b) 'Force of Law: "The Mystical Foundation of Authority"', in Drucilla Cornell et al. (eds) *Deconstruction and the Possibility of Justice* (London: Routledge).
—— (1994) *Spectres of Marx: The State of Debt, the Work of Mourning, and the New International* (New York: Routledge).
Docherty, Thomas (1997) 'The Sign of the Cross' and 'Ana-; or Postmodernism, Landscape, Seamus Heaney', in Michael Allen (ed.) *Seamus Heaney* (Basingstoke: Macmillan).
Donoghue, Denis (1986) 'The Literature of Trouble', in *We Irish* (New York: Alfred A. Knopf).
Dorrity, Gerry (2008) 'One Sunday', in Julieann Campbell and Tom Herron (eds) *Harrowing of the Heart: The Poetry of Bloody Sunday*, p. 90.
Dunne, John (2008) 'Tribute to Lord Fenner-Brockway', in Julieann Campbell and Tom Herron (eds) *Harrowing of the Heart: The Poetry of Bloody Sunday*, p. 86.
Farquharson, Danine and Sean Farrell (eds) (2008) *Shadows of the Gunmen: Violence and Culture in Modern Ireland* (Cork: Cork University Press).
Fiacc, Padraic (ed.) (1974) *The Wearing of the Black* (Belfast: Blackstaff Press).
Fallon, Peter and Derek Mahon (eds) (1990) *The Penguin Book of Contemporary Irish Poetry* (Harmondsworth: Penguin).
Fitzpatrick, Lisa (ed.) (2010) *Performing Violence in Contemporary Ireland* (Dublin: Carysfort Press).
Friel, Brian (1973) *The Freedom of the City* (London: Faber and Faber).
—— (1999) *Brian Friel: Essays, Diaries, Interviews 1964–1999* (London: Faber and Faber).
Fukuyama, Francis (1992) *The End of History and the Last Man* (Harmondsworth: Penguin).
Gallagher, Hugh (2008) 'Bloody Sunday', in Julieann Campbell and Tom Herron (eds) *Harrowing of the Heart: The Poetry of Bloody Sunday*, p. 54.
Graham, Colin (2001) *Deconstructing Ireland* (Edinburgh: Edinburgh University Press).
Hayes, Patrick and James Campbell (2005) *Bloody Sunday: Trauma, Pain and Politics* (London: Pluto Press).
Heaney, Seamus (1975) *North* (London: Faber and Faber).
—— (1979) *Field Work* (London: Faber and Faber).
—— (1980) *Preoccupations* (London: Faber and Faber).
—— (1984) *Station Island* (London: Faber and Faber).
—— (1988) 'The Poems of the Dispossessed Repossessed', in *The Government of the Tongue* (London: Faber and Faber).
—— (1995) 'Orpheus in Ireland', in *The Redress of Poetry* (London: Faber and Faber).
—— (2000) *The Midnight Verdict* (Oldcastle: Gallery Press).

—— (2008) 'The Road to Derry', in Julieann Campbell and Tom Herron (eds) *Harrowing of the Heart: The Poetry of Bloody Sunday*, p. 19.

Herron, Tom and John Lynch (2007) *After Bloody Sunday: Representation, Ethics, Justice* (Cork: Cork University Press).

Johnston, Dillon (2003) 'Violence in Seamus Heaney's Poetry', in Matthew Campbell (ed.) *Contemporary Irish Poetry* (Cambridge: Cambridge University Press).

Kendall, Tim (1996) *Paul Muldoon* (Bridgend: Poetry Wales).

Kennedy, Liam (1996) *Colonialism, Religion and Nationalism in Ireland* (Belfast: Queen's University Press).

Kennelly, Brendan (1981) *The Penguin Book of Irish Verse* (Harmondsworth: Penguin).

Kinsella, Thomas (1986) *The New Oxford Book of Irish Verse* (Oxford: Oxford University Press).

—— (1992) *Butcher's Dozen* (Dublin: Peppercanister Press).

Kinsella, Thomas and Seán Ó Tuama (eds) (1981) *An Duanaire 1600–1900: Poems of the Dispossessed* (Dublin: Dolmen Press).

Kirkland, Richard (1996) *Literature and Culture in Northern Ireland since 1969: Moments of Danger* (London: Longman).

Large, Emmylou (2008) 'Let the Stones Speak', in Julieann Campbell and Tom Herron (eds) *Harrowing of the Heart: The Poetry of Bloody Sunday*, p. 70.

Laughlin, Paul (2008) 'Remembering Bloody Sunday', in Julieann Campbell and Tom Herron (eds) *Harrowing of the Heart: The Poetry of Bloody Sunday*, p. 74.

Longley, Edna (1986) *Poetry in the Wars* (Newcastle upon Tyne: Bloodaxe).

—— (1994) *The Living Stream: Literature and Revisionism in Ireland* (Newcastle upon Tyne: Bloodaxe).

Longley, Michael (1979) *The Echo Gate* (London: Secker and Warburg).

—— (1971) *Causeway: The Arts in Ulster* (Belfast: Art Council of Northern Ireland).

Mahon, Derek (1999) *Collected Poems* (Oldcastle: Gallery Press).

—— (2000) 'The Art of Poetry', interview by Eamon Grennan, *The Paris Review*, 82, p. 154, http://lion.chadwyck.co.uk/searchFulltext.do?id=R00804850&divLevel=0&queryId=../session/1214223771_13623&trailId=11A1AE19EEF&area=abell&forward=critref_ft (accessed 13 October 2009).

McCann, Eamonn ([1974] 2006) *War and an Irish Town* (Harmondsworth: Penguin).

—— (2006) *The Bloody Sunday Inquiry* (London: Pluto Press).

McCarthy, Thomas (2008) 'Counting the Dead on the Radio', in Julieann Campbell and Tom Herron (eds) *Harrowing of the Heart: The Poetry of Bloody Sunday*, p. 56.

McCormack, William John (1986) *The Battle of the Books* (Gigginstown: Lilliput Press).

McDonald, Peter (1997) 'Poetry, Narrative and Violence', in *Mistaken Identities* (Oxford: Clarendon Press).

McLaughlin, Declan (2008) 'Running Uphill', in Julieann Campbell and Tom Herron (eds) *Harrowing of the Heart: The Poetry of Bloody Sunday*, p. 81.

Meenan, Sharon and Killian Mullan (2008) 'I Remember', in Julieann Campbell and Tom Herron (eds) *Harrowing of the Heart: The Poetry of Bloody Sunday*, p. 80.

Moi, Ruben (2007a) '"The Cure by Poetry That Cannot Be Coerced": Text, Canon and Context in Seamus Heaney's *Electric Light*', in Bland Crowder and Jason Hall (eds) *Seamus Heaney: Poet, Critic, Translator* (Basingstoke: Macmillan).

—— (2007b) 'Transtextual Conceptualiztions of Northern Ireland', in Anne Rønning and Lene Johannessen (eds) *Readings of the Particular* (Amsterdam: Rodopi).
Montague, John (1972) *The Rough Field* (Dublin: Dolmen Press).
—— (1974) *The Faber Book of Irish Verse* (London: Faber and Faber).
Muldoon, Paul (1973) *New Weather* (London: Faber and Faber).
—— (1981) Interview by John Haffenden in *Viewpoints* (London: Faber and Faber).
—— (1983) *Quoof* (London: Faber and Faber).
—— (1986) *The Faber Book of Contemporary Irish Poetry* (London: Faber and Faber).
Mulheron, Joe (2008) 'Bloody Sunday', in Julieann Campbell and Tom Herron (eds) *Harrowing of the Heart: The Poetry of Bloody Sunday*, p. 35.
Mullan, Don (1997) *Eyewitness Bloody Sunday* (Dublin: Wolfhound Press).
Norton-Taylor, Richard (2005) *Bloody Sunday: Scenes from the Saville Inquiry* (London: Oberon Books).
O'Brien, Joanne (2002) *A Matter of Minutes: The Enduring Legacy of Bloody Sunday* (Dublin: Wolfhound Press).
Ó Dochartaigh, Niall (1997) *From Civil Rights to Armalites* (Cork: Cork University Press).
Ormsby, Frank (1992) *A Rage for Order* (Belfast: Blackstaff Press).
Patton, Kathleen (2008) 'Derry's Thirteen', in Julieann Campbell and Tom Herron (eds) *Harrowing of the Heart: The Poetry of Bloody Sunday*, p. 17.
Paulin, Tom (1984) *Ireland and the English Crisis* (Newcastle upon Tyne, Bloodaxe).
—— (1986) *The Faber Book of Political Verse* (London: Faber and Faber).
Pelletier, Martine (2006) '*Translations*, the Field Day debate and the re-imagining of Irish identity', in Anthony Roche (ed.) *The Cambridge Companion to Brian Friel* (Cambridge: Cambridge University Press).
Pringle, Peter and Philip Jacobson (2001) *Those are Real Bullets, Aren't They?* (London: Fourth Estate).
Richtarik, Marilynn, J. (1994) *Acting between the Lines: The Field Day Company and Irish Cultural Politics 1981–1984* (Oxford: Clarendon Press).
Turner, Scott MX (2008) '1 Para', in Julieanne Campbell and Tom Herron (eds) *Harrowing of the Heart: The Poetry of Bloody Sunday*, pp. 101–2.
Walsh, Dermot P.J. (2000) *Bloody Sunday and the Rule of Law in Northern Ireland* (Dublin: Gill and Macmillan).
Wills, Clair (1993) *Improprieties: Politics and Sexuality in Northern Irish Poetry* (Oxford: Clarendon Press).
—— (1998) *Reading Paul Muldoon* (Newcastle upon Tyne: Bloodaxe).
Wray, Martin (2008) 'The Fateful Day', in Julieann Campbell and Tom Herron (eds) *Harrowing of the Heart: The Poetry of Bloody Sunday*, pp. 87–8.
Ziff, Trisha (1998) *Hidden Truths: Bloody Sunday 1972* (Santa Monica: Smart Art).

5

'The Given Note': Traditional Music, Crisis and the Poetry of Seamus Heaney

Seán Crosson

> The Storyteller takes what he tells from experience – his own or that reported by others. And he in turn makes it the experience of those who are listening to his tale. The novelist has isolated himself. The birthplace of the novel is the solitary individual, who is no longer able to express himself by giving examples of his most important concerns, is himself uncounseled, and cannot counsel others.
>
> (Benjamin, 1968, p. 87)

These remarks from Walter Benjamin provide a useful starting point from which to examine the presence of traditional music in the poetry of Irish poet Seamus Heaney. Much as Benjamin noted the changed relationship between the traditional storyteller and his audience, and that between the novelist and his reader, I want to suggest a parallel differentiation between the creation and communication of traditional music and its emergence and role in the work of Heaney. Furthermore, this chapter proposes that at a time when Northern Ireland increasingly descended into civil strife and crisis, Heaney looked to landscape and, to a lesser but comparable extent, traditional music, to articulate a distinctive voice, beyond the claims of tradition and community, 'to use the first person singular' as he has remarked, 'to mean *me* and my lifetime' (Randall, 1979, p. 20). Indeed, Heaney has faced a crisis of identity that has preoccupied Irish poets since at least the time of Yeats, a crisis brought on by the discontinuity in the Irish literary tradition, by an unresolved postcolonial condition and a struggle between the pull of community and tradition and that of the individual artist. Heaney's poetry has been challenged by the tensions that underlie relations between each of these elements. Within his work, one finds a quest for motifs, including that provided by traditional music, adequate to his own predicament. In this context, while traditional music and song would appear to have provided Heaney with what he interpreted as an appropriate metaphor for artistic inspiration, his portrayal often avoided the political and social complexities associated with this music.

Heaney's engagement with traditional music reflects a recurring engagement with music generally in the poet's work. The titles of poems are themselves suggestive: 'A New Song', 'Serenades', 'Strange Fruit' and 'Singing School', as well as those discussed below. Heaney has also emphasized in his essay 'The Makings of a Music' the music of poetry itself, which he describes as consisting of two features: a poem's 'structure and beat, its play of metre and rhythms, its diction and allusiveness' and the music which is derived not 'from the literate parts of [the poet's] mind but from its illiterate parts [...] what kinds of noise assuage him, what kinds of music pleasure or repel him' (Heaney, 1980b, p. 61). This second aspect might be described as a poem's 'word music'.[1] This music is most apparent in readings of a writer's poetry aloud, or when one listens to a poet performing his/her own work, a feature that has become increasingly important for the public's engagement with Heaney's poetry as indicated below. Indeed, Heaney has himself noted the importance of the poet's speaking voice in his consideration of William Hazlitt's account of a reading by William Wordsworth. For Heaney, it was 'the quality and sway of the poet's speaking voice' that impressed on Hazlitt the importance of recording the event (Heaney, 1980b, p. 64).

Heaney's poetry has itself been described by Harry White as 'so apparently musical that to comment upon it entails the risk of redundancy' (White, 1998, p. 158). White has recognized a significant musical inheritance in Heaney's poetry, sensing a 'bardic impulse' in his work that places him in 'a line of descent from the music and verse of [Thomas] Moore through the reanimated lyric conventions of the Celtic revival' (ibid.)[2] Indeed, Heaney wrote an introduction in 1979 to *A Centenary Selection from Moore's Melodies* in which he conceded the important influence of music on him as a poet, describing song as 'the inspiring medium through which I became initiated into verse' (Heaney, 1979b, pp. 8–9). Moore's engagement with Irish music was also a response to considerable crisis in Irish society in his own time – including a rebellion against colonial rule in 1798 – as it underwent dramatic change culturally and linguistically in the late eighteenth and early nineteenth centuries. In this context, Irish music seemed to offer Moore an authenticity and continuity that allowed him to connect his work to a perceived ancient indigenous tradition while also building a contemporary audience for his poetry, and Irish poetry in English in general, through song.[3] As I argue below, similar inclinations are also apparent in Heaney's engagement with traditional music.

Heaney's approach also shares some significant similarities with that found among Romantic poets in general and their engagement with oral traditions, including traditional music and song, in the late eighteenth and nineteenth centuries. This engagement was itself a response to crisis, brought on by Romantic poets' disillusionment both with the Enlightenment exaltation of human rationalism and the increasing mechanization of society with the arrival of the industrial revolution, a sense of crisis made all the more urgent by the events of the French Revolution in 1789. In this context, Romantics sought to reassert the importance of creativity, imagination and community, while still affirming individual expression, features they associated with the past and primarily oral, and rural, societies and traditions.[4] As Maureen N. McLane has noted:

> It is not an overstatement to say that, in the last decades of the eighteenth and the first decades of the nineteenth centuries, almost every major British literary poet found him or herself engaging with oral tradition, as well as with the figure of the oral poet, his work, his cultural position, and his method of composition. Oral tradition acquired new status not only as a legitimate fund of cultural authority but also a resource for the making and annotating of 'original,' literary poetry. The image of the oral poet, moreover, fired the Romantic imagination – whether this poet was imagined as Ossian, 'the last of his race,' purported bard of third-century Scottish warriors, or as a seventeenth-century 'last minstrel' singing his dying strains to defeated Scots nobles, or as a contemporary Highland lass singing as she reaped.
>
> (McLane, 2002, pp. 135–6)

However, this 'romance of orality' has been criticized, particularly for its association of orality with concepts of the primitive, an over-essentialization of folk and organic culture and this culture's frequent infantilization (ibid., p. 136).

Several commentators have also criticized Heaney for rehashing the Romantic tropes of nineteenth-century nationalism (tropes apparent in Moore's work) while failing to engage sufficiently critically with the contemporary realities of Northern Ireland.[5] David Lloyd, for example, has criticized Heaney's 'rhetoric of compensation [...] uncritically [replaying] the Romantic schema of a return to origins which restores continuity through fuller self-possession, and accordingly rehearses the compensations conducted by Irish Romantic nationalism' (Lloyd, 1993, p. 20). A central trope within Irish Romantic nationalism was that of the land, a land that was often feminized and represented in the form of a woman, sometimes called Cathleen Ní Houlihan, at others the Shan Van Vocht, and often immortalized in song. Land, and above all the bog, is also a prominent trope in Heaney's work, particularly the first four collections, written as the Troubles in the North of Ireland rapidly escalated, including *North*. This focus reflects Heaney's own concerns with the discontinuities of the Irish tradition, discontinuities he has sought to comprehend, and to some degree resolve, through a focus on landscape.

Indeed, a recurrent concern in Heaney's work are the discontinuities he recognizes in himself, both linguistically and culturally. This concern has resulted in many poems in Heaney's oeuvre focused on the names of places, often tracing their etymology to connect with an older civilization.[6] The most famous example is the poem 'Broagh', which reflects on the distinct pronunciation of placenames in the North, sometimes difficult for 'outsiders' to articulate:

> [...] *Broagh*,
> its low tattoo
> among the windy boortrees
> and rhubarb-blades
>
> ended almost
> suddenly, like that last
> *gh* the strangers found
> difficult to manage.
> (Heaney, 1972, p. 27)

The landscape would seem to offer Heaney a means to access his country's past, to overcome the divisions in the present through the continuity he believes it provides. As he wrote in his essay 'Sense of Place'

> [W]hen I look for the history of our sensibilities I am convinced, as Professor J.C. Beckett was convinced about the history of Ireland

> generally, that it is to what he called the stable element, the land itself, that we must look for continuity.
>
> (Heaney, 1980c, p. 149)

The Irish landscape provides that point of continuity for Heaney, to which he has repeatedly returned for inspiration. In the poem 'Belderg' he finds the patterns of settlement in Mayo replicated in the contemporary patterns of stone walls indicating 'persistence, / A congruence of lives' (Heaney, 1975, p. 14). Elsewhere, in the poem 'Kinship', he finds the artefacts of generations, preserved in a bog from the ravages of time and invasion that have influenced the linguistic and cultural changes in Ireland:

> Earth-pantry, bone vault,
> sun-bank, embalmer
> of votive goods
> and sabred fugitives.
>
> (Ibid., pp. 40–1)

However, much as the landscape has provided for Heaney a point of tradition, continuity and stability, traditional music has served a similar purpose in his poetry. In 2003, Heaney recorded an album of readings and traditional tunes with acclaimed uillean-piper Liam O'Flynn. What began as occasional concerts from the mid-1990s onwards in the UK, the USA and Ireland,[7] eventually resulted in the recording of the album *The Poet & the Piper*. The album takes the listener through from Heaney's earliest collections to work from the 1996 volume *The Spirit Level*. The selection of poems included in this album indicate much about Heaney's work but are also revealing with regard to Heaney's relationship with traditional music.

The opening track on *The Poet & the Piper*, 'The Given Note', provided the title for one of O'Flynn's albums, for which Heaney contributed some words for the sleeve-notes. Heaney describes O'Flynn as 'unshakably part of a tradition' (Heaney, 1995), indicating a major reason why this collaboration was attractive to the Derry poet. For a poet who has remarked in poetry and prose on the discontinuities apparent in the Irish past and present, traditional music provides a means for Heaney, similar to that outlined above regarding Thomas Moore, of connecting with tradition while also connecting with a contemporary audience increasingly engaged with traditional music.

The relationship of music to tradition is apparent elsewhere in Heaney's work. He has had a long collaboration with the Belfast folk-singer David Hammond, which includes their involvement in the Field Day group in the early 1980s. Heaney's poem 'The Singer's House' is an appeal to Hammond to 'Raise it again' man, following his friend's reluctance to sing for a recording session after a bombing incident in Belfast. They were both to make some recordings for a mutual friend in Michigan. '[T]he whole point of the tape', Heaney has noted, 'was to promote that happiness and expansiveness which song, meaning both poetry and music, exists to promote in the first place' (Heaney, 1989, p. xi). However, following the bomb attacks, Hammond was unable to sing as 'the very notion of beginning to sing at that moment when others were beginning to suffer seemed like an offence against their suffering. He could not raise his voice at that cast-down moment' (ibid.) But beyond Heaney's call on his friend to continue to sing, to continue to offer hope, there is also a concern in the poem for the loss of tradition. There is a suggestion in the final two verses of 'The Singer's House' that music and song might offer a means through which to connect again with past tradition, to revive and renew a culture that is losing touch with its history while descending into crisis. While the singer's song is 'a rowboat far out in evening', there is the possibility that such a boat may return, a return suggested in the final verse. While the line 'a hint of the clip of the pick' connects this final verse to the 'saltminers picks' of the opening (a reference to a time in the North's history when the saltmines near Carrickfergus were still active), it also suggests the pick used by a guitarist such as Hammond to play his instrument. Heaney also recalls in verses five and six the fading traditional belief in the Selkie – 'People here used to believe / that drowned souls lived in the seals' – legendary creatures in Irish and Scottish mythology that were believed to be capable of transforming themselves from seals to humans. If the singer can 'raise it again', Heaney suggests, there may be a possibility of connecting once more with such traditions since 'we still believe what we hear' (Heaney, 1979a, p. 27).

The theme of tradition and music is explored elsewhere in *Field Work*. Indeed, song, and singing, is a recurring feature of this volume which marked a movement from the 'deeply visceral engagement with the earth and the historical bodies buried in it' apparent in collections up to *North*, 'to a preoccupation with more transcendental matters' (Hart, 1994, p. 33). As Elmer Andrews notes, 'Seeking a renewed lyricism [...] attuned to the natural world, he thinks of his poems as everlasting flowers: in the words of the poem called "Song", they are "the immortelles of perfect pitch"' (Andrews, 1998, p. 144).

'The Singer's House' is followed in *Field Work* by Heaney's most direct poem to a traditional musician, 'In Memoriam Seán Ó Riada', a work that combines personal memory with reflection on the public role of the artist. However, there is also a clear implication here that Ó Riada offered a means to connect to the past through his work, while also providing a sense of community in the present, particularly in the final two verses where Heaney connects the musician to the Jacobite or *aisling* poets of the eighteenth century, including Aogán Ó Rathaille and Eoghan Rua Ó Súilleabháin:

> As he stepped and stooped to the keyboard
> He was our jacobite,
> He was our young pretender
> Who marched along the deep [...]
> (Heaney, 1979a, p. 30)

Heaney has described poetry as also providing 'continuity' and involving a 'restoration of the culture to itself [...] an attempt to define and interpret the present by bringing it into significant relationship with the past', an effort, he argued as the Troubles intensified in the mid-1970s, which had to be 'urgently renewed' (Heaney, 1980a, p. 60). Yet it is not unusual to find this role associated with music and song in Heaney's work. The process is apparent in the poem 'Song', a delicate lyric that recalls Irish mythology in its final line, a line attributed in Irish folklore to Fionn Mac Cumhail the legendary leader of Ireland's ancient military force, the Fianna (Stephens, 1920). With the inclusion of this line 'To the music of what happens' (Heaney, 1990, p. 127), Heaney connects the present to the past through a reference to music.

Heaney's work reveals a sustained engagement with Gaelic texts. For instance, his translation of *Buile Shuibhne* as *Sweeney Astray* in 1983, introduced a character that would return in the 'Sweeney Redivivus' section of *Station Island* (1984). Heaney's adoption of Sweeney as a persona in his work in these years reflected the continuing movement in his poetry from a concern with place and his own community in a time of crisis to a wish to transcend both in a visionary poetic, encapsulated in the poem 'The First Flight' from 'Sweeney Redivivus':

> I was mired in attachment
> until they began to pronounce me
> a feeder off battlefields
>
> So I mastered new rungs of the air
> to survey out of reach
> their bonfires on hills [...]
> (Heaney, 1990, p. 197)

Heaney's use of Gaelic texts as a means of transcending the present, however, necessarily detaches these works from the historical realities with which they are involved. Referring to Heaney's use of the bog motif to explore violence in Northern Ireland, David Lloyd suggests (in an argument also apparent in the work of Ciaran Carson and Patricia Coughlan) that the poet effectively reduces 'history to myth, furnishing an aesthetic resolution to conflicts that are constituted in quite specific historical junctures by rendering disparate events as symbolic moments expressive of an underlying continuity of identity' (Lloyd, 1993, p. 17).[8] Such a process is also evident in Heaney's allusions to traditional music. An examination of one of Heaney's best-known poems referring to traditional music, 'The Given Note', reveals the mystification that Lloyd criticized, the obscuring of the historical and communal realities that music and song often communicated.

Irish music and song provided a crucial outlet for Gaelic communities at a time of colonial oppression. Both acquired increasingly political undertones as the colonial project developed in Ireland. Fellow Northern poet Gearóid Mac Lochlainn has articulated the subversive potential of music and song in his 2004 collection *Rakish Paddy Blues*:

> bards, rhymers, balladeers, armed with pistols, broadsheets,
> bandoliers,
> manifestos of brotherhood, palimpsests and performing
> fleas.
> They emerged from grey drizzled streets
> to speak in secret tongues of flame,
> under wet lashings of archway spliced with whispers of
> insurrection,
> rumours of transubstantiation
> (Mac Lochlainn and Vallely, 2004, p. 34)

Music and song had an inspiring role in both nationalist and unionist traditions in Ireland, a fact recognized in the past and resulting in the oppression of musicians. Indeed, the suppression of Irish music and musicians historically contributed to their politicization within Ireland and provided a point of resistance to the colonial enterprise. The colonial administration in Ireland had long frowned upon the impact of native traditions on colonial culture and the 1366 Statutes of Kilkenny had forbidden contact between native musicians and poets and colonialists (McCarthy, 1999, p. 33). Possibly influenced by the statutes' failure to prevent such interaction, in 1533 a further British statute prohibited the performance of 'the rhymer, the píobaire (piper), the bard, and the aois ealadhn (the artistic class)' because of a fear that by performing to 'gentilmen of the English pale', these poets and musicians might inspire among this gentry 'a talent of Irishe disposicion and conversation' (Ó hAllmhuráin, 1998, pp. 29–30). By 1603, the Lord President of Munster issued a proclamation calling for the execution of 'all manner of bards, harpers, etc' (O'Boyle, 1976, p. 10) due to their perceived role in the Nine Years War that Gaelic Irish chieftains waged against the colonial administration in Ireland between 1594 and 1603. This proclamation was followed shortly after by an order by Queen Elizabeth 'to hang the harpers wherever found' (ibid.) One of the consequences of this persecution was to end the strictly delineated roles of poet and musician under the Gaelic order such that, as Seán O'Boyle notes, 'the harpers and the court poets joined the pipers and the poets of the people in the enforced social uniformity which followed undiscriminating oppression' (ibid.)

Heaney is very aware of this history, apparent in his reference to Seán Ó Riada in the poem, 'In Memoriam Seán Ó Riada', as 'our jacobite' thereby recalling the *aisling* poets such as Aogán Ó Rathaille who articulated a politically engaged voice of protest against the colonial presence in Ireland in the eighteenth century.[9] However, the potential this offers to explore the contemporary political context in which the poem was written, at the height of the Troubles in the late 1970s, is diffused through the final verse in which Ó Riada is transformed into the non-threatening figure of a 'gannet smacking through scales' (Heaney, 1979a, p. 30).

Heaney's references to this tradition give only occasional hints of its subversive potential. Indeed, in his poem 'The Given Note', traditional music is portrayed as mystical and almost otherworldly, idealized, romanticized and fulfilling a primarily aesthetic function. His comments also suggest the importance of music in engaging an audience. His recent collaboration with O'Flynn is revealing in this regard. 'I have a strong sense of pleasure and pride in sitting beside a piper of Liam's mystery', he has remarked, 'The pipes call and raise the spirit. They also quieten and open up the daydream part of people.'[10] In comments regarding an earlier album by O'Flynn, he also observed: 'my sense of [O'Flynn] is well summed up in a couple of lines from the poem which provides the title for this disc: He strikes me as one of those fulfilled spirits who have "gone alone into the island / And brought back the whole thing"' (Heaney, 1995). The album Heaney refers to is *The Given Note,* a title taken from Heaney's poem of the same name. This poem is the opening track on *The Poet & the Piper* but was originally included in Heaney's 1969 collection, *Door into the Dark,* a collection written and published at a time of increasing crisis in Northern Ireland with the onset of the Troubles. Yet Heaney chooses within the poem a motif that avoids social or political engagement while aestheticizing an important communal practice.

It was Seán Ó Riada who introduced Heaney to the slow air that inspired the poem, 'Port na bPúcaí' (variously translated as 'Music of the Spirits' or 'The Tune of the Fairies'). Heaney has described the poem as

> a retelling of a story I heard Seán Ó Riada tell when he was in Belfast a number of years ago as composer at the Belfast festival. He played a piece of music which he called 'music of the spirits' and told a story about a fiddler getting it out of the air on the Blasket Islands and it seemed to me an image of inspiration just, a mighty wind blowing the music to you. So I wrote it down just as a figure of craft and inspiration.
>
> (MacMathúna, 2005)

What is notable in the poem, however, is Heaney's focus on the individual. It is an individual man who gets this 'air out of the night' after going 'alone into the island' and taking it, he suggests, 'from nowhere'. However, the actual history of this slow air is considerably more complex and revealing with regard to the historical dynamic that produced traditional tunes. According to Paul McNevin '[Slow airs derive] from old Gaelic songs sung in the *sean-nós* style (old-style)' (McNevin, 1998, p. 61) and it would appear that 'Port na bPúcaí' too may have had such a history. *Sean-nós* singing is a distinctive and sophisticated form of singing in Irish found primarily in the Gaeltacht (Irish-speaking) regions along the west coast of Ireland and it is believed to offer one of the few surviving examples of the performance style of a much older tradition of poetry and song in Ireland. Irish music scholar Ríonach Uí Ógáin has given a summary of one oral account (associated with the small Blasket island of *Inis Mhic Uibhleáin* [Inishvickillane] off the south west coast of Ireland) of the origin of the song from which 'Port na bPúcaí' may possibly be derived:

> One day three boats from the Great Blasket went to the small Island. A woman called Neans Ní Dhálaigh was there. When they landed they brought up the boats. After a while two of the boats went to the big Island. One of them stayed and after a while the woman was sitting on a stone. She heard the song. She heard it twice. The third time she was singing the song herself along with the voice and the voice disappeared. The man heard it again and he was fearful and anxious. The woman met him and asked him if he had heard the

song. He said he had. The other three came and they didn't hear any voice. They brought down the boat and they were going home. Neans was singing the song in the boat and the song is called 'The Tune of the Fairies'. The others were afraid when they heard it. It can still be heard on the Great Blasket.

(Uí Ógáin, 2003)

Here is one version of the song attributed to the woman:

Is bean ón slua sí mé	I am a woman from the Sí
Do tháinig thar toinn	Who has come over the waves
Is do goideadh san oíche mé	And I was taken at night
Tamall thar lear	For a while abroad
Is go bhfuilim as riocht so	And I am in this state
Fé gheasa mná sí	Under geasa of the fairy woman
Is ní bheidh ar an saol so	And I will not be in this world
Go nglaofaidh an coileach	Until the cock crows
Is caitheadsa féin	And I must go
Tabhairt fén lios isteach	Into the lios
Ní taithneamh liom é	It is no pleasure for me
Ach caithfead tabhairt fé	But I must do it
Is a bhfuil ar an saol so	And all that is in this life
Caithfidh imeacht as	Must leave it
Ach béadsa ag caoineadh'n	But I will be keening
Fhaid a bheidh uisce sa toinn	As long as water remains in the wave
Is ná deinig aon ní	And have no dealings
Leis an ndream thíos sa leas...	With the crowd that is down in the lios [...][11]

There are a number of interesting aspects to this song and the folklore surrounding it that I want to draw attention to and contrast with Heaney's poem. Firstly and most obviously it is from the perspective of a woman, not a man, that the song is sung, while according to the folklore it was also a woman who first heard it. Secondly, the song itself is reminiscent of the Gaelic *caoineadh*, or lament, by one who feels compelled to go into seclusion with the fairies. As indicated above, the *caoineadh* is referred to in the song itself and Irish traditional musician Feargal Mac

Amhlaoibh in a 2009 documentary on music from the Blasket Islands referred to the song from which the tune emerged as having been originally taken, according to local folklore, from a woman 'a bhí ag canadh nó ag caoineadh' (a woman that was singing or lamenting[12]) (Seoighe, 2009). Angela Burke has identified the important function that laments played in the Gaelic tradition. They were one of the few crucial outlets for women expressing their own very personal and deeply felt emotions within a strictly circumscribed patriarchal society. She has described this therapeutic role as 'Síceoilfhilíocht' (literally psycho-poetry) whereby women who may have been suffering from depression or other psychological conditions found an important outlet through song and story to express their concerns, often in allegorical or metaphorical ways.[13] The Donegal Irish-language poet Cathal Ó Searcaigh, for example, has spoken of his own childhood experience of his mother frequently disappearing, sometimes for days on end. These disappearances were explained by her as time spent with the fairies, though he now attributes them to bouts of depression.[14] Therefore, there was a functional, as much as representational or aesthetic purpose in the creation of songs such as these.

Furthermore, a central role of the performance of traditional music and songs such as 'Port na bPúcaí' was contributing to the creation and consolidation of community. As Tomás Ó Canainn has noted of traditional songs in Irish in his seminal study *Traditional Music in Ireland*: '*sean-nós* is only completely at ease [...] where the singer and his listener are in real communication' (Ó Canainn, 1978, p. 49), while Breandán Ó Madagáin has also observed that such 'Songs are not an independent entity in themselves: they are a form of human behaviour. And their vital context is the social life and culture of the community' (Ó Madagáin, 1985, p. 132). John Blacking has described the vital role of the audience in the performance of music and song as 'Creative listening' (Blacking, 1973, pp. 9–10). 'Creative listening' is most apparent in *sean-nós* singing where audiences actively participate in performances not just through encouraging the singer, but also, on occasion, by holding the singer's hand as he or she performs, moving it up and down to the rhythm of the song. Belfast poet Derek Mahon has given us a striking description of this moment in his poem 'Aran':

> He is earthed to his girl, one hand fastened
> In hers, and with his free hand listens,
> An earphone, to his own rendition
> Singing the darkness into the light.
>
> (Mahon, 1991, p. 31)

However, if we turn to Heaney's 'The Given Note', again one is struck by the description of traditional music as 'this air out of the night', something

> out of wind off mid-Atlantic
> Still he maintains, from nowhere.
>
> It comes off the bow gravely,
> Rephrases itself into the air.
>
> (Heaney, 1999, p. 36)

There is little sense here of the communal activity associated historically with the creation and communication of traditional music. If the music comes apparently out of thin air, one need not concern oneself with its relevance to people for whom traditional music was at one time forbidden and suppressed. It is the subversive potential that music and poetry might offer that Heaney suppresses in this poem, a suppression that is all the more apparent in the subsequent poem included on the album *The Poet & the Piper*, 'Digging', 'the first poem' according to Heaney, 'I wrote where I thought my feelings had got into words' (Heaney, 1980a, p. 41). In 'Digging', Heaney reflects on his father and grandfather's use of the spade in their livelihood and views himself as an inheritor of sorts, but through the use of a different implement:

> Between my finger and my thumb
> The squat pen rests: snug as a gun [...]
>
> [...] I've no spade to follow men like them.
> Between my finger and my thumb
> The squat pen rests.
> I'll dig with it.
>
> (Heaney, 1990, p. 2)

As Blake Morrison has suggested, Heaney's poem, like his father's spade, is involved in 'passing on tradition, extracting "new" produce (poems not potatoes) out of old furrows, and enjoying an intimacy with the earth' (Morrison, 1982, p. 27). However, whatever subversive potential the opening lines intimate is deflected in the poem's closing: 'The squat pen rests / I'll dig with it' (Lloyd, 1993, p. 21).[15]

To conclude, while landscape has provided Heaney with a recurring point of tradition, continuity and stability, particularly as Northern

Ireland rapidly descended into political and communal strife and crisis, traditional customs would seem to have played a comparable role in his work. In common with Romantic poets of the eighteenth and early nineteenth centuries who turned to the past and traditional practices in a time of perceived crisis, Heaney's poetry is marked by attempts to connect to figures such as the farmer in 'Digging' and 'Fodder', the Blacksmith in 'The Forge' and 'Poet to Blacksmith'; the 'Thatcher' in the poem of that name; the fisherman in 'A Lough Neagh Sequence'; and in 'The Given Note' the traditional musician. However, each of those he describes operates as a skilled member of her/his community whose work is formed, acknowledged and validated in that context and performs a primarily functional – and communal – rather than representational role. While Heaney attempts to parallel his own poetry with such traditional craftsmen, his is essentially what Walter Benjamin would call a solitary art. Indeed, Heaney's focus generally has been on establishing and developing his own distinctive and personal lyrical voice, 'If I do write something' we are told in 'The Flight Path', 'Whatever it is, I'll be writing for myself' (Heaney, 1998, p. 413). And such is the emphasis of the poem 'The Given Note': the personal act of creativity, separate and distinct from the communal processes that are vital to the composition and communication of traditional music and song. If Heaney's approach does signify a continuity of tradition, it is the tradition of Romantic/Modernist expression of self via lyric subjectivity; the use and influence of traditional music and song in Heaney's work is mediated through this tradition. It is the crisis faced by the Romantic tradition that is echoed in Heaney's poetry, whereby traditional music provides him with yet a further useful motif (paralleled in his use of landscape) for his lyrical voice as he seeks a way to express his own personal identity beyond the communal calls to protest and confrontation.

Notes

1. For more on this aspect of poetry, see Scher (1982) and Garlington (1997).
2. White has updated his arguments regarding Heaney in his later study *Music and the Irish Literary Imagination* (2000) in which he contends that literature for Irish writers such as Heaney has essentially taken the place of an Irish art music reflected in 'a persistent search for music in language' (White, 2000, p. 34).
3. For further on this, see Crosson (2008, pp. 65–72).
4. For more on the engagement of Romantics with oral tradition, see Finnegan (1977, pp. 30–41).
5. Examples of such criticisms are to be found in Lloyd (1993), Fennel (1991) and Wills (1993).

6. In poems such as this, and others including 'Anahorish', Heaney is also drawing inspiration from the early Irish literatary genre *dinnseanchas*, texts that recounted the origins of Irish placenames.
7. Further information on this collaboration is available from the Tara music website at http://www.taramusic.com/biogs/liamobg.htm and http://www.taramusic.com/archive/lofsh.htm (accessed 18 September 2009).
8. See also Coughlan (1991) and Carson (1975).
9. For a fuller discussion of the *aisling* see Murphy (1939–40). Murphy notes that one genre of *aisling*, the 'love' or 'fairy' aisling, dates back to at least the eighth century. See also Ó Tuama (1960) and Ó Buachalla (1996). As Breandán Ó Madagáin has noted, the *aisling* is a tradition that was intimately connected with music as most *aisling* poems would have entered the popular consciousness of their time through song (Ó Madagáin, 2000, p. 89) Heaney has himself translated several of these song poems, including one of the most famous in the tradition, 'Gile na Gile' by Aogán Ó Rathaille, which he translated as 'The Glamoured' and which is included on the CD, *The Poet & the Piper*. Heaney has also translated the eighteenth-century Gaelic parody of the *aisling* form, *Cúirt an Mheán Oíche* by Brian Merriman, one of the finest and most famous poems in Gaelic, as *The Midnight Verdict* (2001).
10. These remarks are included on the Tara music website at http://www.taramusic.com/biogs/liamobg.htm (accessed 18 September 2009).
11. This version is featured on Méav Ní Mhaolchatha's album *Silver Sea* (2002). Lyrics and translation available at http://www.geocities.com/celticlyricscorner/meav/port.htm (accessed 2 October 2008).
12. My translation.
13. For a discussion of this and its use in Cathal Ó Searcaigh's poetry see Ó Laoire (2003, pp. 17–18).
14. Ó Searcaigh has referred to this in Neasa Ní Chianáin's documentary *Fairytale of Kathmandhu* (Vinegarhill Productions, 2007).
15. It should be noted that Heaney has used music, and particularly song, to directly engage with one of the most marked moments of crisis in Northern Ireland. As Ruben Moi notes in his contribution to this collection, his ballad 'The Road to Derry' was written as a highly critical riposte to the events of what has become known as 'Bloody Sunday' when members of the British parachute regiment killed 13 civilian demonstrators in Derry city. However, and significantly, though initially written to be performed by the folk group The Dubliners in 1972 shortly after the event, it would remain unpublished until some 25 years later in 1997 – when the peace process in Northern Ireland had developed significantly, presumably because of Heaney's own reticence towards such a direct engagement shortly after the event.

References

Andrews, Elmer (1998) *The Poetry of Seamus Heaney* (Cambridge: Icon Books).

Benjamin, Walter (1968) 'The Storyteller: Reflections on the Work of Nikolai Leskov', in Hannah Arendt (ed.) *Illuminations: Essays and Reflections* (New York: Schocken).

Blacking, John (1973) *How Musical is Man* (Seattle: University of Washington Press).

Carson, Ciaran (1975) 'Escaped from the Massacre?', *The Honest Ulsterman,* 50, pp. 183–6.
Crosson, Seán (2008) *'The Given Note': Traditional Music and Modern Irish Poetry* (Newcastle: Cambridge Scholars Publishing).
Coughlan, Patricia (1991) '"Bog Queens": The Representation of Women in the Poetry of John Montague and Seamus Heaney', in Toni O'Brien Johnson and David Cairns (eds) *Gender in Irish Writing* (Milton Keynes: Open University Press).
Fennell, Desmond (1991) *Whatever You Say, Say Nothing: Why Seamus Heaney is No. 1* (Dublin: ELO Publications).
Finnegan, Ruth (1977) *Oral Poetry* (Cambridge: Cambridge University Press).
Garlington, Aubrey S. (1997) 'Music, Word, Performance: Sounds of Meaning', in Walter Bernhart, Steven Paul Scher and Werner Wolf (eds) *Word and Music Studies Defining the Field: Proceedings of the First International Conference on Word and Music Studies at Graz, 1997* (Amsterdam and Atlanta, GA: Editions Rodopi B.V.).
Hart, Henry (1994) 'What is Heaney Seeing in *Seeing Things?*', *Colby Quarterly,* 30(1): 32–42.
Heaney, Seamus (1969) *A Door into the Dark* (London: Faber and Faber).
—— (1972) *Wintering Out* (London: Faber and Faber).
—— (1975) *North* (London: Faber and Faber).
—— (1979a) *Fieldwork* (London: Faber and Faber).
—— (1979b) 'Introduction', in David Hammond (ed.) *A Centenary Selection from Moore's Melodies* (Dublin: Gilbert Dalton).
—— (1980a) 'Feeling into Words', in *Selected Prose 1968–1978* (London: Faber and Faber).
—— (1980b) 'The Makings of a Music: Reflections on Wordsworth and Yeats', in *Preoccupations: Selected Prose 1968–1978* (London: Faber and Faber).
—— (1980c) 'The Sense of Place', in *Preoccupations: Selected Prose 1968–1978* (London: Faber and Faber).
—— (1989) 'The Interesting Case of Nero, Chekhov's Cognac and a Knocker', in *The Government of the Tongue* (London: Faber and Faber).
—— (1990) *New Selected Poems* (London: Faber and Faber).
—— (1995) sleeve-note to *The Given Note,* CD by Liam O'Flynn (Dublin: Tara Music Company Ltd).
—— (1996) *The Spirit Level* (London: Faber and Faber).
—— (1998) *Opened Ground: Poems 1966–1996* (London: Faber and Faber).
—— (2001) *The Midnight Verdict* (Oldcastle, County Meath: Gallery Press).
Lloyd, David (1993) 'Pap for the Dispossessed', in *Anomalous States* (Dublin: The Lilliput Press, 1993).
Mac Lochlainn, Gearóid and John B. Vallely (2004) *Rakish Paddy Blues,* ed. Kieran Gilmore (Bangor: Open House Traditional Arts Festival Ltd).
MacMathúna, Ciarán (2005) 'The Given Note', *Mo Cheol Thú,* RTÉ Radio 1, 27 November.
Mahon, Derek (1991) *Selected Poems* (Oldcastle, County Meath: The Gallery Press in association with Oxford University Press).
McCarthy, Marie (1999) *Passing it on* (Cork: Cork University Press).
McLane, Maureen N. (2002) 'On the Use and Abuse of "Orality" for Art: Reflections on Romantic and Late Twentieth-Century Poiesis', *Oral Tradition,* 17(1): 135–64.

McNevin, Paul (1998) *Complete Guide to the Irish Fiddle* (Dublin: Walton Manufacturing Ltd).
Morrison, Blake (1982) *Seamus Heaney* (London: Methuen).
Murphy, Gerard (1939–40) 'Notes on Aisling Poetry', *Éigse,* 1: 40–50.
O'Boyle, Seán (1976) *The Irish Song Tradition* (Dublin: Gilbert Dalton).
Ó Buachalla, Breandán (1996) *Aisling ghéar: Na Stíobhartaigh agus an t-aos léinn* (Baile Átha Cliath: An Clóchomhar).
Ó Canainn, Tomás (1978) *Traditional Music in Ireland* (London: Routledge and Kegan Paul).
Ó hAllmhuráin, Gearóid (1998) *Pocket History of Irish Traditional Music* (Dublin: The O'Brien Press).
Ó Laoire, Lillis (2003) 'Ag Tabhairt Teanga don Tost', in Cathal Ó Searcaigh, *Ag Tnúth leis an tSolas* (Indreabhán: Cló Iar-Chonnachta).
Ó Madagáin, Breandán (1985) 'Functions of Irish Song in the Nineteenth Century', *Béaloideas,* 53: 130–216.
—— (2000) 'Coibhneas na Filíochta leis an gCeol, 1700–1900', in Pádraigín Riggs, Breandán Ó Conchúir and Seán Ó Coileáin (eds) *Saoi na hÉigse: Aistí in Ómós do Sheán Ó Tuama* (Baile Átha Cliath: An Clóchomhar Ita).
Ó Tuama, Seán (1960) *An Grá in Amhráin na nDaoine* (Baile Átha Cliath: Clóchomhar).
Randall, James (1979) 'An Interview with Seamus Heaney', *Ploughshares,* 5(3): 7–22.
Scher, Steven Paul (1982) 'Literature and Music', in Jean-Pierre Barricelli and Joseph Gibaldi (eds) *Interrelations of Literature* (New York: The Modern Language Association of America) pp. 225–50.
Seoige, Máirín (2009) *Ceoil na noileán: an Blascaod Mór,* Scannáin Dobharchú do TG4.
Stephens, James (1920) 'The Boyhood of Fionn. Chapter VIII', in *Irish Fairy Tales* (New York, The Macmillan Company), http://www.sacred-texts.com/neu/celt/ift/ift02.htm (accessed 10 December 2008).
Uí Ógáin, Ríonach (2003) sleeve-notes, *Beauty An Oileáin: Music and Song of the Blasket Islands* (Dublin: Claddagh Records).
White, Harry (1998) *The Keeper's Recital: Music and Cultural History in Ireland, 1770–1970* (Cork: Cork University Press in association with Field Day).
—— (2000) *Music and the Irish Literary Imagination* (Oxford: Oxford University Press).
Wills, Clare (1993) *Improprieties: Politics and Sexuality in Northern Irish Poetry* (Oxford: Oxford University Press).

6

'Crisis first-hand': Seamus Heaney before and after the Ceasefire

Stephen Regan

Among the most striking and memorable poems written by Seamus Heaney over a period of fifty years are those in which moments of profound crisis are clarified and articulated. The poems most obviously coinciding with the intensification of political violence in Northern Ireland – those in *Wintering Out* (1972), *North* (1975) and *Field Work* (1979) – have been given widespread critical acclaim for their achieved obliquity and their potent use of myth and symbol, but what prompts and generates many of the poems of the 1970s is an immediate and potentially overwhelming sense of crisis. Breaking out of the long historical perspectives engendered by contact with Iron Age and Viking cultures creates a powerful momentum and a dramatic sense of return to immediate political actualities, a structure which is implicit in the two-part arrangement of *North*. Within single poems, however, Heaney shows exemplary skill in signalling the shift from long-established and accustomed modes of behaviour to the sudden apprehension of crisis. It happens in 'Funeral Rites' with the deftly placed 'Now' at the beginning of Section II of the poem, preceding the grotesque and intimate alignment of 'neighbourly murder': 'Now as news comes in / of each neighbourly murder / we pine for ceremony [...]' (Heaney, 1998, p. 97). It happens, too, with the sudden, alarming escalation of violence in Derry, recalled in 'Casualty': 'That Wednesday / Everybody held / Their breath and trembled' (Heaney, 1998, p. 155). Even when explicitly denying the experience of registering and recording crisis 'first-hand', Heaney's poetry is vitally attuned to the urgent rhythms of crisis. In 'Station Island', the penitent poet distinguishes his own 'dumb' response to the murder of his cousin from that of other poets reacting to the news: 'But they were getting crisis / first-hand, Colum, they had happened in on / live sectarian assassination' (Heaney, 1998, p. 260). Here, the poem brilliantly dramatizes an attitude to crisis that has preoccupied Heaney throughout his career, both keeping it at a distance and simultaneously acknowledging its imposing and unavoidable actuality.

In the poems written since the IRA ceasefire in 1994, the urgency informing much of the earlier work has been transmuted into a more reflective and tentative mode of enquiry. This is not to say that the later poems are rid of crisis, but rather that they respond to it differently. A number of poems written since 1994 acknowledge the ceasefire with uncertainty and ambivalence. Part of that uneasiness has to do with the recollection of earlier attempted ceasefires and the lingering perception that a ceasefire, rather than signalling an end to crisis, may be a familiar manifestation of it. As Paul Muldoon's 'Lull' reminds us with its cunning 'eternal interim', the fires continue burning throughout a ceasefire, and the lull might lull us into a false sense of security rather than provide the grounds for a lasting peace (Muldoon, 2001, p. 81). Heaney's ambivalence towards the ceasefire is evident in a short article written for the Dublin *Sunday Tribune* just a few days after the event was announced on 31 August 1994. It opens with what looks like unqualified optimism: 'The announcement by the Provisional IRA last Wednesday changed everything for the better.' The effect of that announcement, he confides, was like having a blind lifted in his head:

> I went outside to try to re-collect myself and suddenly a blind seemed to rise somewhere at the back of my mind and the light came flooding in. I felt twenty-five years younger. I remembered what things had felt like in those early days of political ferment in the late sixties.
>
> (Heaney, 2004)

But that feeling of being 'freed up,' as Heaney puts it, turns to anger as he ponders twenty-five years of suffering that have brought the situation to a point that is actually less politically promising than things were in 1968. Even so, the tentative optimism encouraged by the ceasefire is evident a little later in Heaney's Nobel Prize speech in 1995, in which he speaks of 'acts of faith' around the world that 'inspire a hope that a new possibility can still open up in Ireland as well' (Heaney, 1998, pp. 460–1).

With the exception of Edna Longley's sobering essay, 'Northern Irish Poetry and the End of History', very little attention has been paid to the ways in which writers in Northern Ireland have responded to the peace process and whether the general perception is one of crisis over or crisis prolonged. Longley is well used to journalists from abroad asking writers in Belfast, 'What are you going to write about now?' 'One reply', she suggests, is that poetry before the ceasefire 'had never depended either on one theme or on one orchestration of that theme' (Longley, 2000, p. 280). Even so, some crucially important questions need to be addressed about the perceived change of political climate registered in the recent poetry of writers like Seamus Heaney, Michael Longley, Ciaran Carson and Paul Muldoon. Edna Longley's own incisive readings of works produced by these poets between 1994 and 1999 suggests that 'the collective script might be changing', even though she remains wary of simple formulations such as 'post-ceasefire literature' (ibid., p. 315). The various interruptions and deadlocks and the general intransigence of the peace process have tended to undermine the initial promise and hopefulness of 1994, but the possibility of substantial political progress in a more peaceful domain has prompted reflections and imaginings that seem to indicate a new poetic consciousness.

One of the striking indications of a post-ceasefire consciousness in the work of Seamus Heaney is his powerful urge to revisit and revise his own creative achievements. Edna Longley notes 'the accentuated tendency for poets to quote and revise not only earlier poets and each other but also their former textual selves' (ibid., p. 316). In terms of a distinctive preoccupation with memory, forgiveness and reconciliation, and in terms of a sustained intertextual experimentation with language and imagery, it might be argued that there is a significant body of writing that is 'post-ceasefire' in more than just the obvious chronological sense. At the same time, however, this is a body of work in which crisis continues to have a potent force, gradually opening out into the global crisis acknowledged in *District and Circle* (2006). The image of light flooding into the dark places of the mind in Heaney's ceasefire article is anticipated, of course, in a good deal of his writing prior to 1994. This is especially true of the poems in *Seeing Things*, published in 1991, in which Heaney turns away from a 'poetry / sluggish in the doldrums of what happens', towards the visionary mode suggested by the title of the volume (Heaney, 1991, p.50). In the poem 'Fosterling', he writes of 'waiting until I was nearly fifty / To credit marvels. Like the tree-clock of tin cans / The tinkers made. So long for air to brighten, / Time to be dazzled and the heart to lighten' (ibid.) There is no doubt that Heaney's work has recently come out into the light and that it has started to shed the heavy layers of discomfort that have been there since the early 1970s. To appreciate fully the recent lightening in Heaney's work, and the extent to which it has been a matter of intense creative struggle and a continuing engagement with crisis, we need to recall those moments of darkness and near-despair that made the title of his 1969 book *Door into the Dark* seem ironically prophetic. We need to remember, too, those occasions on which Heaney has been moved to speak out forcefully against the British media, the British government and the British Army.

In March 1988, Heaney was invited to London to receive the *Sunday Times* award for excellence in writing. He used what might otherwise have been a pleasantly emollient occasion to express his deep dismay at the British media coverage of events in Northern Ireland, which threatened to undermine recent attempts to establish an Anglo-Irish political agreement:

> I noticed in yesterday's newspapers an inclination to view the British army presence in Ulster once again as part of the solution rather than part of the problem, an inclination to view them as hygienic, rubber-gloved, impersonally motivated technicians operating in polluted ghettoes where indigenous hatreds are cultured in self-induced and self-wounding conditions. I noticed an inclination to think of military funerals as a tribal and undesirable form of solidarity when enacted on the Falls Road, but as somehow immunised against tribal significance when the victims were British soldiers, the mourners were British parents, and the martial music was relayed with deeply emotive effect by the news channels of British television.
>
> (Heaney, 1988, p. 14)

Heaney's bold and uncompromising stance on this occasion was informed by Robert Lowell's assertion that 'every serious artist knows that he cannot enjoy public celebration without making subtle public commitments', but the example of Yeats was also in his mind: 'Yeats's challenge to the writer was to hold in a single thought reality and justice, and the same challenge is in effect in Westminster and Fleet Street' (ibid., p. 14). We cannot embark upon a worthwhile appraisal of Heaney's post-ceasefire writings without giving adequate measure to the gravity of his earlier writings, and without taking into account what he memorably characterizes elsewhere as his own 'responsible *tristia*' (Heaney, 1998, p. 143). That *tristia* is gently self-ironizing, but it adequately points to a pervasive mood and a sense of moral obligation that persist in Heaney's work over a period of some twenty years.

Heaney's 1993 lecture, 'Frontiers of Writing' (the closing piece in *The Redress of Poetry*), recalls an Oxford college dinner that took place a week after the death of Bobby Sands, on the same day that another hunger striker, the son of a neighbouring family of the Heaneys in Co. Derry, was being buried. As the poet circulates among the sherry-sipping crowd, he thinks of a very different crowd in a small house, close to home, where a funeral is taking place. He recognizes acutely a 'moment of conflicting recognitions, self-division, inner quarrel, a moment of dumbness and inadequacy when it felt like a betrayal to be enjoying the hospitality of an Establishment college and occupying, if only accidentally, the room of a British minister.' What he experiences at that moment is 'the classic bind of all of Northern Ireland's constitutional nationalists', caught between 'commitments to cultural and political ideals which are fundamentally Ireland-centred' and 'their disavowal of support for the violent means of the Irish Republican Army, an army which operates with pre-emptive and atrocious force in order to further similar cultural and political ideals'. Heaney's acknowledgement of the 'frontier' and its political, as well as imaginative, consequences is candid but also unflinchingly forthright: 'But whether the north and the south are to be regarded as monolithic or pluralist entities, the fact of the border, of partition, of two Irelands on one island, remains the salient fact' (Heaney, 1995, pp. 188–9). There are other occasions on which Heaney has made his political sympathies and attachments explicit, and his prose writings have been scrupulously frank about their own aesthetic and ideological procedures. To understand the complex shifts that have taken place in Heaney's writings since the ceasefire, however, we need to go back even further, to 1972.

In an essay titled '1972' and published in the *Guardian* that year, Heaney asks how poetry can come to terms with the violence and brutality of the times. He ponders these lines from Shakespeare's Sonnet 65: 'How with this rage shall beauty hold a plea / Whose action is no stronger than a flower?' (Heaney, 1980, p. 33). In a later essay in 1974, Heaney answers that question with the help of Yeats. What he must do, as Yeats does in his 'Meditations in Time of Civil War', is to find 'befitting emblems of adversity': images and symbols that are somehow adequate to the predicament (ibid., p. 57). Those emblems of adversity have steadily given way to emblems of reconciliation and renewal in recent times, but their force and significance are still apparent in Heaney's most recent poems.

The most striking emblems of adversity in the 1970s can be found in the Bog Poems of *Wintering Out* and *North*, in which Heaney establishes a parallel between the sectarian killings going on in his own North and the ritual sacrifices to Mother Earth in the early Iron Age culture across northern Europe. The source for this pervasive anthropological interest was P.V. Glob's illustrated book, *The Bog People*, published in English in 1969. Heaney writes that 'the unforgettable photographs of these victims blended in my mind with photographs of atrocities, past and present, in the long rites of Irish political and religious struggles' (Heaney, 1980, pp. 57–8). Among the first of the bog poems to be written was 'The Tollund Man', which begins with the announcement of a pilgrimage, a desire to visit the peat bogs of Jutland: 'Some day I will go to Aarhus'. The most striking aspect of this and other bog poems is the strange fusing of Christian and pagan ritual. In the third stanza, the meditative line, 'I will stand a long time', suggests a veneration and a reverence usually reserved for the Stations of the Cross, and the second section of the poem explicitly acknowledges that to pray to a pagan saint is to 'risk blasphemy'. The closing stanza of the poem recognizes the paradox of internal exile, of being an inner émigré: 'Out there in Jutland / In the old man-killing parishes / I will feel lost, / Unhappy and at home' (Heaney, 1998, p. 65).

One of the first poems to be written by Heaney after the announcement of the ceasefire at the end of August 1994 was 'Tollund', the penultimate poem in Heaney's 1996 book, *The Spirit Level*. The poem is dated September 1994, as if announcing its presence in a new political dispensation. At the same time, it looks back at 'The Tollund Man', gently suggesting a changed world view in its delicate verbal echoes of the earlier poem. As the new title suggests, the focus now is less on the fossilized sacrificial object than on the broader prospect of the place itself, with its promising 'path through Jutland fields'. The penitential journey envisaged in the earlier poem has now been undertaken; but most importantly, the speaker's solitary and uncertain veneration in 'The Tollund Man' ('I will stand a long time') now gives way to a sense of shared destiny and communion: 'That Sunday morning we had travelled far. / We stood a long time out in Tollund Moss' (Heaney, 1998, p. 443). The familiar yet 'hallucinatory' quality of the place prepares us for the prospect of 'seeing things', for the possibility of the miraculous.

One way in which Heaney is prompted to see a bright utopian vision is through a subtle recall of 'Townland of Peace', part of a sequence titled 'Freehold', written in the 1940s by John Hewitt: 'It could have been a still out of the bright / "Townland of Peace", that poem of dream farms / Outside all contention' (ibid., p. 443). In 'The Tollund Man', Heaney had established a parallel between ancient Jutland and the 'old man-killing parishes' of his own homeland. Now, he establishes a different parallel between the quiet pastoral of the Jutland fields and Hewitt's wartime regional idyll, in which the poet imagines stepping 'clean out of Europe into peace'. As Edna Longley suggests,

> 'Townland of Peace' may have come into Heaney's mind because its images distinguish peace from war so simply and clearly, and because it explains how wartime circumstances stimulated the visionary new history for 'Ulster...my region' that emerges later in 'Freehold'.
>
> (Longley, 2000, p. 307)

At the same time, Heaney's new vision of 'Tollund' is one that is open to change and modernization. His pastoral setting admits 'Light traffic sound', and the generously embracing image of a scarecrow with its arms open is strategically aligned with a satellite dish in a nearby paddock. A standing stone has been 'resituated and landscaped', and the speaker who once felt lost among foreign names now discovers 'tourist signs in futhark runic script / In Danish and in English'. All the signs suggest that 'Things had moved on' (Heaney, 1998, p. 443).

The earlier negative identification that Heaney articulates in 'The Tollund Man', feeling 'lost, / Unhappy and at home', now gives way to a more easeful and open sense of being 'at home beyond the tribe'. The dejected solitariness of the earlier poem is replaced with a more positive sense of companionship and shared endeavour:

> More scouts than strangers, ghosts who'd walked abroad
> Unfazed by light, to make a new beginning.
> And make a go of it, alive and sinning,
> Ourselves again, free-willed again, not bad.
>
> (Ibid., p. 443)

The image of ghosts is momentarily unsettling, since the haunted present usually signifies the troubled legacy of the past, but the facing of the light is a positive indication of a new start and a new determination to go forward, unconstrained by the narrow moral and religious dictates that have previously hindered progress. The willingness to take risks in the interests of change has a formal corollary in Heaney's readiness to employ the rhythms of living speech: 'make a go of it [...] not bad'. Edna Longley notes that the phrase 'Ourselves again' appears to conflate the familiar translation of Sinn Féin ('ourselves alone') with the famous Irish ballad, 'A Nation Once Again', and she concludes: 'Perhaps it is fitting that subtextual irresolution should characterize an "end" that cannot yet generate the language, the tropes and modes, for "a new beginning"' (Longley, 2000, p. 309). Andrew Murphy, however, offers a more optimistic reading of these closing lines, noting that 'By cancelling the "alone" and replacing it with "again", Heaney suggests a kind of rebirth of Irishness and a breaking of traditional isolationist introversion' (Murphy, 1996, p. 103). The closing colloquial summation, 'not bad', is just deflationary enough to caution against wild expectations; it suggests a reasonable start, but it also invites a more generous estimation of human kindness and potential than had previously prevailed.

The most remarkable manifestation of the Tollund Man in recent times, however, has been in 'The Tollund Man in Springtime', a sonnet sequence included in *District and Circle* (2006). As the title of the sequence suggests, the longed-for germination that Heaney sought in *Wintering Out* has now come about and the Tollund Man walks abroad in the rapidly changing contemporary world. The new global order that he inhabits is one in which terrorism is a persistent and widespread concern, and in which new technology drives the increasing need for surveillance. If this seems like a disappointing, dystopian end to all that was hoped for in the earlier poem – as if the violence and terror at the local level have now assumed a worldwide presence – there is also an abiding hope and determination. The persistence of the Tollund Man testifies to the survival and persistence of poetry itself, and now the Tollund Man speaks in his own voice, with a new-found sense of liberation:

> Into your virtual city I'll have passed
> Unregistered by scans, screens, hidden eyes,
> Lapping myself in time, an absorbed face
> Coming and going, neither god nor ghost […]
> (Heaney, 2006, p. 55)

The strong sense of endurance and fortitude that informs the poem derives in part from the anti-totalitarian vision of Heaney's friend and fellow poet, Czesław Miłosz, who died in August 2004: 'The soul exceeds its circumstances'. The presence of the Polish poet reinforces the impression that 'The Tollund Man in Springtime' is a celebration of poetry's 'staying powers'. By the end of the sequence, it seems as if poet and Tollund Man have merged and become one. If the title *District and Circle* brings to mind the London Underground and the hellish circumstances of the terrorist bombings in July 2005, it also suggests Heaney's continuing preoccupation with his own district and his relentless circling back on his own poetic achievements. There is resilience and endurance in the figure of the turf cutter with which the sequence ends: 'I straightened, spat on my hands, felt benefit / And spirited myself into the street' (Heaney, 2006, p. 58).

Stylistically, too, 'The Tollund Man in Springtime' registers a changed world view. For all the deep-seated anxieties that attend the prospect of globalized terror, there is a lightness and deftness in Heaney's handling of the sonnet form. The syntactical fluency and rhythmic buoyancy of the sonnets suggest a recovery of confidence in the lyric mode. In the opening sonnet, for instance, the Petrarchan rhyme scheme is established with an easeful and artful simplicity, allowing words like 'passed' and 'ghost', 'lost' and 'rust', to function as near-echoes of each other, rather than as full-throated rhymes. This sustained experimentation with lyric form takes on a new confidence and adventurousness in the changed political climate of the post-ceasefire period. Between 1972 and 1994, between 'The Tollund Man' and 'Tollund', Heaney had continued to think about the function of poetry, and about whether lyric poetry, in particular, was adequate to the circumstances in which it now had to operate. One of the most revealing instances of Heaney's theoretical manoeuvring can be found in the Richard Ellmann Lectures which he delivered at Emory University in Atlanta in 1988, and which were subsequently printed in a small book titled *The Place of Writing* (1989). In these lectures, Heaney confesses just how difficult it is to carry on writing in a cultural climate where a suspicion of Yeatsian heroics combines with a more general European scepticism about the possibilities of poetry after Auschwitz:

> [...] it all added up to a situation in which the literary intelligentsia of Britain and Ireland were anxious to confine the operations of imaginative writing to a sanitized realm that might include the ludic, the ironic, the parodic, the satiric, the pathetic, the domestic, the elegiac and the self-inculpatory, but which would conscientiously exclude the visionary prophetic, the patriotic witness, the national epical.
>
> (Heaney, 1989, p. 38)

In Heaney's own work, of course, there are many instances of the domestic, the elegiac and the self-inculpatory, but rather less attention has been given to the visionary prophetic, the patriotic witness and the national epical, all of which are also abundantly present in Heaney's work, and which arguably begin to surface more confidently and explicitly in the poetry written after the ceasefire of 1994. The references to 'the ludic, the ironic, the parodic' derive in part from the preface to *The*

Penguin Book of Contemporary British Poetry, edited by Andrew Motion and Blake Morrison, in which Heaney (somewhat reluctantly) had been included in 1982. It suggests the kind of poetry then being written by Paul Muldoon, a poetry that was advertising itself as postmodern in its self-reflexive, allusive, deconstructive energies. Just a little later in the essay, Heaney takes Muldoon to task for seeming to

> deride the notion that poetry might have a desirable, never mind a demonstrable, relation to the life of a nation. To get involved with such ideas, he [Muldoon] implies, is at best to commit a literary offence, at worst to promote dubious mystiques involving race memory and the chosen people complex.
>
> (Heaney, 1989, p. 41)

How, then, to steer a line between patriotic witness and the kind of postmodern playfulness that would seem to abandon any serious commitment to the life of the nation? Heaney has always tried to balance the place of writing in terms of a particular national location with the place of writing in terms of where it exists, theoretically, in relation to other cultural activities and events.

Three poems written by Heaney over a period of thirty years, all of them preoccupied with a particular place – Toome, in Co. Antrim – suggest how pervasive and persistent Heaney's ideas about the 'place of writing' have been throughout his career. All three poems give voice to the urge and necessity of poetry itself, but also reveal distinctive stages of development in Heaney's thinking about the adequacy of his own artistic impulses in the face of crisis. The first of these poems, simply titled 'Toome', appeared in *Wintering Out* in 1972. It is one of a number of sensuous verbal realizations of local places, including 'Anahorish' and 'Broagh', in which Heaney taps a long Irish tradition of placename poems (*dinnseanchas*) and attempts to recover 'forgotten Gaelic music in the throat': 'My mouth holds round / the soft blastings, / Toome, Toome' (Heaney, 1998, p. 53). At a phonetic level, the poem is an exploration of the distinctive music of Gaelic vowel sounds; it exerts a sense of kinship and perhaps a sense of possession in the mouth's prolonged 'holding' to the soundings of the place. As Heaney suggests in his early essays, however, linguistic contours are also geo-political contours. Toome is part of the Bann valley, a site of important archaeological discoveries (and therefore an appropriate place for poetic excavations involving language and memory), but it is also associated with the 1798 Rebellion, and especially with the folk memory, preserved in

Ethna Carbery's song, of the rebel Roddy McCorley: 'For young Roddy McCorley goes to die on the Bridge of Toome today' (Regan, 2004, p. 367). The 'soft blastings' of Toome open up the poem's excavation of the landscape, while subtly hinting at its troubled political history. Heaney's poetic 'prospecting' uncovers, instead of gold, an assortment of objects, including 'musket-balls'. The final prospect is a place of danger, where the speaker acknowledges the risks that accompany his archaeological excavations:

> I am sleeved in
> alluvial mud that shelves
> suddenly under
> bogwater and tributaries,
> and elvers tail my hair.
> (Heaney, 1998, p. 53)

That final image is a Celtic version of the Medusa myth that suggests that Heaney has pushed back well beyond the 1790s into pagan Ireland. If it provides evidence that Heaney has 'located his primeval, preliterate self', it also reminds us of the fossilizing, petrifying consequences of looking too intently into the past (Morrison, 1982, p. 44).

'The Toome Road' provides a striking indication of the colloquial vigour and directness that started to enter Heaney's work between *Wintering Out* in 1972 and *Field Work* in 1979, as well as its powerful capacity for registering and reflecting on moments of crisis. The stylistic transformation in Heaney's work is immediately apparent in the poem's brisk but vivid recollection of a meeting with the British Army:

> One morning early I met armoured cars
> In convoy, warbling along on powerful tyres,
> All camouflaged with broken alder branches,
> And headphoned soldiers standing up in turrets.
> (Heaney, 1998, p. 150)

The echoes of English folk song ('Early one morning, just as the sun was rising') are quickly dispelled, and the image of a singing maiden is displaced by military hardware. In its surveillance of rural Ulster, the army also appears to have displaced the birds and even the trees in which they sing. The broken alder, the darling tree of the exiled Sweeney, is an ominous sign. In Heaney's version of *Buile Suibhne* (*Sweeney Astray*, 1983), the alder has 'some milk of human kindness / coursing in its sap' (Heaney,

1983, p. 196), but here that innocence has been destroyed. The voice of the poem modulates in response to the perceived invasion, asserting territorial rights: 'How long were they approaching down my roads / As if they owned them?' (Heaney, 1998, p. 150). Peter McDonald worries rather too much about this question, suggesting that any answer which attempts to be precise is apt to be 'ludicrous' or 'absurd' (McDonald, 1997, pp. 55, 57). In terms of the kind of voice that the poem constructs – ostensibly that of a local farmer, as amplified in the accompanying concern for fields, cattle and tractors – the question is plausible enough. One doesn't have to be a speech act theorist to see that the function of the question is not to elicit a precise response, but rather to convey exasperation. McDonald's real concern is with the sense of ownership conveyed in the question. He sees the poem as suspect for its 'reliance on one deep narrative – of possession and identity – over the rejected narrative of incursion' (ibid., p. 57), though it is difficult to find anything as coherent as 'narrative' in a poem which, as McDonald notes, begins in a folk or ballad idiom and closes with the idiosyncratic Greek 'omphalos'.

As Neil Corcoran points out, the closing lyrical address to the soldiers, 'O charioteers', is strangely anachronistic, but its function is to expose rather than obscure political power: 'the British soldiers become, briefly, continuous with the forces of the Roman imperium' (Corcoran, 1986, p. 134). That backward historical look might seem to deflect from the urgent needs of the moment, but it nevertheless presents the British army as an aggressive, occupying presence. The poem gathers to a climax as it sets against the passing image of violence an enduring image of artistic inspiration: 'The invisible, untoppled omphalos'. The Greek omphalos is a crucially important word in Heaney's lexicon, as it is in that of James Joyce. It appears as the first word in the opening essay of his first collection of essays, *Preoccupations*, associating the navel and the centre of the world with the sound of water being pumped in the yard of the farm where he grew up in Co. Derry. McDonald questions both the poem's 'deep narrative' and what he sees as a 'forced' combination of 'ballad rhetoric' and 'lexical idiosyncracy' (McDonald, 1997, p. 57), but his reading is so wilfully intent on exposing what he regards as a suspect preoccupation with identity and possession that it fails to do justice to the poem's capacity to speak eloquently beyond its own specific place and time. This is ultimately the force and power of the seemingly idiosyncratic 'omphalos'. The poem's claim that it 'stands here still, stands vibrant as you pass' is a defiant recognition of art's resistance to brutal pressures, whatever the context, and (as the repetition suggests) a bold acknowledgement of all that poetry stands for.

From the outset, the poet's imagination has set the assuaging rhythms of water being pumped in the yard – 'omphalos, omphalos, omphalos' – against a troubling military incursion. The child growing up in the 1940s hears 'American bombers groan towards the aerodrome at Toomebridge', while 'American troops manoeuvre in the fields along the road' (Heaney, 1980, p. 17). In *Electric Light* (2001), Heaney returns to the early places of the imagination, but with a new sense of energy and insight. The opening poem, 'At Toomebridge', gathers up Heaney's earlier interests in local topography and replays them with a new suddenness and a new sense of the marvellous:

> Where the flat water
> Came pouring over the weir out of Lough Neagh
> As if it had reached an edge of the flat earth
> And fallen shining to the continuous
> Present of the Bann.
>
> (Heaney, 2001, p. 3)

The title and the repeated anaphoric emphasis on 'where' (four times in a poem of ten lines) are strong indicators of a persistent interest in places and placenames in Heaney's work. The technique of finding verbal equivalents for features of the landscape is reminiscent of the earlier 'Toome', while the speaker's excited apprehension of the world recalls some of the early poems in *Death of a Naturalist* and *Door into the Dark*. Even so, there is a distinct and decisive change of perspective. The typographical indentation and the syntactical disconnectedness create the impression that the poem has been extracted from some larger sequence. The movement of water sets up a complex interplay of spatial and temporal effects, as if enacting the processes of memory and imagination as they explore the contours of the earth. The poem acknowledges both the Heraclitean flux that Gerard Manley Hopkins revelled in and the persistent, ineffaceable stuff of history, including the remembrance of 'Where the rebel boy was hanged in '98'. The world is charged with electricity, and poetry is born out of the tension between sameness and difference, between that which lasts and that which changes.

Heaney's renewed engagement with the energies of place in *Electric Light* is undoubtedly prompted by the changing political climate in the late 1990s. A consciousness of the ceasefire and its local consequences becomes apparent in the poem's recollection of 'Where the checkpoint used to be', but this is a post-ceasefire poem in other ways as well. The stylistic corollary of the changed political order is a new willingness to entertain the ludic, self-reflexive, playfully riddling idiom that had previously appeared suspect. Heaney's self-referencing now takes on a slippery, eel-like allusiveness. The closing lines both take us back to the earlier poetry and reassert a sense of changed priorities: 'As once before / The slime and silver of the fattened eel' (Heaney, 2001, p. 3). The expected 'slither' is cleverly transformed into silver, and a subtle subliminal connection is established between electric light and electric eels. We are reminded of the 'prospecting' speaker amidst the elvers in the earlier 'Toome' but also of the phosphorescent eels near Toomebridge in Heaney's early 'Lough Neagh Sequence'. The light that came flooding in with the announcement of the ceasefire in August 1994 now seems to fill the poems with a new political promise and a new stylistic charge and energy.

Since 1994, Heaney's poetry has taken on a more reflective, retrospective disposition; it has steadily, if cautiously, opened itself to the possibilities of reconciliation and peaceful settlement, while remaining alert to the other possibility that the ceasefire might be no more than a brief, illusory resolution of crisis. More recently, in *District and Circle* (2006), the crisis has itself been redefined, so that the political urgencies that had once seemed peculiar to a province have come to be regarded within the context of global terrorism and counter-terrorism. Both before and after the ceasefire, Heaney has credited poetry with the responsibility of being a witness to its times, as well as an impulse for change. To respond imaginatively and sensitively to crisis without yielding to it has been the challenge and achievement of much of Heaney's own work as both poet and critic. It is still too early to tell how Heaney's poetry might develop in the aftermath of new power-sharing initiatives at Stormont, or to anticipate what further crises it might encounter, but there is no doubt, as he himself has recognized, that things have 'moved on'.

References

Corcoran, Neil (1986) *Seamus Heaney* (London: Faber and Faber).
Heaney, Seamus (1966) *Death of a Naturalist* (London: Faber and Faber).
—— (1969) *Door into the Dark* (London: Faber and Faber).
—— (1972) *Wintering Out* (London: Faber and Faber).
—— (1975) *North* (London: Faber and Faber).
—— (1979) *Field Work* (London: Faber and Faber).
—— (1980) *Preoccupations: Selected Prose 1968–1978* (London: Faber and Faber).
—— (1983) *Sweeney Astray* (London: Faber and Faber).

—— (1988) 'Anglo–Irish Occasions', *London Review of Books* (5 May 1988).
—— (1989) *The Place of Writing* (Atlanta: Scholars Press).
—— (1991) *Seeing Things* (London: Faber and Faber).
—— (1995) *The Redress of Poetry* (London: Faber and Faber).
—— (1996) *The Spirit Level* (London: Faber and Faber).
—— (1998) *Opened Ground: Poems 1966–1996* (London: Faber and Faber).
—— (2001) *Electric Light* (London: Faber and Faber).
—— (2004) 'Light Finally Enters the Black Hole', *Sunday Tribune*, 4 September 2004, p. A9.
—— (2006) *District and Circle* (London: Faber and Faber).
Longley, Edna (2000) *Poetry and Posterity* (Tarset: Bloodaxe).
McDonald, Peter (1997) *Mistaken Identities: Poetry and Northern Ireland* (Oxford: Clarendon Press).
Morrison, Blake (1982) *Seamus Heaney* (London: Methuen).
Muldoon, Paul (2001) *Poems 1968–1998* (London: Faber and Faber).
Murphy, Andrew (1996) *Seamus Heaney* (Plymouth: Northcote House).
Regan, Stephen (ed.) (2004) *Irish Writing: An Anthology of Irish Literature in English 1789–1939* (Oxford: Oxford University Press).

7

The Mundane and the Monstrous: Everyday Epiphanies in Northern Irish Poetry

Charles I. Armstrong

In the poem 'The Journey Back', Seamus Heaney uses this closing epithet to sum up his own perspective on Philip Larkin: '*A nine-to-five man who had seen poetry*' (Heaney, 1991, p. 7). Arguably, it captures a crucial dimension of what the first generation of Troubles poets inherited from Larkin and the Movement. There is, on the one hand, the persistence of a Romantic or Symbolist desire to transgress or transcend the bounds of given experience,[1] responding to a crisis of confidence in experience. On the other hand, though, one is simultaneously obligated by the exigencies of the quotidian: the everyday just won't go away.

For some readers, the way in which Northern Irish poets have responded to the gravitational pull of the everyday has been something of an embarrassment: it is has been seen as a somewhat outdated relic of Larkin and his associates,[2] something either to be berated or ignored as one eagerly homes in on the more easily-handled dimensions of textuality or political discourse. Opposing such a view, I will here approach a quartet of Northern Irish poets through an interrogation of what the dimension of everyday life represents in some of their texts. The poets that will be addressed are Seamus Heaney, Paul Muldoon, Ciaran Carson and Leontia Flynn, and emphasis will be given to isolated moments of vision, which either reveal the quintessence of the everyday, or more transcendentally point beyond the routines and rituals of ordinary life. Such everyday epiphanies often take their bearings in a crisis concerning our perceptual access, or sense of belonging, to the world, promising a restoration of sacredness or immediacy in a demystified and objectified existence. Though they frequently promise a sensual relation of organic directness, these poetical revelations are however not, in the long run, immune to ideology and mechanical predictability. The response to crisis thus easily undergoes a crisis of its own, becoming part of – or at least not immune to – the problem, rather than presenting any straightforward solution. Northern Irish poets are, however, frequently self-reflectively aware of this conundrum, and therefore the everyday epiphany will here be placed in juxtaposition with the ways in which these poets engage in a critical interrogation of the quotidian realm, particularly through a questioning of power relations and contemporary consumerism. With regard to this latter dimension, two French theorists of everyday life – Henri Lefebvre and Michel de Certeau – will offer some guidance.

Everyday epiphanies constitute a very important and repeated *topos* in Seamus Heaney's poetry. Volume titles such as *Electric Light* and *Seeing Things* signal towards a pervasive desire to transfigure the quotidian. The everyday epiphany would break through the film of familiarity, restoring a coveted, and temporarily lost, intensity of experience. Readers critical of Heaney have indicated, however, that more than this may be involved: they see in such epiphanies a desire to revivify atavistic dreams of origin, whether these be of a political or poetical order. Certainly the repetitiveness of Heaney's desire to sense the world anew comes with risks, including that of poetic predictability. Already in the preface for the *Lyrical Ballads*, Wordsworth was expressing a desire that 'ordinary things should be presented to the mind in an unusual way' (Wordsworth, 1977, p. 869), and to engage in a similar practice some two hundred years later is obviously to risk not only poetic cliché but also the transformation of the promise of organic immediacy into something not only mechanical but also highly mediated.

Heaney has pursued the idea of poetry as a revivifying of the everyday with obsessive single-mindedness, something which again has led to an increasingly acute self-consciousness. He lays bare his craft with exemplary clarity in the poem 'Making Strange' from the *Station Island* volume – the very title of this poem indeed being fraught with significance. In literary theory, 'making strange' has long figured as a favoured English translation of the Russian term *ostranenie*. In Victor Shklovsky's early article entitled 'Art as Technique', *ostranenie* was presented as a typical poetical device, by which authors such as Pushkin and Dostoyevsky broke through the film of habitual monotony and abstraction with which everyday life had imbued existence (compare Shklovsky, 1965). Thanks to these acts of productive alienation, authors could return the world to its original sensory immediacy. Later, Shklovsky and other members of the Russian formalist school exposed this concept to generalization and transformation, so that it included all means by which a writer could self-consciously lay bare the fundamentals of the artistic process. Heaney's text nicely balances early and late Russian formalism. As Michael Parker has pointed out, the 'occasion for the poem was a guided tour of the home-ground for the Jamaican-born poet, Louis Simpson' (Parker, 1993, p. 189). Heaney the tour-guide mediates between the native and the cosmopolitan by listening to the voice of a *genius loci*. On the one hand, he gives expression to the singular sensuous detail, both through his voice that is 'adept at dialect' and through its evocation of detailed objects – including sweetbriar, snowberries, 'puddles and stones' (Heaney, 1984, p. 32). On the other hand, the poem insistently signals towards its own status as an aesthetic work of art: through its title, a clear nod to the *aisling* genre, and in the concluding stress on the word 'recitation' through which it meta-poetically lays bare its own artistic DNA.

Thus 'Making Strange' is an epiphany of both the sensuousness of an Irish landscape and of the poem's own underlying poetical structure. More implicitly, the poem also suggests that nature and art here encroach upon the process of commodification, a dimension that may be at loggerheads with other facets of the ideology of the aesthetic. As a native but well-travelled guide, the speaker is a constructer of commodified objects: both art and nature become vehicles of tourism, of aesthetic enjoyment of the exotic. Seen within Heaney's larger oeuvre, this is actually the strangest aspect of the poem. Even if he resists a fully-fledged transcendence of the everyday, Heaney's imaginative recalibrations of the given tend towards the withdrawal of both objects and artistic subjectivity from much of their socioeconomic context.[3] Commodification, when it occurs, is figured as a movement from without, threatening the immediate relations found in traditional, rural workmanship. As such, Heaney's usual version of quotidian existence bears some resemblance to the Romantic version criticized by Richard Kirkland, who claims that the everyday is characterized by a 'rural, countrified version of history' that elides political division into a notion of timeless tradition (Kirkland, 1996, p. 21). Insofar as Heaney approaches this latter model, there is little common ground with the more modern, subversive and historically inscribed versions of the everyday presented by thinkers such as de Certeau and Lefebvre.

Heaney's faith in the aesthetic realm's ability to transcend the given should, however, not be exaggerated. This becomes evident if one turns to the sonnet that concludes the first part of his 1991 volume, *Seeing Things*. 'Fosterling' stages an awakening out of a state of inertia. It is a typical crisis poem of Romantic provenance, signalling a rebirth of the poetical consciousness from a state of fallenness and inauthenticity.

In the final lines, the poet conjures a vision that is tentatively poised between expectancy and achievement. He has now arrived at a point in life where he is ready

> To credit marvels. Like the tree-clock of tin cans
> The tinkers made. So long for air to brighten,
> Time to be dazzled and the heart to lighten.
> (Heaney, 1991, p. 50)

Is the temporality of the everyday here left behind, or is transcendence merely wished for and projected? Even if the poet draws inspiration from the travellers, the original materials of their 'tree-clock' made out of 'tin cans' are not transformed beyond recognition. Similarly, the reader is left undecided whether the phrase 'Time to be dazzled' evokes a complete changing of the temporal order, whereby time itself is dazzled or confused beyond its quotidian shape,[4] or whether this merely signals that the poet's age of fifty signifies that he has arrived at a fitting temporal crossroads for a change in perspective. Similarly, the penultimate line balances desire and gratification in the words 'So long for air to brighten': although the reader may be tempted to overlook the undecidability at work here, 'So long' may just as well indicate an imperative (with 'long' functioning as a verb) as an accounting of lapsed time.

'Fosterling' can be seen as exemplary of how the openness of Heaney's everyday epiphanies makes for a tight-rope walk between immanence and transcendence, between the mundane and the numinous. At his least dogmatic, he makes us unsure whether the promise of poetry is an alternative to, or an intensification of, our ordinary lives. In this respect, as in many others, Paul Muldoon's voice represents a sceptical alternative. The fourth poem of Muldoon's sequence entitled *The Prince of the Quotidian* pokes fun at Heaney's claim that he has started 'walking on air' in his poetry (Muldoon, 1994, p. 14). In this collection, Muldoon very decidedly walks on the ground, offering a down-to-earth riposte to this particular poetical forefather. *The Prince of the Quotidian* includes one poem written per day, during the month of January 1992. The result is an unreservedly low-key affair, in which Muldoon himself anticipates critically disparaging epithets such as '"humdrum", "inadequate", // "inconsequential journalese"' (ibid., p. 29) and a dismissive shrug at 'laundry-lists and tax-returns' (ibid., p. 40). In this account of everyday life, transcendence is rendered acutely problematical. One poem takes place on the day of the Feast of the Epiphany. At first it might seem to be leading up to some striking everyday vision, starting as it does with evoking the possible present of finches and deer in the poet's herb-garden. But the final lines change focus from natural epiphany to the bathos of everyday technology:

> In the mean-time, my lemon-peel
> and bacon-rind mobile
> is losing something of its verve.
> I wait in vain for some small showing forth.
> (Ibid., p. 17)

In *The Prince of the Quotidian*, Muldoon makes do without any transfiguring illuminations, proffering highly mundane details from one month of his life. He is shown to be constantly travelling around the United States, particularly in the area around his east coast home, entertaining and being entertained at get-togethers of varying formality. What can be gleaned from this insistently oblique look on the poet's daily existence? The way in which Muldoon presents himself as constantly interacting with friends and family, shows that the poet is not to be conceived of here as a solitary genius, but rather as a social being. In addition, the poet is presented as a situated being – most of the short poems of *The Prince of the Quotidian* include references to specific places or travel. Travel here overrides any sense of settledness or rootedness. This is emphasized not only by references to highways and traffic signals in the environs of New Jersey and New York, but also by constant allusion to Muldoon's past and his contemporaries in Ireland.

Another striking feature of Muldoon's collection is the extent to which it highlights consumerism. Yeats famously insisted upon the unbridgeable gap between the poet and the man who sits down for breakfast (compare Yeats, 1994, p. 204), but the very first lines of *The Prince of the Quotidian* present the poet as having just completed 'breakfast with Belinda and Philip Haas' (Muldoon, 1994, p. 11). The remainder of the volume is chock-a-block with references to shared meals – including a meringue enjoyed during the interval of a performance of the *The Ghosts of Versailles* at the Metropolitan Opera (compare ibid., p. 18).[5] Muldoon also flaunts his consumption of musical and filmic commodities. A particularly striking and teasing instance of this is included in a poem that allusively juxtaposes the due date of Muldoon's daughter, the twelfth of July, with Neruda's birthday anniversary rather than with the Orange marches and their prehistory. Brief nods to poetical colleagues bring the Northern Irish context back into focus, however, only for the seriousness to be apparently punctured by these two concluding lines: 'I spend the evening transferring the new Lloyd Cole / and *Cajun Classics* from CD to tape' (ibid., p. 33).

Such a gesture might be interpreted as a cheeky and deflationary one, but I believe more is involved here than dismissive irony. *The Prince of the Quotidian* presents the poet as a mobile, sociable consumer, implicitly arguing that even the transferring of one's favourite music 'from CD to tape' involves a salutary act of positioning. Rather than just responding negatively to Romantic transcendence, this volume also tries to find affirmative positions in the face of the crisis of subjectivity that has followed in the wake of the industrial and other technological revolutions. In this respect, Muldoon's volume can be productively compared with Michel de Certeau's study *The Practice of Everyday Life*, which evokes consumerist lines of resistance in a technologically sophisticated society. According to de Certeau, consumers are 'unrecognized producers, poets of their own acts, silent discoverers of their own paths in the jungle of functionalist rationality' (de Certeau, 1984, p. xviii). One of the ways in which such subversion occurs is through the transformation of monolithic places into manifold and heterogeneous spaces. While de Certeau privileges the Baudelairean *flâneur* of big cities rather than anything straightforwardly resembling Muldoon's commuting poet, both celebrate the ways in which everyday spaces are less unified and overseeable than the monuments of dominant ideologies.

De Certeau claims that consumerism can be transgressive if it adheres to particular kinds of usages: that is, if it deploys ruses that fragment rather than unify the order made out of its used objects. He is particularly attuned to how immigrants overturn the native systems that are thrust upon them (compare ibid., p. 30). Something similar occurs when Muldoon conflates the experiences of a Pennington car wash with his reading of Nuala Ní Dhomhnaill in the following image: 'my windshield was a tangle / of eel-grass and bladderwrack' (Muldoon, 1994, p. 38). Comparable encounters with the everyday are evident throughout Muldoon's other volumes. With regard to the Troubles, he has developed a mode of what might be called negation of the everyday epiphany, an epiphany of the monstrous behind the mundane. In poems such as 'Ireland' (from *Why Brownlee Left*) and 'A Trifle' (from *Quoof*) he has taken the *topos* of poetical revelation and linked its paradoxical transcendence of the everyday to the violence of random political force rather than to the numinous.

This mode has been deftly appropriated by Ciaran Carson. Published in 1989, Carson's volume *Belfast Confetti* constantly approaches the moment of violence, where the speaker or his associates might become the victims of seemingly unpredictable force. Yet the actual violence is, typically, either deferred, elided or covered in mists of rhetoric and mythology. Particular emphasis is placed on the ways in which everyday life during the Troubles is affected by a temporality of violence: the damage is always in the offing, always a risk lurking just out of earshot. In poems such as 'Gate', 'Last Orders' and 'Punctuation', Carson allows the body's premonitions of imminent violence to articulate themselves, spelling out a temporality of the everyday where dismemberment and loss are always an incalculable risk that one nevertheless tries to calculate and prepare for in one's actions. Violence is the other embedded in the everyday. If there is any transcendence, it is not a religious form of transfiguration or apotheosis, but only a hairline crack that allows possible futures to reverberate in, and transform, the mortal present.

Belfast Confetti includes a lengthy quotation from Jeremy Bentham's description of the panopticon, on the basis of which Temple Cone has drawn a justified parallel between Carson's evocation of the Belfast cityscape and Michel Foucault's theory (inspired by Bentham) of the incarceral nature of modern society (see Cone, 2006). The Bentham quotation takes place in the little prose piece 'Intelligence', where the speaker claims that 'Everyone is watching someone, everyone wants to know what's coming next' (Carson, 1989, p. 78). Still, he points out, the deployed technology is not flawless: 'the glitches and gremlins and bugs keep fouling-up, seething out from the hardware' (ibid., p. 79). In this volume, surveillance is ubiquitous, even if it is not subject to one monolithic force as in Foucault. Yet Carson's insistence upon how the city resists a totalizing view points in another direction: here Henri Lefebvre's understanding of the everyday constitutes just as relevant a frame of reference as that presented by Foucault. Poems such as 'Turn Again' and 'Question Time' use maps to demonstrate how everyday life in the city escapes formalization and overview. In the words of 'Question Time', 'Maps and street directories are suspect. [...] No, don't trust maps, for they avoid the moment: ramps, barricades, diversions, Peace Lines' (ibid., p. 58). This comes close to Lefebvre's understanding of the city as a place of 'effective resistance' to the powers of surveillance and domination, this resistance being embodied in 'not the morphological town mapped out on the ground and embodied in symbols and signs, but city life and society' (Lefebvre, 2000, p. 124). According to Lefebvre, everyday life is 'a compound of insignificances' which is 'practically untellable' (ibid., p. 24). Unlike the religious concept of the numinous, the everyday elusively resists representation due to its very triviality. For Carson, this is particularly brought home by the ephemeral nature of the Northern Irish capital, which he calls 'this brick-built demolition city' (Carson, 1989, p. 82). In Belfast, both memory and maps are always playing catch-up with the constant process of change. This is not progress or a circular return to originary places, but a ceaseless turmoil without any inherent teleology. In 'Revised Version', Carson puts it this way: 'everything is contingent and provisional' (ibid., 67).

As in Muldoon's *The Prince of the Quotidian*, the speaker's ability to circumvent institutionalized or overly rigid delimitations of the everyday is linked to his spatial mobility: Carson presents himself constantly on foot, traversing the pubs and streets of Belfast according to a seemingly aleatory and haphazard trajectory. Here he follows in the footsteps of the *flâneurs* of Baudelaire – a poet not only translated by Carson, but also of vital inspiration to later French celebrants of the everyday such as Lefebvre and de Certeau.[6] In *Belfast Confetti*, though, Carson's relative freedom is also strongly linked to his handling of maps: precisely by showing how differing maps of Belfast contradict one another, and often include buildings and streets that are either demolished or non-existent, he resists the ideological monologues of place. This echoes the inventiveness of traditional music, as depicted in Carson's *Last Night's Fun*. In the latter book, the reuse of traditional songs is interpreted as a radically innovative action: 'the tune can never be perfected or complete: each time it is played it is only a rehearsal for the next time, when it will open up under new management, or take "another handling", as they say' (Carson, 1996, p. 120). Like the playing of a tune, the map rearticulates reality. In this respect, the map is also an analogue for the poem's possibility of performative transgression, and the concluding and italicized epigram of 'Revised Version' – '*The city is the map of the city*' (Carson, 1989, p. 69) – becomes an index of the poem's ability to transcend the commodified state characteristic of consumerist objects.

A younger contemporary of Carson's, Leontia Flynn, enacts her own version of the theme of everyday life. Flynn published her first volume of poetry, *These Days*, in 2004. As one could perhaps expect from a poet who only turned thirty in the same year, the collection is very much focused on processes of maturation and initiation. As is the case with Medbh McGuckian, on whom Flynn wrote her PhD, many of Flynn's poems focus on private life. More specifically, Flynn addresses the private life of students and young adults who haven't settled down. The dichotomy between private and public life is established in the first of a series of poems titled 'Without Me'. With typically grim humour, we are told that the speaker's lover or alter ego spends days 'walking the public sector – / the parks, the museums and the libraries / with the mad old fuckers muttering into the microfiche'. This is contrasted with 'the dark pools of our nights' (Flynn, 2004a, p. 5).

Flynn has claimed that the volume reflects the results of a conscious decision 'to write about day-to-day things' (Flynn, 2004b), and most of the poems include poetical snapshots, as it were, of particular places or events of the speaker's life – a technique that also characterizes the many poetical postcards from foreign cities in her next volume, *Drives* (2008). In *These Days*, such snapshots typically depict either habitual periods of stasis or heightened moments of crisis. Everyday life can be repetitiously banal, as in 'The Amazing, Disappearing', which starts off by evoking 'A morning routine, anaesthetic / as passing your finger through a candle / if you can just do it quickly enough' (Flynn, 2004a, p. 12). It can, however, also be revelatory: in 'What You Get', the speaker is suddenly caught off-guard by a vision at the South Gyle Industrial Estate:

> One afternoon you watch
> as a host of Styrofoam balls comes billowing through
> and covers the close: a great Andrei Tarkovsky
> slo-mo, and you're pleased with it –
> its basic wage, take-what-you-get epiphany.
>
> (Ibid., p. 24)

As in Heaney, who is evoked directly in Flynn's poem 'When I Was Sixteen I Met Seamus Heaney', the poet handles this privileged instant with pronounced self-consciousness. The mention of Tarkovsky is typical of Flynn's collection, which includes several references to popular music, primetime television and classic films. In this poem, the comparison with the Russian filmmaker functions to create an explicit moment of aestheticization. Furthermore, the reference to pleasure (in 'you're pleased with it') can be taken as a staple of aesthetic experience, but arguably brings with it Flynn's typically self-ironic humour. Together with this humour, the references to a 'basic wage' and an industrial setting point away from Heaney and towards concerns characteristic of Flynn's writing.

According to Michael Sheringham, the everyday is 'Frequently associated with the domestic sphere', and can therefore 'be seen as antithetical to politics and the public domain' (Sheringham, 2006, p. 24). Although this is far from true for someone like Ciaran Carson, it largely fits the bill with Flynn. As is the case with many of her poems, the epiphany of 'What You Get' takes place in a personal context. The poem that precedes 'What You Get' in *These Days*, one of the series 'Without Me', evokes a similar everyday epiphany as occurring when the speaker and a friend throw a plastic lid like a frisbee back and forth, somewhere 'down Eskra's lorryless roads' (Flynn, 2004a, p. 23). Only the opening line's mentioning of 'the hiatus of a difficult July' hints at a possible political context. Elsewhere, in the poem 'Holland', the speaker seems to be caught between shamefacedness and mute protest when a doctor generalizes her nervous ailment:

> The Dutch doctor with the brunette handlebar moustache
> smiles sadly as he prescribes Oxazypam
> (are these *cow* tranquilisers?), giving a little shrug
> at his own proposal to 'avoid these with alcohol',
> then taking your grime-stained urchin's hand, he adds
> 'If I live in Belfast, I also perhaps feel bad'.
> Now even your *neuroses* are unoriginal.
>
> (Ibid., p. 39)

Even if Flynn thus hints at a possible overlap between private and political malaise, her first book largely avoids overt mention of the Troubles or other political issues.

Instead there is a sustained focus on the personal life of the speaker, its routine worries, illnesses and neuroses only occasionally finding release in everyday epiphanies. In the sonnet 'The Magician', a child's combination of ingenuity and creativity makes rich and wonderful the otherwise neglected objects of domestic life. Flynn includes several poems about childhood, and even when focusing on adult life she seems rather to be looking back over her shoulder at a sense of lost liberty than relishing the prospect of adult responsibility and experience. The most static poems cultivate a sense of regression into an infant-like inertia. In 'bed Poem', the speaker generalizes this temptation:

> Surely, at some stage – perhaps
> down the black pits of winter mornings – everyone
> has felt the urge to go Florence Nightingale: just
>
> forget this whole business of penetrating
> and directing a day. Take to our lazy beds.
> Let the days have their way with us.
>
> (Ibid., p. 32)

Although personal, Flynn's vision here is not private: everyday life seems to include within itself a general promise of escape from modernity's demand for productivity. De Certeau has claimed that 'If it is true that the grid of "discipline" is everywhere becoming clearer and more extensive, it is all the more urgent to discover how an entire society resists being reduced to it' (de Certeau, p. xiv). Flynn's speaker presents one mode of resistance: retreating to her lazy bed, she resists the teleological thrust of public life.

The bed is arguably the main object of the resulting, semi-autonomous world of unproductive pleasures, which is evoked again and again in *These Days*. All the objects of Flynn's typically intimate, closed spaces have, however, the potential of being derailed from usefulness into an economy of wasteful splendour. The opening stanza of 'Satis House' sketches a catalogue of a typical collection of everyday bric-a-brac, wasting away in a setting of seemingly slothful intimacy:

> Late summer light is slanting through the glass:
> a frieze of light on the carpet, an indiscreet freeze-frame
> of all the junk and clutter of this place –
> something is playing out, and we have set the scene:
> a column of smoke rising up from an ashtray
> then stuttering out: the sunlight's indiscreet snapshot
> of slumped clothes and old newsprint, of ring-pulls and
> bottle caps,
> loose change, the last of your Lustral – spilled salt.
>
> (Flynn 2004a, p. 41)

The same poem ends on what must be interpreted as a tacitly moralistic note. The withdrawal of the speaker and her partner from productive relations amounts, it is implied, to 'the path of least resistance' (ibid., p. 42). Like Tennyson's lotus-eaters, the inhabitants of 'Satis House' are satiated in a problematical way. 'Satis House' thus paves the way for the title poem, which concludes the volume, and which enacts a leave-taking from infantile regression: even if there may be some remnant of irony involved, a sea-change of sorts is indicated by the fact that 'these days I'm serious' (ibid., p. 54). On the evidence of her next volume, *Drives*, such seriousness may not amount to more than an ironic awareness of the insufficiency of escapism, immaturity and the personal realm. A characteristic poem from the latter book, 'Don't Worry', ends with the words: 'but don't worry / about famine or war, here in our world / of love. Okey dokey?' (Flynn, 2008, p. 40).

Leontia Flynn's poetry outlines one possible way of addressing the legacy of the everyday in the post-Troubles era. Where Seamus Heaney gives everyday life a quasi-religious sanctification, Paul Muldoon shows ordinary life as being inescapable, yet also potentially transgressive, through his oblique adaptation of consumerism. Ciaran Carson, for his part, demonstrates how everyday life constituted a vulnerable dimension during the Troubles, but also how the urban *flâneur* can resist the violence of monological ideologies. The careers of three of these poets – Heaney, Muldoon and Carson – will always be linked with the Troubles. If the political context will no longer aggravate or inspire Leontia Flynn and other upcoming generations of Northern Irish poets in quite the same way, it remains an open question whether the realm of everyday will become emptied of content or merely abstractly contrasted with the civic responsibilities of the public realm. Without a sense of political crisis, either in the margins or at the centre of their texts, Northern Irish poets risk being engulfed by the more insidious kind of crisis that arguably has challenged English poets since the Second World War.[7]

In any case, it is evident that the concept of everyday life inhabits an ambiguous place with regard to the many crises to which these poets respond. In 1947, in the first of his three instalments of the *Critique de la vie quotidienne*, Henri Lefebvre presented a shared sense of the everyday as a possible solution to the pervading sense of existential crisis following the Second World War (compare Sheringham, 2006, p. 134). In Northern Irish poetry, a sense of day-by-day normality or business as usual is, in a similar way, frequently presented as a salutary alternative to the unpredictable violence of the Troubles. Yet the ideological underpinnings of the everyday are not unequivocal, and interpretations of it as something sanctified, politically questionable or innately personal contrast and contest each other. The powerful attraction of the quotidian is, it would seem, more than matched by its terminological slipperiness and ideological versatility.

Notes

1. For a philosophical reading of the relationship between Romanticism and the everyday, see Cavell (1994).
2. Other sources for this preoccupation with the everyday, outside the Movement, might be cited – the most important of which is probably Louis MacNeice. Edna Longley has described MacNeice as being 'humanistically absorbed by everyday life' (Longley, 1988, p. 45).
3. For a reading of how the processes of withdrawal and transcendence are set to work in his verse, see Armstrong (2006).
4. Compare the following lines from the same volume: 'There was fleetness, furtherance, untiredness / In time that was extra, unforeseen and free' ('Markings' in Heaney, 1991, p. 8).

5. Muldoon frequently refers to meals; see for instance Hancock (2006).
6. On Baudelaire's importance for the French tradition of *la vie quotidienne*, see Sheringham (2006, pp. 61–2). Translations of sonnets by Baudelaire are included in Carson (1998).
7. According to Randall Stevenson, 'English literature was never more static than under the influence of the Movement: if the later twentieth century proved a difficult period for poetry, it was in large measure because it took so long to realize this, and move on' (Stevenson, 2004, p. 270). Stevenson points out that much of the work of the Northern Irish poets of the Troubles 'embodied a tragic urgency – a compelling need for the voice of poetry, in encountering intolerable events – which English writers could scarcely share directly' (ibid., 255).

References

Armstrong, Charles I. (2006) 'Touch and Go: Seamus Heaney and the Transcendence of the Aesthetic', in Irene Gilsenan Nordin (ed.) *The Body and Desire in Contemporary Irish Poetry* (Dublin: Irish Academic Press).
Carson, Ciaran (1989) *Belfast Confetti* (Oldcastle: The Gallery Press).
—— (1996) *Last Night's Fun: About Music, Food and Time* (London: Pimlico).
—— (1998) *The Alexandrine Plan* (Oldcastle: The Gallery Press).
Cavell, Stanley (1994) *In Quest of the Ordinary: Lines of Skepticism and Romanticism* (Chicago: University of Chicago Press).
Cone, Temple (2006) 'Knowing Street Map by Foot: Ciaran Carson's *Belfast Confetti*', *New Hibernia Review*, 10.3 (Autumn), 68–86.
De Certeau, Michel (1984) *The Practice of Everyday Life*, trans. Steven Rendall (Berkeley: University of California Press).
Flynn, Leontia (2004a) *These Days* (London: Jonathan Cape).
—— (2004b) 'Youth Worker', *Poetry Book Society Bulletin*, 201 (Summer), 10.
—— (2008) *Drives* (London: Jonathan Cape).
Hancock, Tim (2006) 'Dining Out with Paul Muldoon: Poetic and Personal Relations in the Restaurant Poems', in Elmer Kennedy-Andrews (ed.) *Paul Muldoon: Poetry, Prose, Drama: A Collection of Critical Essays* (Gerrards Cross: Colin Smythe Limited).
Heaney, Seamus (1984) *Station Island* (London: Faber and Faber).
—— (1991) *Seeing Things* (London: Faber and Faber).
Kirkland, Richard (1996) *Literature and Culture in Northern Ireland since 1965: Moments of Danger* (London and New York: Longman).
Lefebvre, Henri (2000) *Everyday Life in the Modern World*, trans. Sacha Rabinovitch (London: Continuum).
Longley, Edna (1988) *Louis MacNeice: A Critical Study* (London: Faber and Faber).
Muldoon, Paul (1994) *The Prince of the Quotidian* (Oldcastle: The Gallery Press).
Parker, Michael (1993) *Seamus Heaney: The Making of a Poet* (Basingstoke: Gill and Macmillan).
Sheringham, Michael (2006) *Everyday Life: Theories and Practices from Surrealism to the Present* (Oxford: Oxford University Press).
Shklovsky, Victor (1965) 'Art as Technique', in L. Lemon and M. Reis (eds) *Russian Formalist Criticism: Four Essays* (Lincoln: University of Nebraska Press).

Stevenson, Randall (2004) *The Last of England? The Oxford English Literary History, volume 12, 1960–2000* (Oxford: Oxford University Press).

Wordsworth, William (1977) *The Poems*, Vol. 1, John O. Hayden (ed.) (Harmondsworth: Penguin).

Yeats, William Butler (1994) *Later Essays*, William O'Donnell (ed.) with assistance from Elizabeth Bergmann Loizeaux (New York: Charles Scribner's Sons).

Part III
Situated Words: Place, Ecology and Landscape

8
'The memorial to all of them': Landscape and the Holocaust in the Poetry of Michael Longley

Brendan Corcoran

I

> In the hedges of the fields just a few hundred yards from our house, there was a lovely old crab-apple tree. I used to climb it. You could lie down – it was so hammocky. I disturbed a blackbird on her nest and she took off. I was furious with myself for having disturbed her – I was only about seven. I gazed at these beautiful blue eggs. I thought, about a week later, dare I go back? I didn't want to disturb her again. I returned. Louts, bastards, had ripped the tree to pieces and there was the nest and the eggs broken and one or two little fledglings lying on the ground. It sounds awfully pathetic, but in some ways I'm still getting over that. I realized there were people around capable of that. It's nothing at all compared to Auschwitz, of course – but Auschwitz begins there.
>
> (Corcoran, 2007, p. 119)

Michael Longley's life-long fascination with the natural world stems, in part, from a number of crucial childhood incidents that serve as 'terrible revelations' of the 'pitiless' predation in nature (ibid., p. 118).[1] He describes how a hawk with a sparrow in its claws, got tangled in a sheet hung out to dry, but escaped with the smaller bird still shrieking in its clutches. He then tells of a long-tailed tit's dome-shaped nest, 'so secure and cozy', being 'wrecked by a magpie or a crow' (ibid., p. 119). And finally he presents an account of an un-natural but commonplace – and quintessentially human – scene of perfectly gratuitous violence. In

Longley's testimony, the curious child occupies a 'hammocky' niche in this very local ecosystem, but his seemingly benign presence disturbs the natural order as the frightened blackbird flies away from the nest revealing her eggs beautiful and intact. The seven-year-old is chastened by his impact on this world. Nonetheless, having fought his curiosity for a week, the child returns to the tree only to witness a previously unimaginable level of specifically human destructiveness. The poet's anger remains visceral over sixty years after this event, which impressed upon him both the human capacity for depravity and the ubiquity of such violence. The child's encounter with these broken eggs and the fledglings' bodies strewn in the aftermath of such 'louts' anticipates some of the most powerful scenes in Longley's poetry addressing war and human life in war's wake.

In Longley's 2006 interview account of his early contact (circa 1946) with gratuitous human violence, the poet from the twenty-first century overtly situates the Holocaust alongside his own childhood awakening to the kind of casual and normalized barbarity that enables genocide. Primo Levi, one of Longley's most cherished writers, introduces *Survival in Auschwitz* by also noting that genocide begins with the lamentably commonplace: that 'many people – many nations – can find themselves holding, more or less wittingly, that "every stranger is an enemy"'(Levi, 1996, p. 9). Levi says that 'for the most part this conviction lies deep down like some latent infection; it betrays itself only in random, disconnected acts, and does not lie at the base of a system of reason. But [...] when the unspoken dogma becomes the major premise in a syllogism, then, at the end of the chain, there is the Lager' (ibid., p. 9). In Longley's account of the nest's violation, the gratuitous destruction of nature as both source and otherness is itself symptomatic of the 'latent infection' described by Levi, in which 'every stranger is an enemy'. As a nature poet preoccupied with war, the Holocaust and its deepest origins have infiltrated Longley's own sense of nature and the human element in nature.

Longley's three principle themes are war and its traumas, love and nature, especially the environs of the Irish townland, Carrigskeewaun, on the west coast of county Mayo, where fully a third of his poems are set.[2] While much criticism of his writing focuses appropriately on the importance in his poetry of the Trojan War, World War I and Northern Ireland's Troubles, the Holocaust has also saturated his body of work as an extreme sense of limit and an unalloyable part of our human and poetic condition.[3] This chapter reads Longley's poetry and, ultimately, his relation to the lyric under the sign of the Holocaust's dark star (compare Blanchot, 1995, p. 2).

Longley, in that 2006 interview, also comments on Philip Larkin's 'The Explosion', stating that the final ghostly gesture of a killed miner holding out unbroken lark's eggs after the underground disaster is 'the image I most envy' among his twenty-two most valued poems (Corcoran, 2007, p. 104). Longley's poetry is poised between the actuality of that blackbird's irrevocably violated nest – those broken eggs – and Larkin's image of a not illusory but nevertheless haunted (the miner is, after all, killed) vision of unbroken eggs. The momentary spectre of tentative wholeness frames the unremitting brokenness before us. Both conditions are suspended necessarily together. In other words, both states exist simultaneously yet independently, even as each is shot through with the other. Furthermore, the pause or stay engendered by this state of suspension – which preserves the intensity and reality of both conditions – creates a space for the apprehension of a different kind of mourning. Crucially, the idea of desired wholeness contained by Larkin's poem (in the intact eggs) does nothing to counter the fact of the dead miner or destroyed nest. Instead, the facts of desired wholeness and invariable brokenness insist on a human scale that enables the transmission of the grief suffusing that miner's lyric return and Longley's recollection of those louts' handiwork.

Contrary to assertions by Stan Smith and others that he possesses a too-ready faith in poetry's compensatory power in the face of atrocity, Longley's work testifies to the joint human responsibilities to know (and let in) the world's literal brokenness as well as to desire, through various forms, the ultimate impossibility of wholeness (compare Brewster, 2006, p. 25). For example, in describing the affective beauty of various World War I battlefield cemeteries, Longley suggests that ideally the aesthetic project responding to history will 'both unsettle and console' (Longley, 1997a, p. 102). In these cemeteries, 'the atmosphere aches with pain and anguish [...] The rows of the war graves amount to a huge, silent lamentation' (ibid., p. 102). Longley is attentive to how such sites express the desire for consolation and the fact, especially where the horror of war is concerned, of consolation's inaccessibility. In another 1997 essay on Remembrance Day, Longley describes the dead in the mass graves beneath the ordered rows of headstones as having died 'in an obscene folly, an abomination from which Europe is still recovering' (Longley, 1997b, p. 121). Chastising the purveyors of easy, self-satisfied remembrance of horror, Longley goes on to protest that

> the Remembrance Day ceremony encourages us *not* to remember how shrapnel and bullets flay and shatter human flesh and bones, how continuous bombardment destroys minds as well as bodies,

> how poison gas causes 'froth-corrupted lungs' and 'guttering, choking, drowning'.
>
> (ibid., p. 122)

He asks: 'On Remembrance Day let us try to recover as many details as we can. Let us really and truly remember' (ibid., p. 123). Similarly, Longley invokes Wilfred Owen's 'Preface' to his posthumously published *War Poems* as he defines – in the 2006 interview – poetry's role in the face of atrocity:

> '[...] All a poet can do today is warn'. I don't go to poetry or write poetry for consolation. It's some kind of protest. Poetry is like a beautiful and rare orchid growing up through the tar macadam in a car park. That's what poetry does; there's nothing consolatory about that: a little plant creating its own revolution. Here in Ireland, people think that the elegies one writes are a consolation but they are not a consolation – they are part of a profound protest against cruelty, the cruelty that has its roots in superstition and ignorance and distrust.
>
> (Corcoran, 2007, p. 116)

In his translation, 'Remembrance Day', written after the Dutch poet Ida Gerhardt's poem about the failure to remember the names of World War II's dead after the assault of oblivion's inevitably overwhelming force, Longley transforms the commemorative gesture of a Remembrance Day into the reconstitution of the enormity of such loss in or as part of nature itself:

> The names of the fallen,
> names we forgot so soon,
> are sometimes lamented
> by the howling stormwind.
>
> Put your ears to the poles.
>
> That din overwhelmed me
> below Zalk and Veecaten –
> too much for poles to bear
> almost, and metal wires.
>
> (Longley, 2009, p. 27)

Here, mourning resides in the human apprehension of nature's 'stormwind' – not as mere objective correlative or elegiac apotheosis but as the presence of absence everywhere. The poem, like the telephone or transmission lines, vibrates with the emptiness marked by the need to mourn the nameless dead, including victims of the Holocaust. Above all, Longley's free translation demands that we put our 'ears to the poles' upholding those quotidian but also macabre wires, so as to hear the lamentation that reverberates through our world.

The responsibility to bear witness begins with the perception of a command to listen to the world's lamentation that, like a simultaneous curse and benediction, appalls and allures. Using Julia Kristeva's characterization of abjection as 'a vortex of summons and repulsion', Scott Brewster points out how in Northern Irish poetry (including Longley's) death is suspended before us *as* atrocity set alongside or within an artistic frame that offers the allure of balm (Brewster, 2006, p. 22). Particularly interested in Longley's advocacy for the presentation of horror as part of any honest mourning or remembrance, Brewster also recognizes that, even as Longley's elegiac poetry desires wholeness, it opposes a conventional belief in the accessibility of simple consolation:

> This desire to know, catalogue and remember risks lapsing into memorial history, where commemoration can entomb and obliterate the past yet it also implies a process that lays trauma to rest only in the acknowledgement that accounts cannot be fully settled. Longley's elegies articulate a way of living through the experience of abjection in a way that neither heals nor abandons the 'missing' body.
>
> (Ibid., p. 26)

Longley's life and poetry are fundamentally situated in the aftermath of the blackbirds' destruction, to which the poet remains a perpetual witness, one for whom there is no 'getting over' the originary violence. While rejecting any straightforward compensatory logic, Longley's explicit linking of the Holocaust to the image of the violated nest recalled from childhood acknowledges that the Nazi genocide of European Jews and others is an indelible and pervasive part of his experience and knowledge of the world. As historical fact and imaginative limit, the Holocaust, to a remarkable degree, demarcates Longley's place in the world. Like the revenant of Larkin's poem, Longley's poetry in response to the Holocaust, while offering no explanation or consolation, stays in – indeed, *with* – this broken world of loss, remembering what happens alongside a hope for healing. Ultimately, his poetry is a quiet gesture of accompaniment for a brutal and maddening world. Such a poetry of accompaniment goes beyond the representation of history: it suspends together the human voice of poetry with the vastness of atrocious death, not to redress such death but to imbricate human presence with its absence.

II

In drafts of the two-line poem 'Terezín', Longley alternates between 'Terezín' and 'Silence' as the poem's title. The haunting fact that much art was produced in the Terezín (Theresienstadt) ghetto ties the poem's singular image of violins to the particular place-name. The Nazis used the Terezín 'model' ghetto to distract Red Cross observers from the operations of the killing centres further east; with the place-name title gesturing to this fact, the alternative, unpublished title – its unsettling literal and thematic silence – broaches the magnitude of the whole Nazi operation. From Terezín to Silence, from the particular to the universal – and back again – this poem completes a tiny circuit of quiet horror that actively remembers the dead and exemplifies the lyric endeavour to apprehend a history that, like silence itself, resists containment. 'No room has ever been as silent as the room / Where hundreds of violins are hung in unison' (Longley, 2006, p. 186). Just as the silent violins, like the draft titles, are suspended together, so too is the place of silencing (the 'Lager', in Levi's parlance, always just beyond the ghetto) 'hung in unison' with poetry. Giving voice to this silencing, the poem insists that the silencing persists.

Perhaps because of its exquisite brevity, 'Terezín' succeeds in breaching that vast silence – of the dead and the living – that suffuses the aftermath of atrocity. In tapping this silence imagistically, Longley channels a terrible presence of absence into poetry and, further, into our own hollowed-out hearing. Thus, Fran Brearton remarks that this, like other Longley elegies, 'reverberates beyond its own limits in the space outside' (Brearton, 2006, p. 183). Rejecting any sense of consolation or escape from the image's impact, this couplet of a broken sonnet – it is published with three other quatrain poems each dealing with World War II – posits the aftermath of the Terezín ghetto's infernal limbo (ibid., p. 181).[4] However, the miniature's density strategically fails to contain the silence it renders as the extreme surplus of orchestras of *silenced* violins hung together. The poem about the presence of these memorial objects suspended 'in unison' is grounded on the perverse fact of the instruments' disconnection from their human players. Drafts indicate that 'Terezín' was originally a quatrain, where the final two lines acknowledge the absences declared by the violins' silence: 'Parted from the bows and cases, from the hands / That carried the cases and played the violins' (Longley, 'Terezín', MARBL, 23:30). The excision of these lines further suggests that the violins' silence redoubles the human absence central to the poem's image of 'Terezín'. The poem's presence itself accompanies these objects' incompletion and the death that inheres; crucially, this witnessing of loss represents a concentration of loss, not its alleviation.

'Terezín' is important because it models Longley's strategy of suspending catastrophic death with impossible-to-fulfil desire for consolation: would that those violins might sound! It also evokes the experience of his friend Helen Lewis who, as a young girl, was sent to Terezín before finally entering the black hole of Auschwitz. Speaking at an event honouring her contributions to the cultural life of Belfast, where she was settled after the war, Longley, in the shadow of the Rwandan and Bosnian genocides, reminded the audience of the ubiquity of the 'infection' that Levi says spawns genocide:

> These chilling pages [of *A Time to Speak* (1992)] remind us that the Final Solution was, among other terrible things, a bureaucratic triumph; that it was carried out by people like ourselves. They show how one lie leads to another lie until the hugeness of untruth overwhelms a continent. If enough small compromises with evil are allowed to cluster, we end up in the death-camps.
>
> (Longley, 'Helen Lewis', MARBL, 35:26)

Longley's haunted acknowledgement that the Nazis' 'bureaucratic triumph' depended on 'people like ourselves' is echoed, of course, in his suggestion that 'Auschwitz begins' with the banal, *human* maliciousness figured in a destroyed tree and broken nest. Atrocity can happen anywhere, and none of us who remain untested can be sure of the role we might play. Writing about Longley's 'The Butchers', a poem that 'raises questions about civilization and barbarism' while reaching back from the Troubles through the Holocaust to the home-cum-abattoir that is Ithaca after Odysseus' homecoming, Brearton says that the poem 'is prepared to confront human atrocity without presuming such atrocity to be remote from or incomprehensible to the self' (Brearton, 2006, pp. 176, 177). Such a harrowing notion of aftermath broadens the reach of the Holocaust while in no way diluting the Holocaust's traumatic intensity.

No matter how its ungraspability is approached – as a limit to understanding, a rupture in human history, a time out of time – the Holocaust remains death or, as Susan Gubar puts it, a '*dying*' (Gubar, 2003, p. 7).[5] Thinking it through this enigmatic present progressive undermines conventional lyric memorialization that yearns for finality, in which the past stays in its place. The 'dying' that does not die acknowledges the traumatic reality that the Holocaust remains with us as more than an indelible stain upon European and Western culture. With the other genocides that originally enabled and subsequently spun out from the European and American colonial projects, the Holocaust's persistence as a dying constitutes part of the shadow of atrocity cast into both past and future by this culture of domination. It is a part of *us*:

> I see them absentmindedly pat their naked bodies
> Where waistcoat and apron pockets would have been.
> The grandparents turn back and take an eternity
> Rummaging in the tangled pile for their spectacles.
> (Longley, 2006, p. 254)

Longley's four-line poem 'The Exhibit' concludes with an image evocative of a museum exhibit in which the sheer volume of commonplace items, as in 'Terezín', creates an uncanny sense of absence despite the haunted surplus of items absent their persons. While such exhibits present spectators with indirect though affective glimpses of horror, they are usually contained by the literal structure of the museum that memorializes traumatic history even as it both introduces us to and distances us from the horrors being presented. Longley's poem *exhibits* (as in exposes) the exhibition itself, making it personal by acknowledging that the once-curated image, now free from the museum, is the fallout of an unimaginable moment that haunts the poet. Here, the memorial's aim to keep horror at a safe remove from the secondary witness breaks down. A poet and a poetry are possessed not just by the fact that bodies such as these stood before the showers/gas-chambers, but by the simplest and most creaturely of gestures – the absentminded patting where something should be but isn't. With such revenants searching for their spectacles, the poem ends with something that shouldn't be but is: mass death. While the forced 'exhibition' of their nakedness generates a perversity that clings to the poem like a taint, these spectres remain, figuring traumatic poetry as a haunting.

Again, Longley's instinct is to acknowledge with poetry that the Holocaust, as a wound, stays with us. In response to a question about Adorno's 1949 statement, now reduced to a cliché, that 'to write poetry after Auschwitz is barbaric', Longley says: 'Auschwitz is what poetry, even if it doesn't deal with it directly, has to face. It's *got* to be there in the background [...] I think we are duty bound to try and work out how we got there' (Brearton, 1997, p. 39). The geographical, historical and metaphysical reality of Auschwitz conserves it as a terminus to which we remain 'duty bound' to imaginatively and morally arrive at and depart from – albeit with 'imaginative restraint' (Corcoran, 2007, p. 118). Having shaped our world, even as our world spawned it, the Holocaust is in us. Poetry remains 'duty bound to try' not to understand the Holocaust itself, as the claim of understanding genocide is, according to Claude Lanzmann, 'obscene', but rather to face the horror and the fact that 'we got there' and that *we* now live in the aftermath (Lanzmann, 1995, pp. 206–7; Brearton, 1997, p. 39).[6] For Longley, how we got there is less a historical than an ontological question. Auschwitz may be a black hole, but it is still a constituent part of our poetic universe.

In manuscript drafts of the uncollected poem, 'My Jewish Great-Grandmother', Longley writes that his maternal grandmother Jessica Abraham's Jewish identity is found in 'the debris of my past [...] at the back of my mind' (Longley, 'My Jewish Great-Grandmother', MARBL, 32:7). Here, Longley demonstrates a mode of witnessing catastrophe through the location of the dead in some essential aspect of himself:

> Since each time I forget her she must die
> As with her people she goes underground
> And, pulling over
> The manhole cover,
> Prepares to die without a sound
> And even beyond my mind's eye,
> I must hear Jessica Abraham's shout,
> Search the debris of my past to find
> Artillery putting her eyes out,
> Her ghetto crumbling at the back of my mind.
> (Longley, 'My Jewish Great-Grandmother',
> MARBL, 32:7)[7]

The poet's connection to the grandmother he never knew is at once tenuous and overwhelming. Longley repeatedly acknowledges that, though he knows little about Jessica Abraham, what traces of her that exist are hidden amidst his 'debris' or are too easily forgotten. Indeed, her actual grave – her 'mislaid whereabouts' – is lost (Longley, 2006, p. 157).[8] Not only is 'Her ghetto crumbling at the back of [the poet's] mind', but this final stanza of 'My Jewish Great-Grandmother' opens by declaring: 'Since each time I forget her she must die'. In light of 'a terrible century' with the Holocaust at its epicentre, the failure to remember gestures to the traumatic repetition of dying that temporally structures lyric mourning (ibid., p. 157). Though dead before World War II, Jessica Abraham ties Longley to 'her people', whose later deaths in the Holocaust cannot be forgotten. The implicit command to remember remains palpable, though Longley admits the difficulty of this task: despite the fact that he 'must hear Jessica Abraham's shout', he nonetheless must also 'search' the depths of his 'past' and 'mind' to find her whom he can never know. The poem demonstrates that Jessica Abraham, her death, and the associations she invokes are in him and his poetry. Longley's responsibility as a poet is to 'hear Jessica Abraham's shout' as a call to bear witness and resist the 'crumbling' of personal memory with a poetry that, instead of being a silent (and silencing) memorial, persists to transmit the truth of her absence. The poem suggests that this absence is conveyed paradoxically in a listening for 'impossibility' as the shout that cannot really be heard (Caruth, 1995a, p. 10).[9]

When Longley describes Jessica Abraham's 'ghetto crumbling at the back of [his] mind', her place (a lacuna and scene of desolation) is in him. Longley also finds her ghostly presence in the imaginative locus of World War I's no man's land. The poem 'No Man's Land', from *Poems 1963–1983* (1985), emerged from another poem about Jessica Abraham, 'Granny', from *Man Lying on a Wall* (1976).[10] Given its prominence throughout his poetry, no man's land is a sort of first-place, a disembodied and haunted home-ground, especially before his encounter with Carrigskeewaun. In his early elegy 'In Memoriam', Longley describes his father, a World War I veteran, surviving an explosion at the front in which 'shrapnel shards [...] sliced [his] testicle' (Longley, 2006, p. 30). The poem continues:

> That instant I, your most unlikely son,
> In No Man's Land was surely left for dead,
> Blotted out from your far horizon.
> As your voice now is locked inside my head,
> I yet was held secure, waiting my turn.
>
> (Ibid., p. 30)

This 'nightmare ground' is thus figured as a species of *terra natal*, the place where the poet's 'far horizon' was seemingly lost but then, quite miraculously, found thanks to skilful medics (Longley, 'Review',

MARBL, 36:28; 2006, p. 30). Like Longley's dead Jewish Granny, the dead father, survivor of no man's land, remains a voice 'held securely' inside the poet's head. No man's land, so central to Longley's father's experience of the rest of his life, defines the son's sense of the father and, thus, part of the poet's own origin.

In undated notes for a reading, Longley introduces 'Granny' as written in memory of Isaac Rosenberg. He says: 'Jessica Abraham, died when my mother [was] a baby. I introduce her to the ghost of Rosenberg. A working class London Jew. His difficult poems / carrier pigeons' (Longley, 'Notes', MARBL, 38:14). Their Jewish identity constitutes the initial connection between the two figures (Longley's grandmother and the World War I poet) occupying equally balanced stanzas of the later poem, 'No Man's Land', but Longley's reference to 'a terrible century' at the centre of 'No Man's Land' (the phrase comes from 'Granny'), emphasizes that the Holocaust itself haunts Longley's sense of no man's land. The lost corpses of Rosenberg and Abraham, like so many of the six million – and millions more – literally embody absence, and Longley's poetry repeatedly acknowledges this pervasive absence as a constitutive part of the poet's most important places and of the poetry itself. Robert Jay Lifton speaks of a kindred process when commenting on an admired line by Heinrich Böhl: 'The artist carries death within him like the good priest his breviary' (Caruth, 1995b, p. 141). Lifton says, 'death is constitutive in this sense for all of us. That's not the only thing it is, but if we're to be constitutive in our work we need death' (ibid., p. 141). Just as Longley finds personal and haunting ties to the Holocaust in his biography and in the dystopic origin that is for him World War I's no man's land, he also locates the Holocaust within his own personal Helicon – Carrigskeewaun.

III

In *The Corner of the Eye: Michael Longley, a Poet and his Landscape* (1989), a documentary made by naturalists Michael Viney and David Cabot, Longley states that, as an urban or suburban Protestant poet from Belfast, his relationship to the land itself is richly 'provisional' and non-identitarian (Longley, 2005, p. xv).[11] He says: 'Heaney has his Bellaghy, Montague has his Garvaghy, Muldoon the Moy; coming from Belfast, from suburban Belfast, I've had to borrow Carrigskeewaun as it were and gradually to learn how to read the features of the place' (*Corner*, 1989). Longley's self-identified gesture of *borrowing* the landscape acknowledges radical difference and respectful distance. The place is other; it is not home per se, and neither is it coextensive with the self. It is a venue for encountering the self. Longley's borrowing of Carrigskeewaun recognizes a temporary relationship, no matter if life-long. Temporality implicitly involved, a sense of finitude or '*moralia*' clings to the place and the relationship (Heaney, 2001, p. 9). Death's limit hangs in the air, even in a place that, with all its natural beauty, seems to share nothing with the quintessentially deathly and human landscape of no man's land. Longley may begin with a sense of no man's land as poetic source, but once he comes to know Carrigskeewaun – and know himself through this coastal Mayo townland – it becomes unequivocally his spiritual and poetic home.

Though Longley's Carrigskeewaun poems are suffused with nature, human absence or the evidence of past human presence in this rugged landscape remains a lodestone orienting the poet in what he describes as a 'vast empty space' (Longley, 2005, p. xv). One site where this emptiness is concentrated is the famine village on the shoulders of Mweelrea Mountain just above Carrigskeewaun. Longley describes having a 'sense, in the middle of that silence and desolation, of a bustle, of a liveliness of people moving to and fro and living there, say 200 years ago' (*Corner*, 1989). Its emptiness comes alive almost as a haunting. *Ghost Orchid* (1995), down on the coast, what remains of a shipwreck lies exposed in the middle of Thallabaun strand, the wooden spars in the sand offering the poet a 'blue-print / For the ship of death' (Longley, 2006, p. 232). Later, in 'Level Pegging' from *Snow Water* (2004), Longley further personalizes the disappearing wreck, saying to the poem's dedicatee: 'There are fewer exits than you'd think fewer spars / For us to build our ship of death and sail away' (Longley, 2006, p. 305). At the northern and southern ends of this broad strand close by the Longley cottage, two further traces of human life and death mark the landscape with a poetic Ley line: the 'wind-encircled' (ibid., p. 62), 'tide-digested [...] almost gone' (ibid., p. 288), 'vanishing' (ibid., p. 290), or even 'gone' burial mound at Templedoomore (ibid., p. 305) – and, a little over a mile further south, the cairn on the Dooaghtry headland. Quite literally, in this poetic and spiritual home and source, 'the dead [are] suspended in the scenery' (ibid., p. 292).

The image of the eroded burial mound is found in some form in each of Longley's volumes after *No Continuing City*. Indeed, in *The Corner of the Eye*, this structure within reach of very high tides serves as a focal point for the examination of poet and place. It was once the graveyard – used even into the nineteenth century – of a now-disappeared twelfth or thirteenth-century monastery. In the early 1990s, storms split the mound, accelerating its erosion 'from a lofty pyramid of sand to a disk of anonymous slabs of stone' today (personal correspondence with Ethna Viney; Viney, 2009, p. 121). In 'Spring Tide', from *The Echo Gate* (1979), Longley describes this inexorable process of erasure:

> It isn't really a burial mound
> Reflected there, but all that remains
> Of a sandy meadow, a graveyard
> Where it was easy to dig the graves.
> The spring tide circles and excavates
> A shrunken ramshackle pyramid
> Rinsing cleaner scapulae, tibias,
> Loose teeth, cowrie and nautilus shells.
> (Longley, 2006, p. 124)

Brearton notes how the burial mound's decreasing presence and corresponding increase in symbolic value captures 'the play between absence and presence, preservation and erosion', that runs through the Carrigskeewaun poems (Brearton, 2006, p. 138). This poetry exposes 'the tentative wish that the "art of losing" could become an art of healing' (ibid., p. 138). While Longley 'desire[s]' that nature or poetry might possess the power to console or heal, this 'is never something to be taken for granted' (ibid., p. 138).

The conclusion of 'To Seamus Heaney' extends a ritualistic invitation to visit this place of the dead. This 'sad recital [...] leaving careful footsteps round / A wind-encircled burial mound', is an invocation of human presence against the irreducible fact of absence (Longley, 2006, p. 61). Over thirty years later, 'Petalwort' returns to the image as Michael Viney's declared future gravesite: 'You want your ashes to swirl along the strand / At Thallabaun [...] / Around the burial mound's wind-and-wave inspired / Vanishing act' (ibid., p. 290). For a poet whose work is 'about loss' (as he says in his 2006 interview), the image of the burial mound in the landscape – an omphalos in Longley's most cherished, poetically resonant place – comes to figure not only a mourning and memorialization of the dead by the living, but also the long-term occupation of a part of the world (like the poet's imagination) by the dead (Corcoran, 2007, p. 120).

In *The Lake Without a Name: Poems of Mayo*, Longley says that 'the human habitat in that part of Mayo is precarious, isolate and vulnerable; its history complex' (Longley, 2005, p. xv). He adds that 'the countryside is haunted by grown-over potato-drills, the ghosts of lazy-beds abandoned during the Famine [...] The bones of the landscape make me feel in my own bones how provisional dwelling and home are' (ibid., p. xv). A place 'haunted' by history, Carrigskeewaun maps the invariable suspension of death amidst life's vibrancy – the way death, as much absence as temporal gap, is sustained within (and by) the living world. However, the human intrusion into this natural world brings with it not just natural death but catastrophic death and suffering.

While a steady onslaught of poems calls forth the disappearing/disappeared burial mound, another substantive trace of human death in the Carrigskeewaun landscape – the cairn on the Dooaghtry headland – is referenced sparingly, most notably in 'The Cairn at Dooaghtry' from *Gorse Fires* (1994). Very little is known about the origins of this dilapidated structure. Some locals say that the cairn marks the site of a murder, but others say that the pile of stones, harking back to at least Famine times, memorializes the souls of unbaptized infants and children. Longley says that each time he walks by it, he tosses another stone onto the cairn that never seems to grow; this humble, ceremonial gesture recalls for Longley the dead children of this place – and others (personal email correspondence with Longley). As a memorial for the child-victims of the Irish Famine – perhaps apocryphally – the site marks a remote human community's confrontation with catastrophic death. The cairn's continual decay offers a macabre reminder of the wasting that crushed the native Irish here. While this pile of stones inexorably eroding into a headland of the poet's most sacred space raises the spectre of the 1840s ruination, it is simultaneously haunted by the Holocaust:

> Children lie under the cairn, unhallowed souls
> Whose playground should be the duach and the dunes.
> No higher than little children walking on tiptoe
> Past SS guards at the selections in Terezín,
> The cairn has become a scree, the scree a landslide
> And a raised beach the memorial to all of them.
>
> (Longley, 2006, p. 191)

Comparing the height of the Dooaghtry cairn memorializing anonymous child-victims of the Irish Famine to the height of anonymous children selected for deportation to Auschwitz, the poem evokes the spectres of children like Helen Lewis, caught in the Jewish ghetto of Terezín and trying to avoid the 'selections' for deportation to the death camp. It also situates the Holocaust and its victims within the most beautiful and poetically sustaining place in Longley's universe. Like other Longley poems that transmit one distinct catastrophe through or with another (such as 'Wounds', 'No Man's Land', 'Argos', 'Ceasefire', 'Buchenwald Museum' and so on), this poem models a larger sense of the unbridgeable scope of human suffering. 'The Cairn at Dooaghtry' unconsolingly elegizes the Irish Famine *and* the Holocaust, demonstrating the Famine's abject pervasiveness throughout the Irish landscape and cultural memory as well as the Holocaust's omnipresence in Longley's imaginative life and our world. The poem does not 'entomb or obliterate' traumatic history (Brewster, 2006 p. 26), but presents instead a haunted vision of how 'in a catastrophic age [...] trauma itself may provide the very link between cultures' (Caruth, 1995a, p. 11).

Another example of this phenomenon of traumatic linkages registered at the site of memory itself may be found at the northern edge of Doolough, just east of Dooaghtry and Carrigskeewaun, on the other side of Mweelrea Mountain. A corollary to the inter-connectedness of human catastrophes and the continuity of responses to such catastrophes, the cairn-like memorial bears two plaques. The first reads: 'To commemorate the hungry poor who walked here in 1849 and walk the Third World today. Freedom for South Africa 1994. "How can men feel themselves honoured by the humiliation of their fellow beings". Mahatma Gandhi in South Africa'. The second states: '"In 1991 we walked AFrI's Great Famine walk at Doolough and soon afterwards we walked the road to freedom in South Africa". Archbishop Desmond Tutu.' As surprising as finding the Holocaust in 'The Cairn at Dooaghtry' is the encounter with the leaders of the South African anti-apartheid movement, first Gandhi then Desmond Tutu, in this remote Irish landscape. This recent memorial reminds us that catastrophic suffering remains pervasive today and that the germ of resistance, like hope, is embedded in memory.

'The Cairn at Dooaghtry' connects two distinct catastrophes in a single image of a wasting pile of stones. While the ethical dimension of Longley's work might be represented by Wilfred Owen's notion of 'the eternal reciprocity of tears', shared suffering is not the only basis for aligning the Famine and the Holocaust (Owen, 1963, p. 38). This poem suggests that just as the Irish Famine pervades this part of Ireland, the Holocaust for Longley is everywhere. And, the Holocaust, like the Irish Famine, is not the only catastrophe that the poet in this place (as in any place) must necessarily confront as a witness. Poet and poem alike recognize the site (the Dooaghtry cairn) as laden with an extreme legacy of grief. To the degree this memorial is also degrading physically, it is imaginatively intact precisely because it is situated at the very heart of Longley's most revered landscape – Carrigskeewaun. As with the

Thallabaun burial mound, the literal remains of the numberless, anonymous dead may be gone but their deaths, like Jessica Abraham's 'shout', persist in the poem, in this poet – as his 'unrestricted tenants, fingerprints / Everywhere, teeth-marks on this and that' – and ultimately in *us* as knowledgeable witnesses to the deaths of innocents despite our temporal or spatial remove (Longley, 2006, p. 61).

'The Cairn at Dooaghtry' marks a place in the world and in the imagination occupied simultaneously by the dead children of the Famine and those from Terezín who did not escape the selections. As a 'memorial to all of them', the only true differentiation in the poem involves that between the living and the dead. The memorial itself, reduced by natural forces to child-height, humanizes the victims of unimaginable disaster in much the same way that addressing 'all' of these children hinders any privileging of one set of victims over another. None are exceptional; all are equally innocent and dead and worthy of a place in our most personal and sacred spaces. Longley's admission of the dead into the very source of his poetry – Carrigskeewaun – defines the intensity of his poetry of witness. These innocents are all 'unhallowed' – unconsecrated – precisely to the extent that they are not rarified out of our world by mourning 'songs' or commemorative gestures towards transcendence (Longley, 2006, p. 61). In conversation in 2003, Longley stated that, 'Carrigskeewaun provides me with the template for experiencing all other places and keeps me sensitive, I hope, to the nuances of locality' (Randolph, 2004, p. 27). Longley's work asserts that all such victims of catastrophe remain suspended *in* the world, as well as at the site of the poem that accompanies them. As heterogeneous remainders of cataclysm, these figures insist on being not just seen or heard in their anonymity but also recognized as constitutive parts of a poet and a poetry.

Notes

1. Michael Longley is one of the major contemporary Irish poets. Born in 1939, he has lived most of his life in Belfast, where he witnessed the denaturation of Northern Ireland's civil society during the years of sectarian violence from 1968 to 1998. Along with various selected and collected editions, he has published eight collections of poetry that have won numerous international awards.
2. Three limited edition selected volumes are arranged thematically around these constants: *Cenotaph of Snow: Sixty Poems about War* (Enitharmon, 2003), *The Rope-Makers* (Enitharmon, 2005) and *The Lake without a Name* (Blackstaff Press, 2006). A fourth such limited edition thematic volume, *Wavelengths* (Enitharmon, 2009), focuses on Longley's long-standing commitment to the art of translation.

3. Little criticism of Longley's work exclusively addresses the place of the Holocaust in his writing. Jerzy Jarniewicz's 'Home, Displacement, and Deprivation in Michael Longley's "Ghetto"' (2005) is a notable exception. Fran Brearton, one of the finest critics working on Longley, considers Longley's poetry addressing war, including the Holocaust, in various essays and her invaluable *Reading Michael Longley* (2006). This chapter seeks to add to Jarniewicz and Brearton's fine readings.
4. Popularly called the 'anteroom of hell', between 1941 and 1945, the Nazis deported 140,000 people to Terezín where 33,000 died and 90,000 were transported to the death camps. Fifteen thousand children went to Terezín and around 100 survived (United States Holocaust Memorial Museum).
5. 'We must keep it alive *as* dying. Since not-writing about the Shoah would constitute a Nazi victory, one way to evade indulging in self-serving forms of recollection involves taking seriously the idea that our stake in the fates of the murdered must be considered along with the stake they have in us' (Gubar, 2003, p. 7).
6. Lanzmann's interview and speech called 'The Obscenity of Understanding: An Evening with Claude Lanzmann' unequivocally reifies the Holocaust – he states that 'the Holocaust was a pure event, an unbreakable event, *infracassable*' (Lanzmann, 1995, p. 207). In his film *Shoah*, Lanzmann has produced a *work* that powerfully re-inscribes the limits of representation in its effort to present and transmit something of the Holocaust, notably its quality as an unbridgeable 'abyss' (ibid., p. 206).
7. Longley misidentifies the subject of the poem as his 'Great-Grandmother'. Jessica Abraham (who is also named Braham in *Tuppenny Stung*) is actually Longley's maternal grandmother according to several later references both published and unpublished including *Tuppenny Stung*, 'Granny', 'No Man's Land', and reading notes introducing 'Granny'. Longley's maternal grandmother, 'a beautiful Jewess called Jessica Braham', is a somewhat mysterious figure because, as he says in *Tuppenny Stung*, she 'died at the age of twenty when my mother was still a baby' (Longley, 1994, p. 19). Longley adds that she was rarely spoken of by his maternal grandfather, whose second wife, Maud, 'was insanely jealous of her stepchild' (ibid., p. 19). His grandfather George 'referred once or twice, tearfully, to Jessica Braham and seemed after all those years [by the mid- to late 1940s] to be still in love with her' (ibid., p. 23).
8. This phrase regarding the lost remains of Longley's grandmother – the 'mislaid whereabouts' – appears in the poem 'No Man's Land' that is, in part, a composite of other poems attending to the poet's 'Jewish granny' (2006, p. 157).
9. Fundamental to the survivor's experience of trauma as a death encounter is what Cathy Caruth describes as 'a temporal delay that carries the individual beyond the shock of the first moment', such that the survivor apprehends the event not simply in its repetition but in the failure to witness the event at all (Caruth, 1995a, p. 10). Caruth adds that 'by carrying that impossibility of knowing out of the empirical event itself, trauma opens up and challenges us to a new kind of listening, the witnessing, precisely, *of impossibility*' (ibid., p. 10).
10. We know this because the central act of 'Granny'– 'The echo of splintering / Glass when my grandfather, // In the one story he told / About her, tossed a brick // Through the parlour window / Of rowdy neighbours as she // Lay

dying' – bridges both the first and second sections of 'No Man's Land', the phrase, 'echo of splintering glass', being embedded in the second stanza introducing Rosenberg (Longley, 1976, p. 36; 2006, p. 157).

11. The word 'provisional' is explicitly drawn from the introduction to *The Lake Without a Name: Poems of Mayo* (2005), which, like the film, considers the poet's ties to this place.

References

Blanchot, Maurice (1995) *The Writing of the Disaster* (Lincoln: University of Nebraska Press).

Brearton, Fran (1997) '"Walking Forwards Into the Past": An Interview with Michael Longley', *Irish Studies Review*, 18 (Spring 1997) 35–9.

—— (2006) *Reading Michael Longley* (Highgreen: Bloodaxe Books Ltd).

Brewster, Scott (2006) 'Abject State: Ritual, Waste and the Exile of the Body in Northern Irish Poetry', in Irene Gilsenan Nordin (ed.) *The Body and Desire in Contemporary Irish Poetry* (Portland, OR: Irish Academic Press, 2006).

Caruth, Cathy (1995a) 'Trauma and Experience: Introduction', in Cathy Caruth (ed.) *Trauma: Explorations in Memory* (Baltimore: Johns Hopkins University Press).

—— (1995b) 'An Interview with Robert Jay Lifton', in Cathy Caruth (ed.) *Trauma: Explorations in Memory* (Baltimore: Johns Hopkins University Press).

Corcoran, Brendan (2007) 'Interview with Michael Longley', *An Sionnach: A Journal of Literature, Culture, and the Arts*, 3(2) (Fall) 102–20.

The Corner of the Eye: Michael Longley, a Poet and his Landscape (1989) Michael Viney, dir., Wildgoose Films, Radio Telefís Éireann.

Gubar, Susan (2003) *Poetry after Auschwitz: Remembering What One Never Knew* (Bloomington: Indiana University Press).

Heaney, Seamus (2001) 'Poetry Special: *Lux perpetua*', *Guardian*, 16 June, p. 9.

Jarniewicz, Jerzy (2005), 'Home, Displacement, and Deprivation in Michael Longley's "Ghetto"', in *Ironies of Art/Tragedies of Life: Essays on Irish Literature* (Oxford: Peter Lang, 2005).

Lanzmann, Claude (1995) 'The Obscenity of Understanding: An Evening with Claude Lanzmann', in Cathy Caruth (ed.) *Trauma: Explorations in Memory* (Baltimore: Johns Hopkins University Press).

Levi, Primo (1996) *Survival in Auschwitz*, trans. Stuart Woolf (New York: Simon and Schuster). [Published in Britain as *If This is a Man*.]

Longley, Michael (1976) *Man Lying on a Wall: Poems 1972–75* (London: Victor Gollancz Ltd).

—— (1994) *Tuppenny Stung: Autobiographical Chapters* (Belfast: Lagan Press).

—— (1997a) 'The First and the Twelfth of July', in Gordon Lucy and Elaine McLure (eds) *The Twelfth: What It Means To Me* (Armagh: Ulster Society Publications Ltd).

—— (1997b) 'Say Not Soft Things', in Gordon Lucy and Elaine McLure (eds) *Remembrance* (Armagh: Ulster Society Publications Ltd).

—— (2005) *The Lake without a Name: Poems of Mayo* (Belfast: Blackstaff Press).

—— (2006) *Collected Poems* (London: Jonathan Cape).

—— (2009) *Wavelengths* (London: Enitharmon Press).

—— 'Helen Lewis', Michael Longley Papers, Manuscript Collection No. 744. Manuscript, Archives, and Rare Book Library (MARBL), Emory University. Box 35, Folder 26.
—— 'My Jewish Great-Grandmother', Michael Longley Papers, Manuscript Collection No. 744. Manuscript, Archives, and Rare Book Library (MARBL), Emory University. Box 32, Folder 7.
—— 'Notes for Poetry Readings [undated]', Michael Longley Papers, Manuscript Collection No. 744. Manuscript, Archives, and Rare Book Library (MARBL), Emory University. Box 38, Folder 14.
—— Personal email to the author, 9 September 2009.
—— 'Review of *A Time to Speak* by Helen Lewis', Michael Longley Papers, Manuscript Collection No. 744. Manuscript, Archives, and Rare Book Library (MARBL), Emory University. Box 36, Folder 28.
—— 'Terezín', Michael Longley Papers, Manuscript Collection No. 744. Manuscript, Archives, and Rare Book Library (MARBL), Emory University. Box 23, Folder 30.
Owen, Wilfred (1963) *The Collected Poems of Wilfred Owen* (New York: New Directions).
Randolph, Jody Allen (2004) 'Michael Longley in Conversation', *PN Review*, 31 (2), 21–7.
United States Holocaust Memorial Museum, 'Theresienstadt', *Holocaust Encyclopedia*, http://www.ushmm.org/wlc/article.php?ModuleId=10005424#RelatedArticles (accessed 6 January 2010).
Viney, Michael (2009) 'Michael in Mayo', in Robin Robertson (ed.) *Love Poet, Carpenter: Michael Longley at Seventy* (London: Enitharmon Press).

9

'Toward a Brink': The Poetry of Kathleen Jamie and Environmental Crisis

Lucy Collins

Kathleen Jamie's significance as a writer has, to a large degree, been predicated on the fortunate coincidence of the precision and clarity of her art and her engagement with important issues of identity in Britain today. A Scottish poet at a time when debates on the role of Scotland are to the fore in British culture, she has raised the awareness of readers not through polemics but with a minutely detailed approach to language and form. Her writings on ecological themes reveal a similar attention to acts of observation and representation, asking questions about the relationship between the interconnectedness of the natural world and the individuality that is necessary for creative work.

The particularity of place is an important facet of contemporary poetry, not least because of its peculiar concentration on identity politics. For Scottish writers the question of national identity has a particular resonance, given how closely cultural and political affairs are intertwined. What Christopher Whyte has called the 'transitory but intense love affair' that took place between writers and intellectuals and the nationalist movement reached a peak in the 1990s and remains an important critical framework within which such poets as Robert Crawford, W.N. Herbert and Liz Lochhead are read (Whyte, 2004, p. 210).[1] The nation, however, has both a recognizable particularity and a contingent aspect, as Cairns Craig points out. It is an institution 'whose elements are continually changing but which constitute, by the nature of the issues which they foreground, and by their reiteration of elements of the past, a dialogue which is unique to that particular place' (ibid., p. 31).

In interviews, Kathleen Jamie shows herself wary of the emphasis that falls on regional and gendered identity in her work. She feels confined by 'the assumptions and the baggage' that these definitions suggest (Scott, 2007). Nevertheless, her early work interrogated these subjects, and while changed priorities can indicate a resistance to categorization, there is also a sense of continuity and overlapping influences in her career to date. The poems of *Jizzen* (1999) were written in the five-year period between 1995 and 1999 during which Jamie's two children were born. Though these experiences formed the basis of much of this work, nature also figured, exemplifying the formative connection between human and natural worlds. A poem such as 'The Tay Moses' explores this link through its governing metaphor:

> What can I fashion
> for you but a woven
> creel of river –
> rashes, a golden
> oriole's nest, my gift
> wrought from the Firth –
> (Jamie, 1999, p. 19)

Many of the poems in this collection have a similar celebratory tone, without sacrificing the sense of watchful responsibility that marks Jamie's engagement with the environment. The moral potential of writing is very important to Jamie: 'I do still believe that there is value and worth in trying to move towards something which is true or good in the arts. All the arts ought to act as a conscience, a human conscience' (Fraser, 2001, p. 16). Though Jamie is not an activist, she recognizes the relationship between action and reflection in her work and her commitment to explore ideas of national identity and gender remains linked to her appreciation of nature and her involvement with it. It could be argued that Jamie's body of work demonstrates the interwoven aspect of ecological concern, its connections to social structures and personal events that indicate the resonance of these debates in the wider world.

The political effects of poetry are debated in many contexts, but few can posit a clear role for the poem as an agent of change. Some approaches offer opportunities to read poetry as an important element in the matrix of power however: 'It is not that poetry makes nothing happen', Peter Middleton argues, 'it simply takes a long time and its influences are subterranean' (Middleton, 2008). He goes on to quote J. Bernstein's view that poetry is a 'cipher' for 'an absent politics'. This suggestion of a concealed role for poetry throughout a process of change affirms the poem's ability to interrogate loss of meaning without necessarily providing clear alternative messages. This need not limit poetry's powers of relevance for contemporary society, however. As Jamie herself comments, 'poetry's not very good at getting out there fighting, but it's very good at holding the last line of defence' (Fraser, 2001, p. 20). She also sees poetry playing an important connective role:

> Poetry is the place where we consider or calibrate our relationships – with ourselves, our culture, history. However, with the natural world, many of our approaches have been infantalised [sic], or cauterised. 'We have forgotten the language needed for such communication' writes Thomas Berry, who calls our situation 'autistic'.
>
> (Jamie quoted in Rees-Jones, 2005, p. 199)

An alternative reading of this dissociated position is that our relationship with nature offers opportunities for new moral engagement with the world. The idea of nature 'as potential action, possible location of human reform' (Thompson, 2002, p. 36) gives voice to the dynamic aspect of the relationship between the natural and human worlds and affirms the close connection between their acts of representation. Thus, as Jonathan Bate (2000) has established, a concern for nature need not be seen as a retreat from politics but instead as itself a form of political engagement.

Central to the human relationship with the natural world is a dynamic of power, in which human concerns tend to become paramount, overwhelming any sense of order beyond their own structuring principles. The question of whether human intervention in ecological matters is a necessary responsibility or a damaging intrusion is one that Kathleen Jamie explores in her prose, both implicitly and directly:

> They say the day is coming – it may already be here – when there will be no wild creatures. That is, when no species on the planet will be able to further itself without reference or negotiation with us. When our intervention or restraint will be a factor in their continued existence.
>
> (Jamie, 2005, p. 79)

While for Jamie the relationship between the human and the natural represents a form of ongoing exchange, for many philosophers the affirmation of human primacy remains a governing principle – to deny hierarchy would be to deny human distinctiveness and the rational capability that is central to it. For others, such investment in power is an instrument of environmental exploitation: Warwick Fox goes so far as to argue that excessive personal attachment is the root cause of 'possessiveness, greed, exploitation, war and ecological destruction' (quoted in

Plumwood, 1993, p. 17). That ecological balance can only be achieved once power relationships between humans have been addressed is an important dimension of this argument. Fundamentally, though, the humanity versus nature binary is a false one, because it suggests that all humans are equally responsible for the destruction of the environment, and that all benefit equally from the effects of technological development (ibid., p. 13). For this reason the issue of human agency must always be critically examined in the course of environmental debate. For readers of poetry, such an examination often focuses on the representation of the subject position in the poem. How can the observing speaker address the contexts and responsibilities of their own subject position in relation to the natural world they encounter and depict?

The title poem from the collection *The Tree House* is one that explores this intersection of human and natural in particularly meaningful ways. At the opening of the poem the speaker hoists herself up into the tree and into the tree house – 'Here / I was unseeable' (Jamie, 2004, p. 41).[2] Immediately, perspective becomes important, she is not invisible but 'unseeable', emphasizing the role of the watcher rather than of the watched. Her own new viewpoint is significant in incorporating what is close to ('a bletted fruit') and far away ('the firth drained / down to sandbanks'). The syntax transposes to archaism in the next stanza, drawing attention to the primal aspect of the experience:

> I lay to sleep,
> beside me neither man
> nor child, but a lichened branch
> wound through the wooden chamber,
> pulling it close;
>
> (p. 41)

Here human and natural substance are entwined – the living branch almost inseparable from the wooden planks of the house. The poem as a whole conjures with possibility, so that the infinite array of choices ('we might have lived / a hundred other lives') exist simultaneously, from attic rooms open to the moonlight to taxis that 'head for elsewhere' (p. 42). Yet the inevitability of existence is finally affirmed; the likelihood that even in the face of great choice, the life that has been arrived at by chance would be the one deliberately chosen. This suggests that human existence may be following an inclination so strongly asserted as to make it inescapable, yet such a dynamic also contains the possibility of change. Within the inexorable movement toward environmental disaster, then, is always the forming consciousness of the individual, open to influences, to suggestion and learning. This doubleness has a cost, though. It is ultimately painful to maintain – an idea suggested by the final image of the poem, where the wooden tree house is 'a gall / we've asked the tree to carry / of its own dead' (p. 43). The interdependent quality of the human and natural processes of the world is finally affirmed here; this interdependency continues through the seasons and just as humans are required to consider the place of nature, so nature can adapt to our behaviour and persist.

The opening poem of the collection introduces this resilience through a metaphorical reading, within which, we could argue, are the seeds of Jamie's later realism. 'The Wishing Tree' is both real tree and folk emblem and, as such, is suggestive of our mixed responses to the natural world. At first the tree resists mythical situation: it is neither 'in the wilderness / nor fairyland' (p. 3), but is associated with boundaries, of the parish, of land and sea. In the tree is concentrated the power of human wishes: it seems to exemplify the pastoral mode, being a part of nature that must bear human meaning. Yet though the tree is 'poisoned' by human hope, it not only survives but even thrives. This endurance is also figured through the subject position here, for it is the tree that speaks throughout the poem; so it is the experience of nature, not of the human that is paramount:

> To look at me
> through a smirr of rain
>
> is to taste the iron
> in your own blood
>
> (p. 3)

The tree's projection of a human perspective here significantly reminds us of the need to reconsider the dynamic of human mastery over nature. In this poem there is a touch of the primeval about the relationship – it is not the twenty-first-century human that is necessarily under scrutiny, but the human through time, repeating fears and inclinations, adopting nature to bear these meanings.

For many ecocritics, there is a crisis of representation at the core of the debate. The tendency to examine the depiction of nature in literary texts has been challenged by those who believe that – since all texts are created – nature cannot be found 'in' literature, though texts can provide a space from which a consideration of nature might grow.[3] Pastoral poems are now seen as exemplifying an attitude towards nature that privileges human desires and actions, but elements of this mode can be reworked in innovative ways. In 'Alder' the poet apostrophizes the tree: 'Are you weary, alder tree, / in this, the age of rain' (p. 7). When the poet asks the tree to teach her 'a way to live / on this damp, ambiguous earth' the nuances of climate change are extended to a world struggling with the burden of meaning. For Jamie, ecological debates are not an end in themselves – no matter how important nature is to her individual understanding and her poetic reach – they are part of a larger enquiry into meaning that is endlessly woven through her work in different forms and using different materials.

So, there remains a strong link in Jamie's poetry between her passionate attachment to that natural world and her acknowledgement that poetry has a further role in exploring the most difficult transitions in human life. The relationship between individual and collective experience has special bearing on the response to environmental crisis, which demands a global commitment to change. The uses of poetry speak to this dynamic in important ways, as Jane Hirschfield suggests: 'Poetry enacts a recovering of wholeness, of emotional and metaphysical balance, whether in an individual (the lyric poem's task) or in a culture (the task of the epic)' (Hirschfield, 1998, p. 29). The way in which a poem's form may signal a different 'task' for the work is only the first stage of the process. The most subtle and attentive poets will manipulate the possibilities of form to yield new approaches to topics of urgency: Jamie uses the lyric to combine individual perspectives with material of deceptive cultural weight. The impact of scarcity on environmental balance demands that the fulfilment of real need should be given priority over consumerism. In Jamie the articulation of scarcity is to be found in language itself, in the lack of superfluity and ornamentation of both poetry and prose. In spite of the simplicity of form evident in many of the poems in *The Tree House*, though, Jamie uses traditional modes in highly sophisticated ways, turning self-reflexive poetics to philosophical use when she considers how metaphor reconstructs the natural world for the poet.

The flow of water through channeled terraces opens 'Water Day' (p. 8). This containment gives way to freer movement, as the poem traces the journey water makes, through 'clay- / lined channels', 'sluice gates' and 'weedy gullets'. This rhythmic verisimilitude leads to speculation on the meaning that might be derived from this movement:

> Proof of remote
> beneficent mountains; the mind's

release from silence, the boll
and eagre of sex, perhaps,
or poetry?

(p. 8)

Always attuned to the familiar connection between nature and creativity, Jamie here allows free play between the worlds of nature, the intellect, the body and creative art. The interrogative form sharpens our awareness of the voice in this poem and introduces a playfully direct address. Again Jamie uses metaphor yet questions its overdetermination of meaning, suggesting instead freedom of action and interpretation. That the natural world must play a role in human explanation is fundamentally undermined here.

In so many of Jamie's poems the voice is at once resonant and tentative. This is partly to do with her willingness to draw on closely observed experience at the same time as she questions the unitary aspect of such a standpoint. The imposition of a human perspective on nature is pivotal to ecocritical study, yet by interposing the subject position between the reader and the material world the relationship to nature is inevitably changed. In order to render this relationship in complex ways, Jamie seldom locates the self definitively in her poems, preferring instead to explore the connections between being and dwelling more loosely. Heidegger's preoccupation with the question of being – with what it is to exist in the world – is obliquely relevant to ecological debates:

> Mortals dwell in that they save the earth [...]. Saving does not only snatch something from a danger. To save properly means to set something free into its own essence. To save the earth is more than to exploit it or to even wear it out. Saving the earth does not master the earth and does not subjugate it, which is merely one step from boundless spoliation.
>
> (Heidegger, 1993, p. 352)

To free the non-human to realize its own essence means resisting the imposition of human will – and the primacy of individual human identity – in the world. Yet human selfhood cannot be denied without falsifying the unique perspective that makes writing possible in the first place. So, it is important for Kathleen Jamie to acknowledge the problematic aspect of contextualized identity in her work, since so much of it engages with the changing relationship between self and environment. Northrop Frye's contention that the question 'Who am I?' is often subservient to the question 'Where is here?' is especially relevant to Jamie's negotiation of selfhood in her poetry.[4] Multiple perspectives are often adopted – such as in 'Frogs' and 'The Cave of the Fish' – and she also uses language in more radical ways to indicate the unfixed nature of being and, further, its freedom of self-expression. Sometimes the 'space' of the poem is rendered literally in her depiction of air, of suspended states of being, of creatures in flight. 'Pipistrelles' marks just this kind of process. The first observation in the poem is of a space between trees; next – as though the speaker is drawing closer – comes the realization that this space is both altered and created by the presence of the bats:

> a single
> edgy intelligence, testing their idea
> for a new form
> which unfolded and cohered
>
> before our eyes.
> (p. 30)

The energy at the core of this poem is both one of non-human activity (the bats are following their normal pattern of existence) and human creativity (in doing so they alter the speaker's perception of the trees). This kind of energy provides a vital dynamic to the collection as a whole, which is shaped by the idea that human understanding can be fundamentally altered by renewed attentiveness to what already surrounds us – a core prerequisite of environmental reform.

This question of relationship is crucial: elsewhere in the volume it is the connection between air and earth which proves important. In 'Basking Shark' Jamie explores being-in-space using syntax and line-breaks to disturb the reader's sense of balance and perspective. The speaker lies at the cliff-edge looking down at the shark below: 'Behind me peat moor / careered inland. I gripped / sweet rock – but it was only / resting' (p. 23). Rock, moor and shark create an unexpected contrast of the dynamic and the motionless; what is apparently solid is no longer experienced as such. The interrelationship of these various parts of nature is crucial to how understanding is reached, since it is only through proximity to the cliff that the shark can 'come to sense the absolute / limits of its realm'. The overlapping examination of different natural elements in this poem, and in *The Tree House* as a whole, indicates Kathleen Jamie's understanding of the relationship between the dynamics of the poetic process and those of the natural world.

The observation of limits, with which this poem ends, also marks a recognition of the partial nature of all experience. The individual's relationship to place is an important element of Jamie's investigation of environmental concerns, and this relationship is particularized by the nature of her own experience.[5] Throughout her work the difference between inhabiting and visiting a place is drawn attention to by the poet. This happens, for instance, in the essays of *Findings* where the temporary nature of her engagement with some environments is interwoven with the enduring links she has to her home place. The importance of land as home, highlighted by such a figure as Mary Austin, a canonical writer of American wilderness, is resonant for Jamie, yet in questioning the necessity of reading her work within a Scottish nationalist framework, she is not disavowing the significance of community, but rather finding ways to connect to a global context.

'When we write poetry, an exchange is operating between self and others' (Jamie, 2000, p. 278): it is in this way that Jamie's poetry, and indeed her prose, speaks to a community of readers without relinquishing the highly individualized use of language that makes her work remarkable. Collective experience and responsibility are important dimensions of reading Jamie's work that draw us in to an important relationship with the poem. The subtlety of this poetry avoids the pitfalls of too clear a message: to end a poem such as 'Landfall' with the question 'can we allow ourselves to fail?' (p. 15) is both to stress the urgency of environmental preservation and to pose a philosophical question in which the returning swallow offers a model of tenacity and endurance for speaker and for reader.

Human destructiveness overshadows all ecological engagement, including the literary representation of nature. Jamie is attentive to the connections between these damaging acts and the range of their consequences, yet she is also aware of her own dual role as reflective observer and implicated participant. Her use of shifting perspectives is key to this realization. The poem 'Frogs' opens with a close examination of two mating frogs that 'became, // as you looked, almost beautiful' (p. 5). This act of observation enhances their significance and draws attention not just to the two creatures under scrutiny, but to the motivation behind the examining eye. The differentiated detail of the female frog's 'mottled' back and the male's 'marked with two stripes' is undone by human destruction, by '[t]he car // that would smear them / into one'. This act grotesquely enforces their intimacy ('belly / to belly, tongue thrust / utterly into soft brain') while it also forever destroys their beauty and, more importantly, their autonomy. The pun formed by the repetition of the phrase 'press on', in the sense of both 'to bear down on' and 'to continue', does not prepare us for the surprising final image: 'the woman by the verge / with her hands cupped' (p. 6). This figure may represent the speaker herself, marking a shift in perspective – and the necessity of such a shift – as the poem closes. It also affirms that the 'slow creatures' here are both human and animal, showing Jamie to be attuned to the ecocritical turn that also sees poor and marginalized peoples as victims amid the careless actions of the more powerful.

Jamie's art has always prized such close scrutiny and *The Tree House* is full of poems named for creatures: 'Swallows', 'White-sided Dolphins', 'Basking Shark', 'Pipistrelles'. She views the world in microcosm, so that by intimate attention to the single living thing, the entire ecosystem may implicitly be encountered. 'Flight of Birds' is a moving poem that is frank in its exploration of human responsibility for ecological disaster: 'There is no Paradise, / we've humiliated living creatures' (p. 39). The unwillingness to differentiate between the needs of other creatures and the failure to be watchful of their presence gives rise to terrible loss. It is a loss that can only be rectified by attentiveness and, further, by the power of language itself:

> – Suppose as a last ditch, we gathered
> empty-handed at the town's edge and called
> each bird by name
>
> (p. 39)

This act of naming is essentially a spiritual one, which involves a stripping away of pride and greed ('empty-handed') and trusting all to the expression of intention in language. In her own personal life, Jamie has recognized similar dynamics at work. During her husband's illness, she questioned the fact that she did not pray for his recovery, but considered the fact that such a prayer might instead be found in the act of close observation:

> But I had noticed, more than noticed, the cobwebs, and the shoaling light, and the way the doctor listened, and the flecked tweed of her skirt, and the speckled bird and the sickle-cell man's slim feet. Isn't that a kind of prayer? The care and maintenance of the web of our noticing, the paying heed?
>
> (Jamie, 2005, p. 109)

The 'web of noticing' that she refers to here makes the act of observation not just prayerful but fundamental to engagement with the wider world. It is illuminated by Heidegger's consideration of the sensuous in art: 'what is sensuous about the artwork is that it is in the artwork: it exists for the nonsensuous and the suprasensuous, for that which is also named the spiritual or spirit' (Heidegger, 2004, p. 249). This connection between the world of the senses and that of the spirit is fundamental in Kathleen Jamie's art. Her own position privileges the role of subjectivity in this act of connection and, in doing so, it calls attention to the responsibility of the individual in the business of 'paying heed'. The practice of attentiveness – which W.B. Yeats saw as crucial to the poetic process – is also a means of apprehending the greater pattern of the world, so that to scrutinize the smallest part of life is to know much of its entirety. The poem 'Moult' uses the image of seabirds' feathers washed ashore to explore this relationship. Once part of a bird's 'outstretched wing', they speak of both the mechanical operation of flight and its experience:

> What
> can one frayed feather
> tell of that design,
>
> or the covenant they undertake,
> wind and kittiwake?
>
> (p. 38)

The web of nature, which is an important dimension of Jamie's thinking and writing, is at the core of the shaping of this collection too, since reading demands that we pursue understanding by means of connection, as well as by interacting with the poems as single organically-sustained objects.[6] Imaginatively, this process of correlation continues to be important for the poet, as she turns towards microscopic scrutiny of human cells to extend her awareness of the similarities between different parts of the ecosystem and to push the boundaries of her own powers of observation:

> I drove home along the river I fancied I'd seen in the poor man's liver cells. The tide was in, no sandbanks. The inner body, plumbing and landscapes and bacteria. The outer world had also flown open like a door and I wondered as I drove, what it is that we're *just not seeing*?
>
> (Jamie, 2008, p. 46)[7]

Jamie is concerned here with the ways in which the human mind seeks patterns in order to make sense of what it sees. Yet the vastness of the unobserved world limits human knowledge and brings the relationship between actual and imagined into sharp relief.

This particular relationship has been important to Jamie over the course of her career to date: many of her earlier poems combine the magical and the real in interesting conjunction, drawing both on the folk dimensions of Scottish heritage and the gritty realism of contemporary writing. Perceived links exist between nature and spirituality – especially in contexts where the connection with nature suggests new ways of living – and these links have an important role in her work. Two adjacent poems from *The Tree House*, quite at variance stylistically, use the twilight and the dawn to figure moments of awakening that might be seen as spiritual. In 'The Blue Boat' the title itself is a metaphor for the dying light: 'slung from its mast, a lantern / like our old idea of the soul' (p. 19). The transition from day to night can be understood as a microcosm of the journey towards death; a meaningful spiritual moment is created here through familiar imagery made original by the juxtaposition of telling detail. 'Gloaming', which follows, is almost a prose-poem, unusual for this poet in its use of long lines:

> We are flying, this summer's night, toward a brink, a wire-thin
> rim of light. It swells as we descend, then illuminates the land
> enough to let us name, by hill or river mouth, each township
> below.
>
> (p. 20)

These lines mimic the gradual landing of the plane; the slow dawning, not just of the new day, but of recognition as the contours of the land become visible and the speaker can 'place' herself on the map – 'This is the North' (p. 20). As well as night becoming day, air becomes earth as the plane lands. There is a feeling of discovery here that is enhanced by long lines attentive to the processes of movement, as well as to observed detail. This is also a discovery of the fragility of this world, of the proximity of 'the brink', of the tenuous aspect of the coming light.

The fragile aspect of acts of representation seems always in view in this collection. In spite of the more forthright voices of Jamie's earlier poems, here impressions are fleeting and language is muted, as though the more combative stance of the younger writer must yield to reflective, contingent positions. 'Stane-raw' enacts aspects of this transition in fascinating ways. The title of the poem is the Scots for common lichen – often seen growing on rocks at the shore but also found inland. The poem is concerned with how widespread and tenacious this organism is, and in the use of dyes derived from it. Humans throughout history could not leave their mark without recourse to these natural resources, showing that even self-conscious bodily expression can be linked to nature:

> a bruise-
> coloured tattoo, hidden
> beneath our clothing, like this
> indelible dog rose
> inked on my shoulder,
>
> (p. 35)

Here ink is the medium of text, as well as of art. Though human artifice ('clothing') may cover the manifestation of nature, the speaker writes her own 'text' on the body – a text of self-representation and one that cannot be removed. The interdependence of different forms of representation here, linguistic and visual, is a position that Jamie has taken some time to move towards:

> I used to think that language was what got in the way, that it was a screen, a dark glass. That you could not get at the world because you were stuck with language, but now I think that's wrong. Now I think language is what connects us with the world.
>
> (Scott, 2007)

The suggested struggle with language is implicated both in the creative progression of the poet and in her metaphysical shifts. The extent to which these move in tandem is of particular significance here, given that Jamie's increasing mastery of form is matched by the sophistication of her thought; what some critics have seen as a development of her philosophical training.[8] Her cultural identity is pertinent to this issue, since Scotland offers the richness of possibility that all multilingual regions share: 'Anyone who stays here and is interested in the spoken or written word is constantly aware of being on the edge of another tongue' (Crawford, 1993, p. 161). This sense of being 'on the edge' links language and geography, so that opportunities for transition between places are implicated in similar shifts in language.

Changes in register are further complicated by Scotland's dual-language position. A number of contemporary poets such as Iain Mac a'

Ghobhainn and Aonghas MacNeacail write and publish in two languages; in such cases, there are sensitive decisions to be made concerning the creative preferences of the writer, and how they position themselves in relation to their audience. Contemporaries of Jamie's such as Robert Crawford and W.N. Herbert are clearly identified as Scottish poets working in English, but do use some Scots in their writings. Christopher Whyte sees Jamie's use of Scots as 'more natural and convincing', though she retains 'a cautious, experimental air' (Whyte, 2004, p. 208). The poet herself agrees:

> If you feel duty-bound to use Scots to uphold the language, that's no reason to use the language at all, you use it because it's present in your mouth and in your ear and because it can do a job that standard English can't do, reach parts that language cannot reach.
>
> (Fraser, 2001, p. 22)

Only four of the poems in *The Tree House* are written in Scots: '"For when the Grape-vine's Sap"', 'Speirin', 'Selchs' and 'Hame', the first and last of which are versions of poems by Hölderlin. Though their congruence with the recurring themes of the book is immediately obvious, these texts nonetheless offer specific challenges to the non-Scots speaker already absorbed in the vivid simplicity of many of the other poems. The issue of language is significant in ecocritical terms too, in drawing attention to the particularity of place and the endurance of that place – and of its forms of expression – to the present day. Yet, for a collection preoccupied by what it is to dwell, completely and ethically, on this earth, the influence of Hölderlin is instructive and a concern with 'hame' and with belonging is crystallized here:[9]

> – here whaur jags o roses
> and gean-trees
> pit oot thur sweet air,
> aside the birks, at noon
>
> (p. 28)

The specificity of the natural world has always been important to Jamie and nowhere is this more evident than in the precision of the Scots language, invoking cherry trees and birches in terms that contextualize them not through geographical description but through the chosen language of composition. It is through language, through the 'translation' of a German poet to a Scottish world, that the power of the local to speak of the universal finds particular form. Yet Heidegger's denunciation of symbolic readings of Hölderlin's natural imagery may have a particular bearing on Jamie's language choice here. If, as Heidegger argues, it is the *concealment* of nature's activities that the German poet is concerned with, then the elusive quality of the Scots language to many of Jamie's readers may enact a similar refusal to offer simplified readings of the natural world.[10] This testing of the act of representation itself confirms the important relationship that these poems bear to the achievement of the book as a whole.

The Tree House is ultimately a contemplative collection, in which Jamie takes stock of her growth as poet and as human being and fashions this exploration from the natural world that so significantly shapes her vision. This act of fashioning leaves other possibilities open, for nature – as Jamie's book of prose pieces *Findings* reveals – is about venturing beyond what is known and comfortable, to explore new territories. Fellow-poet Jane Hirschfield observes:

> The world's beauty continually surprises, in no small part because it's not controlled by self or what self knows. Even a sand grain or pebble, considered closely, can liberate us from conscious mind's constriction, from our close-held embrace of ego's dominance over things.
> (Hirschfield, 1998, p. 50)

To know the self, and further, to represent the self, is to push the boundaries of experience so that new encounters can clarify existing views of identity and belonging. It is in this crucial respect that Jamie can remain an important Scottish poet while still challenging us to consider our responsibilities to the whole of nature.

Notes

1. Though Kathleen Jamie herself resists the centrality of identity politics in the critical reception of her poetry, she has acknowledged the personal significance of political change: 'The referendum on the issue of the Scottish parliament was held in '97, and this year we took the two infants to Edinburgh on the day of its opening. Births of children and of nations. Acts of Union and of Separation. New life' (Jamie, 2003, p. 127).
2. All subsequent poetry quotations are from *The Tree House* (Jamie, 2004) and are given by page numbers in the text.
3. Two of the major protagonists in this debate are Lawrence Buell, among the most prominent figures in American ecocriticism, and Dana Phillips, who has written in response to Buell (1995). See Phillips (2003).

4. Richard Hunt (2002, p. 232) investigates Frye's observation in relation to Margaret Atwood's poetry in 'How to Love This World: The Transpersonal Wild in Margaret Atwood's Ecological Poetry'.
5. Jamie was born in Renfrewshire, brought up outside Edinburgh and now lives in Fife. She has travelled widely and her experiences of visiting Tibet and Pakistan, among other countries, have formed an important part of her prose writings (see Jamie, 2002).
6. Deryn Rees-Jones attributes Jamie's use of the concept of the web of nature to her reading of Jonathan Bate's *The Song of the Earth*; she argues that this work has had a profound influence on Jamie's engagement with environmental issues. See Rees-Jones (2005, pp. 199–202).
7. A recent essay by Kathleen Jamie – 'Pathologies: A Startling Tour of Our Bodies' (Jamie, 2008) – is an account of her exploration of human disease and infection under the microscope in a hospital laboratory. It was prompted by her awareness of particular circumstances in which nature threatens individual survival.
8. Jamie graduated from Edinburgh University with a degree in philosophy. Lilias Fraser (2001, p. 19), in her interview with the poet, draws attention to the role of her philosophical training in shaping her poetic development,.
9. Friedrich Hölderlin (1770–1843) is a German poet whose work reflects a significant interest in the synthesis of classical and Christian influences. Achieving little recognition during his lifetime, his work gained prominence during the twentieth century.
10. Heidegger writes: 'The rivers in Hölderlin's poetry are, however, in no way symbolic images that are merely more difficult to interpret in terms of degree. [...] The lines just cited tell us that the flow of the river that is named here is an activity that takes its own time, and that such activity is concealed. The concealment of its activity signifies that this river has a distinction' (Heidegger, 2004, pp. 250–1).

References

Bate, Jonathan (2000) *The Song of the Earth* (Cambridge, MA: Harvard University Press).

Bryson, Scott J. (ed.) (2002) *Ecopoetry: A Critical Introduction* (Salt Lake City: University of Utah Press).

Buell, Lawrence (1995) *The Environmental Imagination: Thoreau, Nature Writing, and the Formation of American Culture* (Cambridge MA: Harvard University Press).

Crawford, Robert (1993) *Identifying Poets: Self and Territory in Twentieth Century Poetry* (Edinburgh: Edinburgh University Press).

Fraser, Lilias (2001) 'Interview with Kathleen Jamie', *Scottish Studies Review*, 2 (1) (Spring), 15–23.

Heidegger, Martin (1993) 'Building, Dwelling, Thinking', in David Farrell Krell (ed.) *Basic Writings* (Abingdon: Routledge).

—— (2004) 'Three Lectures on Poetry', in Jon Cook (ed.) *Poetry in Theory: An Anthology 1900–2000* (Oxford: Blackwell Publishing).

Hirschfield, Jane (1998) *Hiddenness, Uncertainty, Surprise: Three Generative Energies of Poetry* (Tarset, Northumberland: Bloodaxe Books).

Hunt, Richard (2002) 'How to Love This World: The Transpersonal Wild in Margaret Atwood's Ecological Poetry', in Scott J. Bryson (ed.) *Ecopoetry: A Critical Introduction* (Salt Lake City: The University of Utah Press).
Jamie, Kathleen (1999) *Jizzen* (London: Picador).
—— (2000) 'Holding Fast – Truth and Change in Poetry', in W.N. Herbert and Matthew Hollis (eds) *Strong Words: Modern Poets on Modern Poetry* (Tarset, Northumberland: Bloodaxe).
—— (2002) *Among Muslims* (London: Sort Of Books).
—— (2003) 'Kathleen Jamie', in Clare Brown and Don Paterson (eds) *Don't Ask Me What I Mean: Poets in their Own Words* (London: Picador).
—— (2004) *The Tree House* (London: Picador).
—— (2005) *Findings* (London: Sort Of Books).
—— (2008) 'Pathologies: A Startling Tour of Our Bodies', *Granta 102: The New Nature Writing* (Summer), 35–50.
Middleton, Peter (2008) 'Language Public and Poetry', *PORES: A Journal of Poetics Research,* www.pores.bbk.ac.uk/issues/issue5/poetry-and-public-language/middletonlanguagepublicandpoetry (date accessed 6 June 2010).
Phillips, Dana (2003) *The Truth of Ecology: Nature, Culture and Literature in America* (Oxford: Oxford University Press).
Plumwood, Val (1993) *Feminism and the Mastery of Nature* (London: Routledge).
Rees-Jones, Deryn (2005) *Consorting with Angels: Essays on Modern Women Poets* (Tarset, Northumberland: Bloodaxe Books).
Scott, Kirsty (2007) 'In the Nature of Things: Kathleen Jamie', *Guardian Unlimited,* 18 June 18 2005, http://books.guardian.co.uk/poetry/features/0,12887,1508838,00.html (accessed 8 November 2007).
Thompson, Roger (2002) 'Emerson, Divinity, and Rhetoric in Transcendentalist Nature Writing and Twentieth-Century Ecopoetry', in Scott J. Bryson (ed.) *Ecopoetry: A Critical Introduction* (Salt Lake City: University of Utah Press).
Whyte, Christopher (2004) *Modern Scottish Poetry* (Edinburgh: Edinburgh University Press).

10

Sounding the Landscape: Dis-placement in the Poetry of Alice Oswald

Janne Stigen Drangsholt

In *The Last of England?* Randall Stevenson (2005) points to the way in which the mid-century renunciation of empire was followed by changes that need to be understood primarily in terms of *loss*. Each of these losses is conceived of as marking the last of a certain kind of England, and, while another emerged, this was a nation far less unified by tradition and more open in outlook, lifestyle and culture than before. The problems that are thus seen to be connected with the contemporary idea of England are even more pressing in relation to the concept of 'Britain', or 'Britishness'. In Sarah Broom's recent study of contemporary British and Irish poetry, she problematizes the way in which 'Britain' acts as shorthand for a multiplicity of regions and nations with histories that have varied and diverged enormously over the last four or five decades, and points to the growing uncertainty about the significance of 'Britishness' in relation to the strong connections felt towards the different regions (Broom, 2005, p. 2). As a result, Britishness loses its significance as a unifying concept and comes closer to being a perfunctory gloss over regional, national and even global characteristics that refer to a place which does not sound like home to everyone.

In terms of poetry, this problem was clearly voiced in 1982, when Blake Morrison and Andrew Motion placed Seamus Heaney as the most important new poet of the last fifteen years in *The Penguin Book of Contemporary British Poetry*. In a letter published a year later, Heaney dissociated himself from the anthology because of the use of the designation 'British'. Heaney emphasized a 'deep design / To be at home / In my own place', which made it impossible for him to accept the designation 'British' (Heaney in Stevenson, 2005, p. 177). Among the Northern Irish poets in the same anthology, including Medbh McGuckian, Paul Muldoon and Michael Longley, many shared the same view.

While this incident emphasizes the failure of 'Britishness' to provide the individual with a sense of identity, it also raises the question as to what might aid the individual in forging some kind of self in relation to a community, or even a nation. When Seamus Heaney talks of 'home', it is not primarily on the basis of structures of national identity, but in reference to a certain kind of landscape that keeps on 'pulling a man back into the ground', to use the words of Alice Oswald (Oswald, 2005b, p. x).[1] For poets like Seamus Heaney and Ted Hughes landscapes were still vital in the construction of a sense of identity and self, confirming a strong link between human subjectivity and the places we inhabit. With the rise of the postmodern idiom, however, the idea of forging a home through a connection between nature and self was once again threatened. To a large extent this resulted in a kind of 'crisis-poetry', in which the poetic subjectivity struggled with the thought of placing itself in any kind of 'scape'. While one problem was the perceived impossibility of finding a self to place, another was a failing sense of stability in the exterior surroundings. Thomas Docherty points to the disjunctive relationship between landscape and subject in Heaney's poem 'The Grauballe Man' and calls it 'a poetry which lies uncertainly between image [...] and memory [...], between history and its representation' (Docherty, 1997, p. 208). In a contemporary literary and theoretical context, it seems, landscapes have become increasingly difficult to map, threatening to render cartography a meaningless exercise and simultaneously divesting the subject of any stable sense of place.

Nevertheless, the thematization of landscape remains important in some registers of contemporary poetry, particularly recognizable in a continuous effort to construct a place which feels like home. Interestingly, writings by Eavan Boland, Jo Shapcott, Lavinia Greenlaw and Alice Oswald all deliberately stage crisis by trying to articulate landscape or a sense of place. In some poems this effort manifests itself as the construction of a 'site', poeticizing a location which allows the subject to envision a space open enough to allow a selfhood to be formed, language to be said and a journey to be undertaken, or, alternatively, interrupted. In other texts, the subject fails to conceive of place as anything other than an absence. In Jo Shapcott's poem 'On Tour: In the Alps', the lyrical I is faced with an auditory obstacle when attempting to relate herself actively to her surroundings:

> [...] it's hard to tune my ear to it
> against so many men's voices shouting
> all the names they know, at the dark
>
> (Shapcott, 2000, p. 64)

The dialogue between self and place, it seems, depends on a kind of silence that is made impossible by the established truths of history. Home has already been appropriated by someone else, a problem that is also raised in other poems by Shapcott. In 'Motherland' words like 'England' and 'Home' only invoke 'Distance' as 'Degree / of remoteness, interval of space' (2000, p. 124). What we see here is a perception of space as an absolute 'interval' rather than a clearing in which a connection can be made.

Shapcott's poems present us with a poetic persona who is travelling in the Alps or migrates into the form of another being: a cow ('The Mad Cow in Space'), cheetah ('Cheetah Run') or goat on a 'Dusk, deserted road' ('Goat') (Shapcott, 2000, p. 48). Another poet who employs motion in order to explore a sense of place is Alice Oswald, who frequently concentrates on repositionings that allow for true encounters. This happens in the poem 'Woman in a Mustard Field', where the subject only comes 'to sense again' by fleeing 'your house to meet the space / that blows about my head' (Oswald, 1996, p. 16). In her introduction to the poetry anthology *The Thunder Mutters,* Oswald emphasizes the importance of movement, connecting it directly with the kind of nature that pulls 'a man back into the ground' (Oswald, 2005b, p. x). For Oswald, this is a process that is essential for determining what it entails to be human. What is more, such a process seems to be manifested in the kind of poetry that sees neither nature nor landscape as a 'mere conceit', in what Oswald refers to as 'restless poems' that remain open to the many centred energies of the natural world (ibid.)

Such a conception of poetry is relevant to her own work. Instead of presenting us with a poetic subject enjoying a safe distance from its surroundings, Oswald's poems situate themselves on a border on which questions can be asked. This is particularly apparent in *Dart* and *Woods etc.,* which are both inaugurated by interrogations. *Dart* opens by questioning 'Who's this moving alive over the moor?', while *Woods etc.,* pensively asks 'what is water in the eyes of water' (2002, p. 1; 2005c, p. 3). Other questions have to do with location. In the poem 'Field', the poetic subject places itself 'at the centre of all visible darkness' (2005c, p. 25). As suggested by the oxymoron 'visible darkness', the subject does not seek to place itself firmly in the stability of what it can identify and categorize. Rather, it has situated itself in the openness of 'the big field behind the house' on 'Easternight', that is, in a space that is both physical and temporal, and where death and birth seem to coincide. At the same time, the subject is also aware of itself as a corporeal being, as it stands in the field, looking at and listening to its own surroundings. According to Jean-Yves Lacoste in *Experience and the Absolute,* this is an essential point of departure. For Lacoste, the ipseity of the self is that which defines us. A result of this recognition is the accompanying awareness that the question of *where* we are must always precede that of *what* we are (Lacoste, 2004, p. 7). In Oswald's poem, the answer to this question is the large space of a field behind the house, at a time when the universe itself becomes dislocated by the mythical force of 'Easternight'. As the evening approaches midnight, the world goes from being 'wedged / between its premise and its conclusion' to being 'unhorizoned / hung upon nothing, barking for its owner'. The world's displacement from a 'visible darkness' to an 'unhorizoned' nothingness also seems to reflect a change within the poetic subject, however. In the final verses of the poem, light seeps through and the speaker demonstrates an ability to register its surroundings in their absolute presence: 'burial, widowed, moonless, seeping / docks, grasses, small windflowers, weepholes, wires' (Oswald, 2005c, p. 25).

The way in which these individual elements appear in all their presence towards the end of the poem evokes a sense of immanence that Oswald has frequently been lauded for, conjuring some degree of physicality in her presentation of being. In a short prose piece entitled 'Wood Work', Oswald indirectly comments on this aspect of her poetry while discussing her characteristic lack of punctuation. She says that 'I like the look of the words all happening at once and the grammar having no homecoming', and adds that as the poems are not arranged chronologically the reader should immerse herself in 'one poem at a time. or [sic!] better still, in one phrase, one word. Like Stockhausen's music made of single points' (Oswald, 2005a, p. 5). These two statements are important for Oswald's overall project because they signal the way in which the poetic speaker's question of 'Who am I?' is always attended by that of 'Where am I?' through the physical presentation of the poem. In *Dart,* the initial question of 'who' is followed by a relentless movement towards the sea, while the lack of punctuation and capital letters in 'Sea Poem', the first poem of *Woods etc.*, creates the effect of simultaneously pointing back to *Dart* and forward to the other poems in the collection. At the same time, the second verse line heightens the immanence of the words as they appear on the page: 'what is water in the eyes of water / loose inquisitive fragile anxious' (Oswald, 2005c, p. 3). The way these descriptions of being follow each other naturally, yet in a seeming random manner, gives the impression of a single thought that is at once instantaneous, illuminating and strangely transitory.

The kind of movement we see here, which is absolutely present yet firmly dis-placed in its lack of linear purpose, is also interesting to the extent that it amplifies the sense of crisis in Oswald's poetry. In this, Oswald bears a resemblance to the Romantic poets as they are presented in Harold Bloom's *The Ringers in the Tower*. Bloom points to the lack of rectilinear process in Wordsworth and reads this as a sign of crisis. In Wordsworth, Bloom says, the saving moment inevitably comprises a backward glance into a time that has already been lost (Bloom, 1971, p. 17). This displacement strips the text of a proper subject, as well as a firm placement in time and space.

While Wordsworth's poetry appears to end up in crisis through his inevitable focus on the past, Oswald's subject in 'Field' seems actively to seek the displacement of time and place in order to visualize both its interior and exterior surroundings. 'Woods etc.' is another poem structured around an 'I'. Here, the unifying economy of the self is both challenged and constructed through sounds that cannot be determined by sight and which consequently largely go 'unnoticed', like the sound of a 'footfall' in the first stanza (Oswald, 2005c, p. 7). While this metaphor on the one hand points towards the way in which the mind works, continuously linking impressions, sensations and thoughts in an uncontrollable and largely imperceptible stream, on the other hand it also emphasizes the limitless and continuous formation of subjectivity coexisting with that which is fundamentally different and unknown in the self.

While Oswald never allows for what she seems to perceive as the limiting unifying effect of the eye, the mind is nevertheless able to transform the footfall into a perceivable image, 'sweeping together the loose tacks of sound' into an auditory memory: 'I remember walking once into increasing / woods, my hearing like a widening wound'. The woods are a soundscape, a numberless multitude in a state of constant expansion that challenges the idea of a centre, a definite border, and any firm sense of unity. The importance of the idea of a soundscape is suggested by Oswald in an interview where she expresses her preference of sound over sight, saying that 'I'd much rather listen than look' (Oswald, 2003, p. 32). Oswald connects listening to 'that primitive mind [...] where your knowledge is stored' (ibid.) The suggestion here is that listening is distinguished by a greater openness than the empirical coldness of the eye, transcending rather than fixing the boundaries of physical space. And even more than that, listening is connected with origins as the space where knowledge is still attainable.

This focus on the importance of listening also links Oswald to Heidegger and his writings on poetry as a mythical language. For Heidegger, the crisis tormenting Western civilization is grounded in our reliance on metaphysics and the attendant proclivity to favour speech above listening, and vision above hearing. Heidegger points to poetry as constituting a more unified language, in that it involves not only speaking, but also hearing and listening, heeding and being silent and attentive (compare Heidegger, 1962, pp. 55–8). In listening, the need to master the real through naming is loosened, opening up to difference.

In 'Woods etc.' there is no suggestion that this is a straightforward exercise. As the subject walks into the symbolic woods, the very manifestation of difference, hearing itself, is presented as 'a widening wound'. This can be connected to the way in which the woods are constantly 'increasing', thus preventing the subject from landmarking or mapping the territory. When the lyrical subject mentions the sun's position, there is an emphasis on the fact that this is only 'imaginary', the factual indications of place being 'the last glow of rain dead in the ground'. To navigate by means of the rigid rationality of the Platonic sun is not an option, nor is finding one's way by empirical observation of the sun's position in the sky.

The last few verses of the third stanza also negate the possibility of finding the necessary information within the body itself. While the subjectivity hopes that knowledge 'would rise suddenly from scattered parts of my body', there is no sense of an epiphany or moment of illumination. Rather, the final verse of the fourth stanza shows us that only silence endures. There is no 'clearing in that quiet, no change at all'.

The reference to a 'clearing' once again evokes Heidegger's gestures towards a different mode of perception than that which can be identified by the empirical gaze. Like Oswald, Heidegger employs the metaphor of a wood as a space in which understanding may actually be possible: 'the clearing, the open region, is not only free for brightness and darkness but also for resonance and echo, for sound and the diminishing of sound. The clearing is the open region for everything that becomes present and absent' (Heidegger, 2000, p. 442). Heidegger's clearing provides a space which is both landscape and soundscape, opening up to a perception which defies the hegemony of sight. Through this openness, the clearing incorporates both *alètheia* (as that which is not hidden or forgotten) and its counterpart *lèthe* (as that which is hidden or forgotten), rendering it a space which does not distinguish between that which can be seen and that which goes unnoticed. To Oswald's poetic subject, however, there is 'no clearing in that quiet', suggesting the speaker's fundamental inability, or unwillingness, to truly listen. And while the subject is hoping for a vertical illumination that will link the eyes, or the various elements of self, with the movements of the sun in the heavens, we find the opposite taking place as the 'little mercury line / that regulates my speech' starts to fall rapidly and endlessly in the uncomprehending body.

Through the subject's inability to listen to the quiet, the woods are filled with associations of forlornness, as in the first verses of *The Divine Comedy* where Dante finds himself 'within a shadowed forest, / For I had lost the path that does not stray' (Dante, 2008, p. 59). While Dante also employs the woods as a route towards salvation, attesting to his guilt in the form of a sinful nature as an ever-present reality that enslaves the human race, Oswald's poetic subject is unable to take this step. The absolute other in the form of God or the sun remains an impossibility in Oswald's poem, where the whole world is made up of metonymies. Instead of selfhood and identity there are 'upturned apses' and a 'little mercury line'. In this sense, the poem is not so much structured by the metaphorical 'woods' as by the metonymical diffusion of the 'etc.'

If the sense of crisis in Wordsworth stemmed from a recurrent focus on an impossible moment, then, the crisis in Oswald can largely be seen in connection with such a metonymical dispersion. Only to refer to such a crisis as 'postmodern' is less than satisfactory, however. In fact, it seems more rewarding to take Charles Taylor's diagnosis of a 'historically limited mode of self-interpretation' as a point of departure (Taylor, 1989, p. 111). This refers to the way in which we distinguish between what is conceived to be 'within' and 'without'; understanding, thoughts, ideas and feelings are to be located 'within' while objects in the world are placed 'without' (ibid.) In Oswald's poetic universe, such a distinction seems connected to the sense of forlornness that we find in poems like 'Field' and 'Woods etc.' However, an awareness of such a lack of orientation can also be employed as a point of departure for a reintegration in a new landscape. The relation between language and landscape is a precarious one, and even though the subject is caught within a static silence, the falling movement of the 'mercury line / that regulates my speech' towards the very end of 'Woods etc.' may suggest the initiation of a process towards the ability to listen.

It is worth noting that while *Woods etc.* questions the human potential for listening and finding itself in a comprehensible landscape, Oswald's earlier sequence *Dart* presents us with a self that moves in tune with spatial and temporal surroundings. We see this in the epigraph, where the poet quotes Ivan Illyich saying that 'water always comes with an ego and an alter ego'. This citation refers both to the divided self of psychoanalysis and Heraclitus' famous fragment L: 'As they step into the same rivers, other and still other waters flow upon them'

(Kahn, 1979, p. 53). With fragment L Heraclitus seems to propagate the idea that a unitary form is maintained while its material embodiment is constantly lost and replaced, emphasizing the cyclical nature of the universe. In *Introduction to Metaphysics,* Heidegger reads this as a characteristic element in Heraclitean philosophy as a whole, saying that it uncovers the gatheredness of such elements as life and death, day and night (Heidegger, 2000, p. 142).

Such a Heraclitean insight can also be found in *Dart,* where a river embraces the various selves and presences encountered along the way, integrating the other voices while remaining incommensurable to the enunciating self. In this, the voices emerge as a mosaic in which it is possible to maintain difference, thus illustrating Illyich's aphorism of multiplicity. This does not mean that *Dart* is pure harmony, however. The presentation of the multitude of voices that are fragmented, linked, gathered and different also functions to highlight many of the crises that are permanently present in our Western culture. One of these has to do with the way the text itself is situated in relation to the extra-textual reality that it (re-)presents, evoking Thomas Docherty's essay 'Ana-; or Postmodernism, Landscape, Seamus Heaney', where he claims that postmodernism's problematization of the relation between the 'real' and its 'representation' has severed the link to the trans-historical or mythical subject of Romanticism and modernism. The reality which is supposed to ground our representations, whether in the form of history as an exterior fact or in 'the presence-to-self' of the supposedly transcendental subject, is no longer available to us except as an image (compare Docherty, 1997, p. 208). In this context, poetry places itself in the precarious space between history and its representation, forming a discourse which presents a highly questionable memory or image.

This latter comment is interesting in relation to Oswald's status as 'nature poet'. Nature poetry, or ecopoetry, is a label which has been much favoured in recent years, and Oswald's name frequently crops up in this context. While the poetic universe has an undeniable basis in the nature that surrounds us on various levels of being, 'nature poet' is also a problematic label in the sense that it evokes associations of a nearness or closeness which seems incompatible with the metaphysical investigations suggested above. Indeed, Oswald herself rejects the label, saying that 'I [...] write about the special nature of what happens to exist' (Oswald, 2003, p. 207). Hence, the question is displaced into an interrogation as to what this 'special nature' refers to, shifting the focus from a Kantian observation of the metaphysical object to a Heideggerean exploration of the thing *as it is* in its presence. The incessant movement in Oswald's poetry suggests that this 'special nature' is a fleeting otherness, a kind of *objet a,* which can never articulated because it exists in the timeless spatiality of that which was always already there.

We can find an example of this towards the end of *Dart,* where the river 'name disappears and the sea slides in to / replace it' (Oswald, 2002, p. 48). This event echoes the Heraclitean fragment cited above, emphasizing the cyclical nature of the universe. The recognition that seems to present itself to the reader is that there is no overcoming the crisis of selfhood as this, perhaps, *is* the core of self. The long poem ends with the river identifying itself to the reader:

> This is me, anonymous, water's soliloquy,
>
> all names, all voices, Slip-Shape, this is Proteus,
> whoever that is, the shepherd of the seals,
> driving my many selves from cave to cave ...
> (ibid.)

The name that the river awards itself is a negation of name-giving in the sense that it refers to the perpetual shape-shifter who has even given his name to the English adjective *protean,* meaning 'polymorphous, ever changing, unstable'. It is also, however, an affirmation of identity as a process of becoming. With the image of the river driving its multiple selfhood 'from cave to cave', time becomes space in the sense that the temporalities of past, present and future are recognized to be equally relevant. Oswald has said that she is fascinated by the 'feeling of movement in Homer', which differs from the writing of later Greek poets which is 'very conditioned through the eye' (Oswald, 2003, p. 31). As a result, the fluid identity of the protean self is also echoed in the language itself. The three dots that end *Dart* manifest the mobility and mutability of a poetic discourse that tries to subvert the eye's demands of linearity. Instead of confirming its own ending and finality, it is subtly altered into the otherness of the page's blankness by a manifested 'etc.' In an interview Oswald says that 'I love etc and dot dot dot. I feel the universe is constructed with an etc.' (Kellaway, 2005), signalling a vision of the universe as a landscape which is constantly crossing its own boundaries.

While the poetic subject of the river remains playful and easy in its flow and flutterings, the kind of selfhood that it represents is based on a crisis in the sense that it manifests a process which is radical, uncompromising and recurrent. In this, Oswald's comprehension of self appears to be very much in line with that of Julia Kristeva, who sees crisis as inherent and crucial to sociality. Crisis, or the unsettling process of meaning and subject, is also fundamental for the human being's recognition of itself, as signalled by Kristeva's concept of 'subject-in-process' (Kristeva, 1980, p. 135). In the essay 'From One Identity to Another', Kristeva describes the 'subject-in-process' as a crisis that is primarily caused by poetic language. Poetic language disturbs the subject because of its alignment with the semiotic aspects of being. Hence, goals such as name-predication and signification are subjacent to processes of condensation and displacement, as can be seen in tropes like metaphor and metonymy (compare ibid., p. 136).

While Oswald's poetic discourse brings the semiotic to the surface through stylistic features such as lack of punctuation and capital letters, the main disruptive element is her use of metonymy and metaphor. In 'Woods etc.' the self is presented as a metonymical structure. *Dart,* however, is characterized by the gathering force of the metaphor, as can be seen in the river's 'I am' statement towards the end of the poem. The river is a protean slip-shape, 'driving my many selves from cave to cave', that refuses to link itself to one absolute identity (Oswald, 2002, p. 48). Hence, the metaphoric river is a trope in continuous movement, process and transformation, rather than a unified entity. It is an act of cartography which comprises a democratic vision of being, through the incorporation of voices and languages of human selves encountered beyond the shores of selfhood. In her introduction to *Dart,* Oswald refers to this as a 'sound-map of the river, a songline from the source to the sea'. While the images of 'source' and 'sea' connote a sense of depth and origin that function to signal that the river is an element of meaningfulness, this is more of a democratic process than something that can be concretely enunciated.

The metaphorical river is a landscape that is both interior and exterior, physical and spiritual, which provides encounters between everything that exists. In this context, it is also significant that the name *Dart* is identified in the notes as 'old Devonian for oak' (Oswald, 2002, p. 11). As in the poetic universe of Ted Hughes, an important source of inspiration to Oswald, the oak seems to connote processes of gathering. The ancient oak presents itself as an act of gathering recollection, as can be seen in the speech of the waternymph, who informs us that 'They say all rivers were once fallen trees' (2002, p. 12). Thus, the poetic discourse makes a link between a mythical place of origins and an organic space in which everything is continuously transformed. The cyclical nature of the universe is emphasized as the waternymph apostrophically calls on Rex Nemorensis, explained in a note as 'the King of the Oakwoods who had to be sacrificed to a goddess', and 'Flumen Dialis', which the note identifies as 'a priest of Zeus [...] the god of the oak' (2002, p. 13). As is also suggested by these names, this part of the poem is a prayer for renewal and resurrection, for continued circularity and the eternal return of everything. While the river takes life, it also gives it back, and the waternymph prays that

> come spring that
> lights one oak
> off the next
>
> and the fields
> and workers bursting
> into light amen
> (2002, pp. 13–14)

The way in which everything becomes unified as it bursts into light is once again reminiscent of Ted Hughes, whose poem 'That Morning' from the sequence entitled *River* (1983), ends with a joyous apprehension of the absolute, as the poetic persona asserts 'So we stood, alive in the river of light / Among the creatures of light, creatures of light' (Hughes, 1993, p. 179). In the same way as the explosion of light envelops every being in Oswald's poem, Hughes's poetic persona takes part in a deeply significant experience in which a moment of oneness takes place between the material and spiritual worlds, as civilization finds its way to the purity of nature. While Hughes centres his poem on a poetic speaker, Oswald's poem is spoken from the polyphonic point of intersection between river and other. This renders *Dart* a greater challenge to the idea of self, which is established as flowing and semiotic, barely audible, and perhaps even indecipherable; 'mutterings' suggesting the distance between such a sense of self and what we experience as a self created by the symbolic order of society and culture. The river being, or fluid being, is an ancient self which simultaneously exists as a 'living presence' in the sense that it constructs, and unceasingly alters, its being in encounters with the other. This is suggestive of an immensely interesting comprehension of the subject as something that only comes into being in a community or a *mitsein,* while at the same time functioning as a self-reflexive comment on the narrative itself as a mobile and mutable process.

The reference to the oak tree is also accompanied by another, more concretely cultural allusion to the landscape of being, however, in the sense that it is England's national tree. As an emblem of England, the oak symbolizes the strength and endurance of the nation, signalling its continued function as a ground of experience and upholder of a heterogeneous and polyphonic, yet strangely unified, identity and sense of self. This is also suggested in the opening of the poem, where Oswald presents us with an old man who is 'seeking and finding a difficulty' (Oswald, 2002, p. 1). The connection between man and river is established through the movement of 'seeking'. As the man consults his map, the river responds to him by issuing the 'sound map' referred to in the epigraph, and calling out to him, something which amounts to a calling out to itself: 'The Dart, lying low in darkness calls out Who is it? / trying to summon itself by speaking…' (ibid.) The implication here is that the river is, unknown to itself, presumably mirroring the old man who is seeking – who is trying to find his way by referring himself to the map, and trying to transform distance into a nearness, where the place sought is the place reached or a shelter which can protect him on his journey. Through the posing of the above-cited question 'who is it?' the swamp landscape is transformed into a room in which the old man is allowed to speak. When he introduces himself, singing his own song, this is also the river singing of itself – as it has, indeed, summoned itself by speaking. In this, we are listening to the simultaneous voices of the ego and the alter ego, the man and the river, the language and the landscape – presented in a simultaneous speech. The voices of the human being and river being intermingle, once again suggesting the separate yet unified process of speaking. The flow of words on the page is also the flow of the language of the beings, and one 'I' follows the other in a natural sequence that challenges yet affirms the distinction between the two.

The way in which the poetic language juxtaposes, intermingles and parallels the river being and the human being suggests that Oswald employs the topography of the landscape not only as a way of exploring the self, but also as a field in which the division between self and landscape is dis-placed so that the lack of autonomy and distance between the two elements may be enunciated, highlighted and elucidated. While the river may have one place of origin, it has innumerable beginnings. Thus, the poem becomes a space for beginnings, encounters, transformations and, above all, movement, rendering it a discourse of crisis only to the extent that it is revolutionary, disruptive and transgressive. Oswald's is what one may refer to as a *transformative discourse,* leading to borderline experiences which dis-place the subject only to the extent that it is able to face an other. In this space, the reader can catch a whiff of 'winter flowers, smelling of a sudden entering elsewhere' ('Sonnet', Oswald, 2005, p. 21), dis-placing, but nevertheless promising, resurrection.

Note

1. It should be noted here that Irish poetry's relationship to landscape does have a quite distinctive history, to which Heaney also relates. Due to the format of this chapter, this will not be a point of discussion here.

References

Bloom, Harold (1971) *The Ringers in the Tower: Studies in Romantic Tradition* (Chicago: University of Chicago Press).
Broom, Sarah (2005) *Contemporary British and Irish Poetry: An Introduction* (Basingstoke: Palgrave Macmillan).
Dante (2008) *The Divine Comedy,* trans. C.H. Sisson (Oxford: Oxford University Press).
Docherty, Thomas (1997) 'Ana-; or Postmodernism, Landscape, Seamus Heaney', in *Seamus Heaney (New Casebooks)* (Basingstoke: Macmillan).
Heidegger, Martin (1962) *Being and Time* (New York: Harper & Row, 1962).
—— (2000) *Introduction to Metaphysics,* trans. Gregory Fried and Richard Polt (New Haven and London: Yale University Press).
Hughes, Ted (1993) *Three Books: Remains of Elmet, Cave Birds, River* (London: Faber and Faber).
Kahn, Charles (1979) *The Art and Thought of Heraclitus* (Cambridge: Cambridge University Press).
Kellaway, Kate (2005) 'Into the Woods', interview with Alice Oswald, *Observer,* 19 June 2005, http://www.guardian.co.uk/books/2005/jun/19/poetry.features (accessed 28 January 2010).
Kristeva, Julia (1980) *Desire in Language: A Semiotic Approach to Literature and Art* (New York: Columbia University Press).
Lacoste, Jean-Yves (2004) *Experience and the Absolute. Disputed Questions on the Humanism of Man,* trans. Mark Raftery-Skehan (New York: Fordham University Press).
Oswald, Alice (1996) *The Thing in the Gap-Stone Stile* (London: Faber and Faber).
—— (2002) *Dart* (London: Faber and Faber).
—— (2003) 'Presiding Spirits. Alice Oswald turns back to Sophocles', *Magma Poetry,* 26 (Summer): 28–32.
—— (2005a) 'Wood Work', *Poetry Book Society Bulletin,* 205 (Summer): 5–7.
—— (ed.) (2005b) *The Thunder Mutters: 101 Poems for the Planet* (London: Faber and Faber).
—— (2005c) *Woods etc.* (London: Faber and Faber).
Shapcott, Jo (2000) *Her Book: Poems 1988–98* (London: Faber and Faber).
Stevenson, Randall (2005) *The Oxford English Literary History: Volume 12: 1960–2000: The Last of England?* (Oxford: Oxford University Press).
Taylor, Charles (1989) *Sources of the Self: The Making of the Modern Identity* (Cambridge: Harvard University Press).

11
Place, Narrative and Crisis in the Long Poems of Paul Muldoon

Anne Karhio

I

Despite the frequent claim that Paul Muldoon's poetry has evaded any profound engagement with the various crises that plague the society around the poet, most famously the Northern Irish Troubles, several of his poems take acts of violence, experiences of loss and separation, as well as the crises of war, terror and the 'war on terror' as their subject-matter. They also display a profound distrust of the kind of language that would offer any simplified explanatory frameworks for the conflicts and acts of violence or oppression depicted. Muldoon's early poetry's perceived political disengagement in the Irish context followed directly from resistance to the very specific kind of political engagement in poetry and literature that Seamus Deane has promoted in the context of late twentieth-century Irish poetry. The critical debate around this topic has been summed up many times during the past couple of decades.[1] For Deane's Gramscian-Marxist position, politics and poetry are to be inseparable if they wish to break the complicity of poetry as an elitist aesthetic practice with the wider oppressive systems of a bourgeois society. The opposing camp to Deane's philosophy, that of practical criticism highlighting the autonomy of poetry as artistic practice, has been represented by Edna Longley, for whom, famously, poetry and politics, 'like church and state', should be separated (Longley, 1986, p. 185). In Colin Graham's words, in the critical climate marked by the political situation of Northern Ireland, the question has been 'the supremacy of either a definitive Irishness or a literariness' (Graham, 2001, p. 55). The trouble with this battlefield, where nationality, culture and politics are set against the formal and aesthetic, as Shane Alcobia-Murphy has noted, is that any agreed definition for the term 'politics' is often missing. Alcobia-Murphy particularly draws attention to the fact that 'politics' is too often simplistically confused 'with propaganda or sectarian ideology' (Alcobia-Murphy, 2006, p. 97) – though it is hard to believe that even more 'engaged' poets would want to become mere mouthpieces for any particular sectarian faction. At times, a 'political' emphasis is one with any degree of societal engagement or historical contextualization, while, at others, it is confined to subscribing to a specific ideological position.

But, of course, the critical division between political and cultural readings of poetry on the one hand, and, on the other, readings emphasizing the formal and aesthetic qualities of texts, is by no means solely an Irish phenomenon. For example Marjorie Perloff outlines, from the perspective of her experiences of American academia, the current situation on the other side of the Atlantic, where the growth and dominance of a politically motivated cultural studies community has challenged the more formalist approaches, now considered elitist and out-of-date:

> in the politicized post-Vietnam era [formalist theory] came under sharp attack from those who take poetics to be essentially a historical or cultural formation. Indeed in this [...] paradigm, formalism becomes a dirty word, a smoke-screen for ignoring the ideology and political ethos of a given work.
>
> (Perloff, 2004, p. 9)

For literary studies in America, the crisis prompting such a shift was the Vietnam War and the consequent mobilization of the 1960s counterculture. Subsequently, the civil rights movement in the North of Ireland gained impetus from the civil rights movement in the USA; as Michael Parker asserts, in the 1960s,

> [The] emergence of the black civil rights movement in the United States [...] possessed a special resonance for a new generation of university-educated Catholics and liberal Protestants and served as an important point of reference in their own politicization.
>
> (Parker, 2007, p. 40)

The perceived parallels between Ireland and America would also have their impact on both poetry and criticism. The 'politicization' of literary and cultural studies is thus a wider phenomenon than one might be led to believe when reading some recent overviews of Irish literature and politics, even if one abstains from compromising the specificities of time and place contributing to an individual poem in favour of any generalizing historical framework.

My purpose here is to focus on one formal aspect of poetry as displayed by one poet, that is, on the narrative elements of Muldoon's long poems, and the ways in which they operate in portraying crisis and place, contexts external to the poems themselves. The challenge, therefore, is to demonstrate how the aesthetic and formal devices – and readings – of the poems contribute to their engagement with the crises they encounter, rather than to their withdrawal to any kind of isolated literary or aesthetic ivory tower. In the case of Muldoon in particular, his technical skill as a poet is at times seen as *dis*engaging his work from the circumstances which (perhaps) it should address.[2] However, a poem's formal qualities should be seen to operate in dialogue with their personal, historical and critical contexts and as generative of meaning, not as mere exercises in technical craftsmanship. How Paul Muldoon's specific use of poetic language and structure relate to the states and events of crisis that appear in his poems will be examined through historical and biographical reference *and* through attentiveness to the singular event of the poem, the exact form or figure it takes and makes.[3]

The concept of the 'long poem' is an elusive one: as Joseph Conte notes, 'the difficulty lies in the apprehension that the term "long poem" refers only to volume, and says nothing about the form or the content of the work' (Conte, 1992); the term poses no absolute requirements other than length itself. The long poem continues to carry echoes of narrative verse belonging to oral storytelling traditions, and their interlocking of narrative and place. For Romantic poets, narratives of past times and distant places would provide material for internalized landscapes of the imagination as well as lyric imagery,[4] thus also contributing to the development of the dominant mode of twentieth-century poetry, the short lyric poem. Both the short Romantic lyric and the long poem's connections to the epic (the Romantics wrote their share of long poems, of course) have persisted to our days. Critics have seen that epic aspirations of cohesion and comprehensiveness in a sense survived the emergence of the modernist collage, which, on the surface at least, aimed at relinquishing narrative continuity and replacing it with the 'doctrine of the Image' (McHale, 2000, p. 250). The 'anti-narrative stamp', as Geoffrey Squires describes it (Squires, 1983, p. 5) of modernist writing is similarly discussed by Marjorie Perloff, who notes that

> As such, story held little interest for the early twentieth-century poets [...]. It was not spurned because poets like Yeats or Stevens or Crane

> questioned, as postmodern writers have increasingly done, the very nature of order that a systematic plot structure implies. Rather, the poetry of modernism was wedded to a sharp distinction between poetry, the lyric expression of personal emotions, and prose, the language of fiction, of the novel.
>
> (Perloff, 1996, p. 158)[5]

However, simultaneously with the structure of the collage (the fragmented, discontinuous and alienated surface of their longer poems), at another level the modernists asserted the significance of the narrative. In the guise of an underlying master-narrative, narrative's invisible gravitational force would bring coherence to the chaos of the poem's disrupted and apparently disconnected surface: 'the more scrupulously one suppresses the master-narrative, the more complete one's dependence on submerged master-narratives' (McHale, 2000, p. 252). Poetic imagination would thus seek to restore order to chaos through lyric craft, and long forms of poetry would typically adopt the form of lyric sequences rather than maintaining surface continuity or linearity within a poem's various parts. For Joseph Conte, 'the modern epic' (he mentions Olson's *Maximus Poems* and Merrill's *The Changing Light at Sandover* as examples), despite its apparent break with narrative forms of epic verse, veers towards completion and coherence, a 'universal statement', and 'retains a hierarchical superstructure' (Conte, 1992) – in other words, the master-narrative of completion and universal design.

In an earlier study, Rosenthal and Gall defined the modern poetic sequence (including examples as diverse as Whitman's *Song of Myself*, Yeats's *Words for Music Perhaps*, Eliot's *Waste Land*, Pound's *Pisan Cantos* and Kinsella's *Notes from the Land of the Dead*, to mention but a few) as 'a grouping of mainly lyric poems and passages, rarely uniform in pattern, which tend to interact as an organic whole' (Rosenthal and Gall, 1983, p. 9). Instead of narrative linearity and formal coherence, therefore, the lyric sequence often confirms a Romantic-modernist sense of subjectivity:

> It usually includes narrative or dramatic elements, and ratiocinative ones as well, but its structure is finally lyrical. Intimate, fragmented, self-analytical, open, emotionally volatile, the sequence meets the needs of modern sensibility even when the poet aspires to tragic or epic scope.
>
> (Ibid.)

In other words, it 'meets the need' for a 'lyric expression of personal emotions'. And while Rosenthal and Gall drew attention to the way in which the poetic sequence relates to 'lyrical possibilities of language', its perceived origin in modernity's 'cultural and psychological crisis' and its gravitation towards an 'emotional center energizing the poem' highlight their own relationship to the Romantic-modernist tradition of poetry. For them, the traditional, narrative long poem was still unable to address the kind of crisis to which the poetic sequence responds:

> [...] it is sheer dogmatism to rule out any form or genre as obsolete [...], and it is always possible that some genius will find a way of writing a long, continuous narrative poem or logically or thematically developed one that will satisfy the most knowledgeable and sensitized of contemporary readers. But a fatal ennui with such efforts does seem to have set in [...]
>
> (Rosenthal and Gall, 1983, p. 6)

The long poetic form of lyric sequence, in other words, has taken the place previously occupied by the narrative long poem.

But if Rosenthal and Gall were somewhat unsure of the potential for the re-emergence of the narrative long poem in the early 1980s, subsequent critics have since registered the 'return of story in postmodern poetry' (Perloff, 1996, p. 155), or the ''Replenishment of Narrative in the Postmodernist Long Poem' (McHale, 2000).[6] Where modernist poets often replaced surface narrative with collage and fragmentation and simultaneously asserted the power of an underlying master-narrative, the situation is, to simplify somewhat, the reverse in the postmodern long poem. Any underlying ordering principle is denied by the play of surface narrative, often by reference to popular and coded forms of storytelling: 'such "stories" foreground the narrative codes themselves and call them into question' (Perloff, 1996, p. 161).

From early in his career, Muldoon has been considered an exemplary postmodernist by virtue of such challenging of master-narratives while portraying a marked interest in narrative in the form of arrested, incomplete and fragmentary elements, through direct quotation and reference or by adopting and mutating the narrative codes of detective stories, adventure tales, epics, Western films and so forth. For many, Muldoon is the poet of Lyotardian *petits rècits* par excellence, manifesting a preference for 'the fragmented and ramifying fictions to image [sic] the unpredictability of life' (Kerrigan, 1984, p. 22). In Ireland, of course, the twentieth-century long poem has developed in a context where the more radical formal experimentation of European modernist avant-garde found less foothold,[7] and the narrative element was never discarded to the same extent as elsewhere on the Continent. Long poems like Kavanagh's 'The Great Hunger', and Montague's 'The Rough Field', as well as more recent examples by Heaney, Carson, Ní Dhomhnaill and Boland (the list is by no means exhaustive) attest to the prevalence of narrative in twentieth-century Irish poetry, as well as to its continuing preoccupation with place. This is also manifested in poets' continuing fascination with the Irish language place-name or *dinnseanchas* tradition.[8]

In a critical climate where poetry's engagement with place is usually seen through a search for origins, a historically inscribed landscape constructed through cultural memory, Muldoon's poetics is seen to strive to free itself from the restraints of place: 'Muldoon relishes the dialogue of difference, enthusiastically mobilizing such potent tropes of modernity as those of displacement, dislocation, and composite, cosmopolitan identities' (Kennedy-Andrews, 2006, pp. 110–11). If not quite placeless, Muldoon's poetry is thus seen as unattached, or even exilic or escapist. For Seamus Deane, his early work was 'poetry of denial', poetry that 'refuses to be locked into the expectations raised by the narrative categories [the poet] invokes', becoming an inscription of 'pure space' (Deane, 1986, p. 245). Deane's criticism of Muldoon is based on a perceived indifference to the background of conflict and oppression, stemming from a purportedly postmodern surface aesthetic. It is the kind of poetry in which 'the postmodernist simulacrum or pluralism supplants the search for a legitimating mode of nominating and origin' and thus also the means to address the foundations of societal crisis in order to imagine an alternative future (Deane, 1990, pp. 18–19). However, the narratives of Muldoon's long poems, including the three poems on which I shall focus here, are nearly always set in very definable (albeit shifting and changing) locations, and are by no means presented as lacking historical context. The crises they address or portray are viewed as events embedded in a material place, even when distanced from the present, characterized by memory and physical remoteness. Instead of airy postmodern 'pure space'[9] or textual *jouissance*, Muldoon is preoccupied with the ways in which a focus on details and quirks of both event and language, on unexpected causes, consequences and connections, enables the poet to portray places in a way that does not fall neatly within any single, explanatory narrative framework. The poetic sequence and its emphasis on lyric subjectivity are also evoked in re-imagining narrative elements in poetry in ways that challenge 'the doctrine of the Image' and the primacy of 'emotional centres', while retaining an awareness of this tradition in twentieth-century poetry. Muldoon's longer poems are often difficult to categorize as long poems or sequences, as they embody elements of both in making most of 'the scope of these larger structures' (Muldoon quoted in Barker, 1998). Crisis and place, or crisis *in* place, inasmuch as it is discussed through the medium of the long poem, will nevertheless have to bring the narrative impulse out into the open by highlighting the constructed nature of any story from the shards and splinters of experience.

There is thus a need to address both a crisis of the narrative and narratives of crisis in poetry: how does Muldoon's poetics re-imagine narrative forms in the long poem to address the crises it depicts, and how does it simultaneously negotiate its relationship to place, or the precise spatial coordinates of any event of crisis that it seeks to incorporate? The three poems I will focus on have appeared in three consecutive decades of the poet's career. 'The More a Man Has, the More a Man Wants' concludes the 1983 collection *Quoof*, and tracks fragmented paths through the Northern Irish land and cityscape that provide the backdrop for sectarian violence and the hunger-strikes of the political prisoners of Belfast. 'Yarrow' is the final poem of *The Annals of Chile* (1994) and, more elegiac in its tone, attempts to come to terms with personal crisis and loss in focusing on the speaker's childhood home. Finally, I will look at the title poem of the 2006 collection *Horse Latitudes*, a sequence which perhaps most explicitly intertwines personal and public upheavals, most notably the US invasion of Iraq and the 'war on terror'.

II

'The More a Man Has, the More a Man Wants' concludes Muldoon's 1983 collection *Quoof*, which many have considered perhaps his most disturbing volume, with its depictions of mutilated human bodies, sexual violence and sectarian acts of terror. It consists of forty-nine sonnets, albeit often disfigured almost beyond recognition (one sonnet/stanza has fourteen lines of one single word each, for example). Set in contemporary Northern Ireland and North America, the poem draws from the anthropologist Paul Radin's 1956 book *The Trickster: A Study in American Indian Mythology* and his translation of the Winnebago tribe's trickster cycle, also consisting of forty-nine sections, on the wanderings of the sexually exuberant, shapeshifting and socially disruptive trickster figure. The poem follows two characters – Gallogly, a terrorist on the run,[10] and Mangas Jones, a Native American seeking to avenge the killings by an Ulsterman at Wounded Knee – through landscapes on both sides of the Atlantic. Through the terrorist acts of Gallogly and the warpath of Mangas Jones, the poem explores the complex relationship between violence and colonial injustice, revenge and retribution. It also situates the events in precise locations, including for example inner-city and suburban Belfast, the Armagh/Tyrone border, the rivers Callan and Bann in Northern Ireland and the New York Museum of Modern Art, 'mountains north of Boston', the Staten Island ferry, Logan airport and a Midwest gas station like the one depicted by Edward Hopper in 'Gas' (1940). Extreme precision of time and place ('Aldergrove [...] at 3.54 a.m.', a bar 'three miles west' from the Stranmillis embankment, a check point 'half a mile across the valley' and so forth [Muldoon, 2001, pp. 128, 132]) only confuses any desire to create coherent meaning through narrative: the more specific the detail, the less evident its meaning within the larger framework of the story. The figures of the poem move through the cities and landscapes in constant chase and escape, neither giving any particular location primacy over another nor offering the reader any centre or point of gravitation from which to view the totality of the poem. The chase ends with an explosion at a gas station, but rather than an epiphanic conclusion, this explosion leads to the discovery of a dismembered hairy hand holding a luminous stone, which, in the words of Robert Frost's 'The Mountain' is 'No bigger than a ... / "Huh"' (ibid., p. 147).

The ending mocks the Romanticism of the American transcendentalist tradition, one referred to in an earlier stanza where Gallogly reads Thoreau's *Walden*:

> *Everyone has heard the story of*
> *a strong and beautiful bug*
> *which came out of the dry leaf*
> *of an old table of apple-tree wood*
> *that stood*
> *in a farmer's kitchen in Massachusetts*
> *and which was heard gnawing out*
> *for several weeks –*
> When the phone trills
> he is careful not to lose his page –
> *Who knows what beautiful and winged life*
> *whose egg*
> *has been buried for ages*
> *may unexpextedly come forth?* 'Tell-tale.'
> (Ibid., p. 140)

American modernists, including Robert Frost and Gary Snyder, have retained an interest in the legacy of nineteenth-century transcendentalism and its possibilities in lyric expression, and Muldoon's own fascination in the coming together of images of enlightenment and the trickster tales of native tribes is perhaps less a manifestation of a postmodern obsession with detachment than of a desire to view the conflicts and acts of terror of the poem in parallel with the American counter-culture's relationship to the Vietnam war: 'Viet-ma-friggin'-*knees*. / He drops a payload of napalm' (ibid., p. 129). Indeed, Deane's criticism of the yoking together of disparate elements (he mentions the Winnebago trickster cycle and the IRA gunman roaming around Belfast as examples) fails to recognize how these narratives of crisis and counterculture in fact *do* acknowledge an origin, or various origins, for both oppression and resistance. At the same time, any possibility of artistic transcendence or moments of lyric intensity in the midst of chaos is made suspect. There is a simultaneous awareness and denial of the traditional lyric process where 'the isolated speaker [...], located in a specific landscape, meditates or ruminates on some aspect of his or her relationship to the external world, coming finally to some sort of epiphany' (Perloff, 1996, pp. 156–7). The relationship to 'truth' of the pebble of quartz, all that is left after destruction (like the pine-cones that survive the apocalyptic destructions of purging forest-fires in Snyder's poetry[11]), exemplifies yet another typically Muldoonesque obsession with the ways in which materiality and meaning constantly circumvent each other – not because there are no possible explanations for historical events, for example, but because they are too various to form a coherent, rational whole. With the encounter of the final image of the pebble, the poem's narrative progression comes to a halt but not to a closure. Focus on the material basis of experience is always complicated by the materiality of language, and the yoking together of the physical detail of place and the formative precision of poetic discourse denies the possibility of a final unity of vision. The 'hyperspecificity'[12] of location and material detail points to the gap which by necessity remains between materiality and meaning. The pebble of quartz's relation to 'truth' will not be revealed. The potentialities of lyric emotional centres to respond to societal crisis, which Rosenthal and Gall see as central to the modern poetic sequence, are undermined by the sequence of sonnets that constructs a narrative, albeit disjointed, of apparently meaningless violence. The disruptive course of events draws on sectarian-ideological motives but reaches no resolution, and violence is constantly portrayed in parallel with images of transcendence, drawn from

Romantic and modernist lyrics, which never quite fulfil their epiphanic potential. Tim Kendall calls the poem an act of 'organized violence' against the sonnet (Kendall, 1996, p. 108); the mutilated sonnet/stanzas follow a narrative that repeatedly fails to offer the kind of continuity a reader might expect, and leaves us hovering between a desire for, and distrust in, a possibility of order underlying the chaos.

III

'Yarrow' concludes the 1994 collection *The Annals of Chile*, and is more autobiographical in its subject-matter and more immediately personal in tone than 'The More a Man Has'. It contemplates death (specifically that of Muldoon's mother, Brigid Muldoon) and memory, and the final unintelligibility of death, be it the result of illness, an accident or a political cause. *Annals*, as Fran Brearton notes, is 'Muldoon's most elegiac collection to date' (the date of publication for Brearton's essay being 2003; elegy later returns in the 2006 *Horse Latitudes*) (Brearton, 2003, p. 11). Brearton draws attention to the parallels between Michael Longley's *Gorse Fires* (1991), dedicated to the memory of Longley's parents, and *Annals*, published three years later (Longley is perhaps the most powerfully elegiac of contemporary Northern Irish poets).[13] 'Yarrow', too, at times points to crises other than personal loss – for example to questions of poetic authorship and politics, as in the figure of S—, a female radical, for whom the ideal is to 'find a pugilist-poet who'd tap into his own prostate gland / for the piss-and-vinegar ink' (Muldoon, 2001, p. 354); any wider societal and/or political conflicts only act to highlight the inexplicable nature of a more personal bereavement.

This time, the poem is a sequence of elaborately rhyming sestinas (the rhyme scheme carrying over to Muldoon's following collection *Hay*), and the highly complex formal control exercised by the poet is curiously juxtaposed with the lack of success the speaker has in retaining a secure foothold in his childhood farmyard, introduced at the beginning of the poem with 'the row of kale', 'the hen-house improvised from a high-sided cattle-truck', 'the pair of angle-iron / posts between which she'll waver, one day towards the end, / as she pins the clothes on the clothes-line' (Muldoon, 2001, pp. 346–7). From this first location, the reader is taken via numerous returns, departures and diversions to the concluding stanza, which finally leaves him or her 'lost with all hands between Ireland and Montevideo' (ibid., p. 392).

Like 'The More a Man Has', 'Yarrow' shifts location between Ireland and America, between the farm in Moy, County Armagh, and 'a den in

St John's, Newfoundland' (ibid., p. 348). The narratives of media and memory are framed by the present-day context of the speaker surfing through television channels, continuously switching from one film or music video to another. 'Yarrow' acknowledges a centre of sorts, with its first-person speaker and with the constant returns to the farm in County Armagh. Joseph Conte has noted that the postmodern long poem is often 'centrifugal' (Conte, 1992),[14] and this seems particularly apt to describe 'Yarrow': from the point of departure from the childhood home, the poem seeks trails in all directions in its hopeless and endlessly deferred desire to arrive at some consoling resolution. But the poem is also centripetal: the pull of the family farm constantly strives towards a centre which slips further away the more the speaker tries to reach it.[15] The repeated phrase 'again and again' blurs any certainty of initial coordinates as he tries to preserve that which is dearest through memory; language mutates the remembered place with each return. Unlike 'The More a Man Has', which never returns to the same place twice in its out-of-breath race, 'Yarrow' always starts its frustrated attempts to put memory and event into some kind of meaningful context from the same coordinates, as if there is a desire at least to be certain of some initial point of origin as a start for narrative progress: 'The bridge. The barn. The all-too-familiar terrain' (Muldoon, 2001, p. 351); 'The bridge. The barn. The all-too-familiar seal-flipper terrine' (ibid., p. 366); 'The bridge. The barn. Again and again I stand aghast / as I contemplate what never / again will be mine' (ibid., p. 387); 'The bridge, the barn: the tongue of a boot once lust- / trous with mink- / oil' (ibid., p. 391).

Repetition as a poetic device has been employed with increasing frequency in Muldoon's later work. In an interview with Lynn Keller, the poet credits this to his increasing engagement with music in the 1990s (Keller, 1994, pp. 8–9), thus drawing attention to the formal consequences of the coming together of two different art forms. If the traditional function of the lyric is to offer some kind of a transcendental epiphany – like the ones to which 'The More a Man Has' ironically refers – the breathless repetition and the attempt to start again in order to match place and narrative only render impossible such revelations: repetition only produces difference. Gilles Deleuze, in *Difference and Repetition*, outlines the relationship between lyric singularity and repetition as a poetic device:

> [In] lyrical language [...] every term is irreplaceable and can only be repeated. Repetition can always be 'represented' as extreme resemblance or perfect equivalence, but the fact that one can pass by degrees

> from one thing to another does not prevent their being different in kind.
>
> (quoted in Perloff, 2004, p. xxviii)

The always slightly varied repetition of the brief statement which should preserve the memory of the family farmhouse and its surroundings only stresses its transience. The singularity of each lyric phrase and the simultaneous 'equivalence' between the recurring phrases underline both a striving for place as a material basis for memory and its ongoing mutation through language: each attempt to narrate the same, or to return to the same place, produces more variation. The poem does not resolve the personal crisis of pain and loss, but instead re-enacts it in each event of recurrence in poetic language. While almost obsessively place-bound, the poem cannot prevent the place that should offer consolation from constantly becoming other.

IV

The final poem I will discuss here, 'Horse Latitudes', is yet another sequence of sonnets, each of the nineteen sonnets being titled with a place-name beginning with the letter B, from Beijing to Burma via Bannockburn and the Boyne, each place the site of a battle. The poem intertwines societal and personal crises; wars and battles are presented alongside the speaker's companion Carlotta's battle with cancer and retrospective allusions to her late grandfather's exploits in the army: the narratives of war and personal struggle intertwine and run across the borders of the individual sonnets. Muldoon himself has explained the history of the poem as follows:

> I started the sonnet sequence 'Horse Latitudes' as the US embarked on its foray into Iraq. The poems have to do with a series of battles (all beginning with the letter B as if to suggest a missing Baghdad) in which horses or mules played a major role. Intercut with those battle scenes are accounts of a battle with cancer by a former lover, here named Carlotta, and a commentary on the agenda of what may only be described as the Bush regime.
>
> (Fenton, 2006)

'Horse Latitudes' is, perhaps most explicitly of the poems discussed here, a poem of place, narrative and crisis. Commenting on Muldoon's collection, Fran Brearton notes that '*Horse Latitudes*, for all its "play", is [...] a deeply political book. It is also, one senses at times, an angry book, whose forms are bound up with its sense of personal trauma and historical crisis' (Brearton, 2007). In line with Brearton's analysis, it is certainly hard to see how Muldoon's perceived postmodernist disengagement (or 'denial') could any longer be considered an issue. The Iraq war makes it impossible for the poet 'to untangle / the ghastly from the price of gasoline' (Muldoon, 2006, p. 9).

Place-names connect the narrative elements of the poem to a 'real-world' basis, and yet the constraint of what might be termed the 'b' structure makes this world strange by imposing on it an almost mechanical order, though one not entirely random, since all these places now acoustically as well as semantically connect with 'battle', as well as the absent 'Baghdad'. The impersonal and mechanical 'b' structure seems cold and relentless in its progression, and offers neither consolation nor potential closure nor end to the violence of history – there will always be another battle. The persistent intrusion of the 'b' title structure also prevents the story fragments of the poem from falling under any invisible master-narrative; a result of the framework of a series of events reduced to a list of place-names, linked by their initial letter – the connective 'glue' of the letter 'b' is both random and meaningful. The dismal tone is underlined by the fact that the repeated 'heehaws' of the mules that occur through the poem are brought to an end in the last stanza, where Carlotta's grandfather is said to have 'cut / the vocal cords of each pack mule / with a single, swift excision' (ibid., p. 21). Battle follows battle, and the intrusive noise of suffering is finally silenced. The historical events relating to each place appear to give each place-name a depth, context and sense of linear progression, providing an illusion of explanation through narrative continuity. The battles are presented in chronological order, yet the linearity implied by chronology is made suspect by the sequence's repetitive pattern: each battle is different, but also another manifestation of the same. The historical narratives referred to are also complicated, interrupted and cut off by the requirements of the sonnet structure and the constraints of the rhyme scheme (end words of the first three lines of each sonnet rhyme with the end words of the three last lines, and the eight lines in the middle are three rhyming couplets accompanied by two lines rhyming with lines in the first and last tercets), but also by breaks in syntax ('whereof ... whereof ... whereof' [ibid., p. 6], 'whereat ... whereat ... whereat ... whereat ...whereat ...' [ibid., p. 20]) and the giving way of the story to acoustic jams that call meaning into question ('*Dust? Fust? Must?*' [ibid., p. 19]). As in 'The More a Man Has' and 'Yarrow', the striving for precision only adds to the confusion.

Muldoon's habit of giving different stanzas of a poem separate titles which seem to have a more or less arbitrary relationship to the lines they precede has puzzled readers for decades. The names of philosophers in the epic long poem 'Madoc' and the alphabets ordering his curious history of Irish literature, *To Ireland, I*, have added to his complex and allusive poetry and prose apparently ordered frameworks which often seem to contradict rather than explain the narrative and dramatic dimensions of the poems. Muldoon's critics, often at loss with his formal and structural experimentation, have repeatedly failed to recognize how his poetics enact a carefully controlled pattern, which generates alternative meanings and draws attention to the fact that structure, sound and meaning in poetry can never be wholly separated. This often leads to his poems being considered 'playful' without further elaboration, or merely clever at the cost of any communicative content: for one reviewer, in 'Horse Latitudes' 'Muldoon tries hard to be clever and fails' (Ward, 2008).

But such formal experiments are hardly lacking in precedents. For example, there are similarities with the French experimental poets of the Oulipo movement[16] and the practitioners of procedural poetry in America where apparently eccentric or haphazard formal constraints or tools (rather than enveloping structures 'containing' the message of the poem) are used as a 'generative device'. Indeed, Marjorie Perloff, in a footnote to her essay on Oulipo and procedural poetics in America mentions Muldoon as one of the writers in the contemporary American poetry scene who counteract the dominant trend of free verse as a façade for the absence of semantic attention to metre and sound pattern (Perloff, 2004, pp. 213, 296). In other words, structures that on the surface seem to be acting as constraints to the free flow of the poem are seen to contribute to its meaning in a way that opens further meanings rather than closing the entire poem into a coherent, independent whole. In 'Horse Latitudes', the repetition of the 'b' pattern and the rhyme pattern of each poem or stanza highlight the material and sonic properties of language and subject referential narrative to the semantic and transformative possibilities of language's materiality. Brian McHale suggests that contemporary writers of long poems tackle the issue of master-narrative by 'practicing "weak" narrativity'; he gives the example of Kenneth Koch's *Seasons on Earth*, where 'weakness is achieved by allowing the vicissitudes of rhyme to dictate the constitution of the world and the direction of the story' (McHale, 2000, p. 260).[17] The claim of any narrative to knowledge or truth is thus complicated by the highlighting of the poetic medium itself. The examination of parallels between Muldoon's work and other examples of poetic avant-garde could help in approaching the function of the more experimental characteristics in his writing as something more profound than mere aesthetic 'playfulness' and trickstery.

V

For Helen Vendler,

> Muldoon's long poems [...] are always a breakneck cinematic reel of truth, fiction, journeys, crossed plots, snapshots, memories, illustrations, quotations and allusions. They can be tiresome or exhilarating, depending on how well their glittering surface coordinates with the momentum pulsating underneath it.
>
> (Vendler, 2006)

Such separation of the 'glittering surface' and a 'momentum [...] underneath' highlights the persistent strain in criticism of Muldoon's work in which the more experimental formal elements are seen as technical virtuosity for their own sake, somehow separate from the poem's 'content'. When it comes to Muldoon's addressing of crisis, however, there is no reason to consider formal elements of the poems as surface ornaments, or as some kind of a clever release from the otherwise atrocious or painful events depicted. As I hope to have shown above, his long poems' addressing of place, narrative and crisis are far from a poetry of 'denial'. Instead of taking evasive action, they narrate place as both linguistically constructed and materially concrete. Their narratives of crisis warn us against accepting any straightforward explanation, any simplistic story behind disruption and violence. Geoffrey Squires has considered the long poem to be particularly suitable for 'expression of conflict, within the society, within the individual, or between individual and the society', and embodying a desire 'to go beyond the episodic, contingent, situational response for which the short poem is the natural vehicle' (Squires, 1983, p. 6). And if (somewhat undefined) length is the only tangible prerequisite for a contemporary long poem, it can still be seen to carry possibilities not available for a short lyric: the complex accumulation of narrative as process and of narrative fragment, extensive use of repetition, the possibilities of the sequence structure or an intertextual engagement with other narrative poems. Not that short poems cannot incorporate narrative or repetition (Muldoon's own work can also be seen as a manifestation of the narrative potential of the short poem);

but they cannot employ them to the same accumulative scale or gather the kind of momentum that seems crucial to their addressing of place as something dynamic, constantly under formation. The copious reasons and consequences of the crises Muldoon's poems depict call for a medium that can reveal some of the complex network of causes, consequences and unexpected occurrences in which these crises take place.

Notes

1. See for example Kirkland (1996), Corcoran (1999), Graham (2001), Alcobia-Murphy (2006).
2. For such critical responses, see for example Alcobia-Murphy (2006, p. 13).
3. I refer here to Robert Frost's preface to his *Collected Poems*, 'The Figure a Poem Makes': 'It should be of the pleasure of a poem to tell how it can. The figure a poem makes. It begins in delight and ends in wisdom' (Frost, 2004, p. 235).
4. Ruth Finnegan, for example, has commented on the coming together of the communal 'folk' tradition of narrative verse in Romanticism, 'which laid such stress on the *individual* artist and his freedom'. As Finnegan observes, 'the feeling that through folk popular art one could reach back to the lost period of natural spontaneous literary utterance as well as to the deep and natural springs of national identity was basic to the romantic attitude, and received extra force through ideological and nationalist references to "tradition"' (Finnegan, 1992, p. 34).
5. Meeting W.B. Yeats in 1930, Virginia Woolf wrote in her diary how the poet noted that in the modern world, he (and Walter de la Mare who was also present at the meeting) 'can only write small fireside poems', as 'most of [its] emotion is outside their scope'. Woolf responded to this by remarking, 'All left to the novelists' (Lee, 1997, p. 575).
6. *Changing Light at Sandover* (which Conte, as noted earlier, considers an example of the modern epic), Edward Dorn's *Gunslinger*, Kenneth Koch's *Seasons on Earth*, and Lyn Hejinian's *Oxota: A Short Russian Novel*. In Perloff's essay (1996), Dorn and Hejinian are joined by Ashbery, Howard Norman and Ursula Le Guin.
7. The story of modernist poetry in Ireland is of course more complex than this, with figures like Beckett, MacGreevy and Devlin, among others, drawing from the trends of 'European' modernism. See for example Davis (2008).
8. Also spelled *dinnshenchas* and *dinshenchas*, the term means 'place lore' or topography. Gerry Smyth writes that '[r]oughly translating as "the traditional, legendary lore of notable places" [...] *dinnshenchas* developed from onomastic (placename traditions) and aetiological (origin legends) discourses derived from early Celtic culture' (Smyth, 2001, p. 47).
9. Deane's criticism of postmodernist theory echoes critics who have seen this kind of textuality as characteristic of nihilistic attitudes to agency and place. For Terry Eagleton, for example, the same stance that produces the constantly shifting surface narratives of postmodernist philosophy is responsible for 'the postmodern cult of the migrant', which he diagnoses as 'a hangover

from the modernist cult of exile' (Eagleton, 2003, p. 21). Similarly, for Caren Kaplan, postmodernist theory 'recuperates such modernist tropes as the "artist in exile"' (Kaplan, 1996, p. 67).

10. Gallogly's name refers to the Irish word 'gallóglach', in English 'gallowglass', meaning in its original context a 'foreign warrior' hired by Irish chiefs in medieval times; 'oglagh' also refers to *Óglaigh na h-Éireann*, a phrase, as Michael Parker notes, 'used by the Provisionals to bolster their claim to be Ireland's defenders' (Parker, 2007, p. 92).
11. Snyder's own adoption of Thoreau's image of the 'beautiful and winged life' emerging from the dormant egg, and its paralleling with Buddhist philosophy, Native American lore (including frequent use of the Trickster myth) and mind-altering substances was familiar to Muldoon, Michael Allen suggests, through Snyder's 'Passage to More than India' (Allen, 2004, p. 75).
12. I borrow the term from Marjorie Perloff, who uses it to describe the function of quotation as 'found text' in Pound's poetics (Perloff, 2004, p. 52).
13. Matthew Campbell notes that elegy is a prominent feature in contemporary Irish poetry, as experiences of exile and societal change in a globalizing world have 'engage[d] the Irish poet [...], still preoccupied with the sense that change may also mean loss, the loss of the traditions and certainties of a recognizable national identity' (Campbell, 2003, p. 3).
14. Conte juxtaposes the modern epic, striving for completion through 'gravitational attraction', with the serial form, where 'individual elements are both discontinuous and capable of recombination. The serial long poem is open, shapeshifting and expansive, i.e. "centrifugal"' (Conte, 1992).
15. For Michael Allen, it is *Annals* that is 'centripetal', whereas Muldoon's 1998 collection *Hay* is 'centrifugal': the latter is keener on following its associative poetics 'to all directions' without repeatedly aiming to return to the same location (Allen, 2004, p. 84).
16. The term was coined by the French poet Jacques Roubaud, for whom extreme formal constraints in poetry are not extrinsic to it, but where 'a text written according to a constraint describes that constraint' (Roubaud, *Oulipo and the Combinational Art* [1991], quoted in Perloff, 2004, p. 208). Muldoon has himself spoken about his fascination with the relationship between formal constraint and linguistic serendipity, or of 'structure and serendipity' (Barker, 1998). On Muldoon and Oulipo, see also Buxton (2004, pp. 144–5).
17. Of course, Koch's attitude to rhyme has been very different from Muldoon's, as Koch puts an emphasis on 'the other kinds of form there are in the rhymed poem' (Kenneth Koch, *The Art of Poetry*, quoted in Allen, 2004, p. 77).

References

Alcobia-Murphy, Shane (2006) *Sympathetic Ink: Intertextual Relations in Northern Irish Poetry* (Liverpool: Liverpool University Press).

Allen, Michael (2004) 'Pax Hibernica/Pax Americana: Rhyme and Reconciliation in Muldoon', in Tim Kendall and Peter McDonald (eds) *Paul Muldoon: Critical Essays* (Liverpool: Liverpool University Press).

Barker, Sebastian (1998) 'A Drink with Paul Muldoon', *Long Poem Group Newsletter*, 7, http://www.dgdclynx.plus.com/lpgn/lpgn72.html (accessed 6 August 2009).

Brearton, Fran (2003) '"Ploughing by the Tail": Longley, Muldoon and Anxiety of Influence', *Nordic Irish Studies*, 2(1): 1–15.
—— (2007) Review of *Horse Latitudes, Tower Poetry*, http://www.towerpoetry.org.uk/poetry–matters/jan2007/muldoon.html (accessed 19 August 2008).
Buxton, Rachel (2004) *Robert Frost and Northern Irish Poetry* (Oxford: Clarendon Press).
Campbell, Matthew (2003) 'Ireland in Poetry: 1999, 1949, 1969', in Matthew Campbell (ed.) *The Cambridge Companion to Contemporary Irish Poetry* (Cambridge: Cambridge University Press).
Conte, Joseph (1992) 'Seriality and the Contemporary Long Poem', *Sagetrieb*, 11 (Spring & Fall), http://www.acsu.buffalo.edu/~jconte/Seriality_Sagetrieb.htm (accessed 9 December 2009).
Corcoran, Neil (1999) *Poets of Modern Ireland: Text, Context, Intertext* (Carbondale: Southern Illinois University Press).
Davis, Alex (2008) 'Is it Really a Revolution Though?', *Masthead*, 10, http://www.masthead.net.au/issue10/davis.html (accessed 19 August, 2008).
Deane, Seamus (1986) *A Short History of Irish Literature* (Notre Dame, Indiana: Notre Dame University Press).
—— (1990) 'Introduction', in Terry Eagleton (ed.) *Nationalism, Colonialism, and Literature* (Minneapolis: University of Minnesota Press).
Eagleton, Terry (2003), *After Theory* (London: Penguin Books).
Fenton, James (2006), 'A Poke in the Eye with a Poem', *Guardian*, 21 October 2006, http://www.guardian.co.uk/books/2006/oct/21/featuresreviews.guardianreview6 (accessed 19 August, 2008).
Frost, Robert (2004) 'The Figure a Poem Makes', in Jon Cook (ed.) *Poetry in Theory: An Anthology* (Malden, MA: Blackwell).
Finnegan, Ruth (1992) *Oral Poetry: Its Nature, Significance, and Social Context* (Bloomington: Indiana University Press).
Graham, Colin (2001) *Deconstructing Ireland: Identity, Theory, Culture* (Edinburgh: Edinburgh University Press).
Kaplan, Caren (1996) *Questions of Travel: Postmodern Discourses of Displacement* (Durham: Duke University Press).
Keller, Lynn (1994) 'An Interview with Paul Muldoon', *Contemporary Literature*, 35 (1): 1–19.
Kendall, Tim (1996) *Paul Muldoon* (Chester Springs, PA: Dufour Editions).
Kennedy-Andrews, Elmer (ed.) (2006) *Paul Muldoon: Poetry, Prose, & Drama: A Collection of Critical Essays* (Gerrard's Cross: Colin Smythe).
Kerrigan, John (1984) 'The New Narrative', *London Review of Books*, February: 16–19.
Kirkland, Richard (1996) *Literature and Culture in Northern Ireland since 1965: Moments of Danger* (Harlow: Addison Wesley Longman Limited).
Lee, Hermione (1997) *Virginia Woolf* (London: Vintage).
Longley, Edna (1986) *Poetry in the Wars* (Newcastle-upon-Tyne: Bloodaxe).
McHale, Brian (2000) 'Telling Stories Again: Replenishment of Narrative in the Postmodernist Long Poem', *Yearbook of English Studies*, 30: 250–62.
Muldoon, Paul (2001) *Poems 1968–1998* (London: Faber and Faber).
—— (2006) *Horse Latitudes* (London: Faber and Faber).
Parker, Michael (2007) *Northern Irish Literature 1956–1975* (Basingstoke: Palgrave Macmillan).

Perloff, Marjorie (1996) *The Dance of the Intellect: Studies in the Poetry of the Pound Tradition* (Evanston, IL: Northwestern University Press).
— (2004) *Differentials: Poetry, Poetics, Pedagogy* (Tuscaloosa, AL: The University of Alabama Press).
Rosenthal, M.L. and Sally M. Gall (1983) *The Modern Poetic Sequence: The Genius of Modern Poetry* (New York and Oxford: Oxford University Press).
Smyth, Gerry (2001) *Space and the Irish Cultural Imagination* (Basingstoke: Palgrave).
Squires, Geoffrey (1983) 'A Short Note on the Long Poem', *Irish University Review,* 13 (1): 5–6.
Vendler, Helen (2006) 'Review of *Horse Latitudes*', *New Republic Online,* http://www.powells.com/review/2006_11_09.html (accessed 19 August 2008).
Ward, Christian (2008) 'Review of *Horse Latitudes*', *Rattle: Poetry for the 21st Century*, http://www.rattle.com/ereviews/muldoon,paul.htm (accessed 19 August 2008).

Part IV
Suspended Judgements: Rethinking Poetic Reception

12

Paul Muldoon: Critical Judgement, the Crisis Poem, and the Ethics of Voice

Guinn Batten

I

The fate of two literary critics, Robert Southey and John Carey, may seem remote from the consequences of culpable ethical judgement that, in Lord Byron's 'The Vision of Judgment' and Paul Muldoon's poetic sequences 'Madoc' and 'Horse Latitudes', create crises in modern states and their empires. Carey, who once called Muldoon a 'pantomime horse' to Heaney's 'Derby winner' (1987, p. 56), perhaps inspired, as Ivan Phillips (2005) has argued, the equine references in 'Madoc', a squibble (as Muldoon might put it), but hardly a geopolitical conflict. Robert Southey's published denunciation of the Satanic School (and more particularly of Byron's morals) in his preface to *A Vision of Judgement*, joined with that poem's panegyric for George III, provoked Byron's 'The Vision of Judgment', an excoriation of the Laureate's endorsement of the king's colonial wars. In the same Byronic spirit Muldoon produced his own parody of the Romantic apostate, 'Madoc'. But does literature respond to 'crisis' in any meaningful way? While we may recall that a Muldoon poem once asked 'if Yeats had saved his pencil-lead / would certain men have stayed in bed', nonetheless his poetry, including the volume that deals directly (or as directly as Muldoon ever does) with the Gulf War, *Horse Latitudes*, suggests that the answer may be 'yes' ('7, Middagh Street', Muldoon, 1987, p. 39).

Southey and Carey are poor judges because as critical readers the aggression that they deploy in their judgements ignores the animus which may likewise drive others' words to their own ends, and lead, through words, to wars. Indeed Carey, had he listened more alertly as a reviewer to the tone of Muldoon's *Meeting the British* surely would have foreseen, perhaps in homonymic reference to his name, any number of Muldoonish beasts of carriage, pantomime and wartime, slouching towards a Middle Eastern city that starts with 'B'. Gypsy Rose Lee is herself, in the 1987 *Meeting the British* poem '7, Middagh Street' partial to pony acts. Two decades later in the Gulf crises of 'Horse Latitudes', in a sequence concerned with the beasts who carry the burdens of wars, and more generally the vehicles by which (and on account of which) wars are prosecuted, the 'car' in 'Carey' is an implied but missing referent. The critic, as might be observed by the reader alert to poetic animus (particularly when the poet is himself alert to the suffering animal), has become the vehicle that carries the poet's tenor. Central to Muldoon's ethics of voice in a time of crisis is not only the observation that references are inevitably missed but also that, and more importantly, sometimes a crucial referent *should* be missed. This holds true for Muldoon, I believe, even if those readers who miss references – Southey and Carey – are doomed to repeat them, visibly in the rearguard of the mock pony act that Muldoon might call, with some mischief, 'the end of the poem'.

'Horse Latitudes' presents one vehicle that Muldoon's readers have seen before: the mule. Here that beast is subject to the censorship of a grammarian who, not so coincidentally, is also a wartime profiteer who takes his granddaughter, a *femme fatale* whose derring-do seems a pointless end in itself, 'for a quick whip / through conjugation, declension, / and those other "crannies of the crammer"' (Muldoon, 2006, p. 18). 'No respite from his yammer / on boundlessness being a bind / and the most insidious kind / of censorship self-censorship.' But to understand fully that last line about censorship, we must turn to the final poem of 'Horse Latitudes': 'Her grandfather's job was to cut / the vocal cords of each pack mule / with a single, swift excision' ('Burma', Muldoon, 2006, p. 21). What has this figure who dates from the American 'Prohibition' ('Burma') to do with the self-censorship to which the poet alludes in 'Basra', and, more particularly, what has the 'position' that he wishes not to 'give away' in the final lines of 'Burma' to do with the voice, and the position, of the poet during the state of emergency?

Critical judgement, however well-honed (or at least well-thumbed) its tools, may not be able to separate itself from the censorship of the emergency legislation introduced during the state of exception, from the Special Powers Act enforced during the Troubles in Northern Ireland to the Homeland Security Act that remains in force in the States. Crisis may become, as Walter Benjamin observes in 'Critique of Violence', the everyday condition of the rule of law that creates what Muldoon would call 'the doldrums' of our times. As Benjamin writes in his fuller study,

On the Origin of German Tragic Drama, 'the most obvious catastrophes did not perhaps impress this experience on men any more bitterly than the changes in legal norms, with their claims to eternal validity which were particularly evident at those historical turning-points' (cited in Santner, 2006, p. 17).

On the face of it, offering examples of poor literary judgement to introduce a discussion of the politics of the crisis poem may seem simply to reinforce the notion that literature, with the other arts, becomes suspect when states are threatened by enemies without, and within. Indeed, one could argue that the specificity of detail with which Muldoon, like Byron, renders the scene of war (including wars by, and against, terror) should in itself deter us from the sleuthing of poems for such missing referents as, say, evidence of a poet's vindictive response to critical judgement. Living in a time of war, even when that war is prosecuted at a distance, reopens the complaint that, given the brute fact of slaughter and the slain, scholars give too much time to the quarrels of literary communities, to the difference, as Muldoon writes in 'Cows', between Celan and Celine (Muldoon, 1994, p. 35). The grandfatherly grammarian in 'Blenheim' spends 'weeks and months in the doldrums // in the hope that something might come to mind, / that he might yet animadvert / the maiden name of that Iron Maiden / on which he was drawing a blank' (Muldoon, 2006, p. 12). Given the pressing need, during the state of emergency, to prevent human suffering, might not the ambitious scholar worry that she distracts, or even excuses, herself from a war fuelled by habits of consumption of which she knows she is guilty by tracking the missing persons in poetic lines – written from the geopolitical hot spots that are the titles of the poems in 'Horse Latitudes' – to which she might 'animadvert'? (We might note a singular missing referent here among these nineteen sites of violence that begin with 'B': 'Belfast'.) As Muldoon hints in the first line of 'Blenheim', an alertness to danger puts even the voices of birds in the daily service of a crisis that feels at once oppressive and salacious.

It is no coincidence that a contemporary poetry of crisis such as Muldoon's might register moral pressure on, and of, the flesh by way of reference to a female figure of sovereignty (Maggie Roberts Thatcher) and also of physical coercion. Were this a scene of interrogation, where the poetic speaker would literally be pressed by that maiden to speak, a failure of words, even if inadvertent, would entail further suffering. The other feminine presence in 'Blenheim' is Carlotta, whose hypersarcoma is a disease in which the flesh presses in on itself. But there is also a verbal pressure from within: her name, like Carey's, carries inside it the word 'car', which evokes metonymically, in her case, drive. More forebodingly, the car in 'Carlotta' homonymically, and metonymically, suggests 'carrion'. That reference recurs later in *Horse Latitudes* literally as road kill, and in the same poem it also carries the reader to the hospital death bed, to a disease fatal to women, ovarian cancer ('Turkey Buzzards'). The carrion who circle road kill, what we might think of as blood for oil, metonymically connect the war in Iraq with an everyday fact of life on the American highway. Each site of violence could, of course, be called a 'crisis', yet one we accept as an inevitable price to pay for vehicular speed, a crisis dealt with daily in courts of law and emergency rooms. The poet-prince of the quotidian, as Muldoon has dubbed himself, links these sites where the biopolitical dimension of contemporary authority is most powerfully enforced. While an ethics, and a poetics, of formal *failure* may seem a difficult task, Paul Muldoon, in his recent writing, shows us how poetry may provide a template, a form, that allows the matrix of captivation, the sovereignty of such female figures in his poems as Sara Fricker, 'S—', and now the hypersarcomic Carlotta, literally to fall apart.

II

Clair Wills, in her astute reading of 'Madoc', rightly observes that there is a 'problem of connection itself' in the crisis conditions of competing colonizations explored in this long poem. Concerning the many dropped keys in the volume *Madoc*, she concludes that the real key is 'language', for a poem is 'a device or machine for generating' the coincidences or correspondences that sustain critical judgement, and also 'for introducing ever further possibilities of meaning and interpretation' (Wills, 1998, p. 154). Yet while the reader of the long poem 'Madoc' surely 'delights', as Wills suggests, in 'linguistic variety', there is a very real problem with what Muldoon himself knows is 'the cyclical nature of creation and destruction': it may lead not only to the reflexive mirrors of his verse forms but also to the powerful image that Wills cites from the poem 'Vico': a 'hand-wringing, small, grey squirrel / plods / along a wicker // treadmill that's attached / by an elaborate / system of levers // and cogs and cranks / and pulleys / and gears [...] // [...] to a wicker / treadmill in which there plods / a hand-wringing, small, grey squirrel' (Muldoon, 2001, pp. 249–50). Wills offers hopefully that 'the exuberance of the language' here 'belies' this closed, 'dreary, despondent cycle', concluding that 'the cycles of conquest and colonisation that Muldoon explores in "Madoc"' ultimately unleash 'new energies' in a 'forward movement of creation which cannot be captured in circular terms' (Wills, 1998, p. 156).

Muldoon has himself until his 2007 *Horse Latitudes* largely adhered to forms that are so constrictive that the 'great Cog' (Muldoon, 1994, p. 189), as he calls it, could not actually slip, so tightly woven and (to use Agamben's term for the state of exception) so closely captive did they hold the poem's content, and its reader. As recently as 2002, in *Moy Sand and Gravel*'s 'At the Sign of the Black Horse, September 1999', we seem to witness, on first reading, an exuberant flood of signifiers down Canal Road. Yet on closer inspection the poem's ending rhyme 'gag' circles back to the opening 'gawk', suggesting yet another cycle (or, given Muldoon's fascination with hurricanes since *The Annals of Chile*, cyclone). 'Gag' and 'gawk' uncomfortably put into the same frame of reference bodily responses – oral and visual – that civilization hierarchizes to keep separate. Muldoon returns to us, in the book's final line, the figure who haunts this volume as what Agamben would call '*homo sacer*', or bare life, a human being whose life is so worthless that his death would not constitute a worthy sacrifice. An Irish refugee from the Famine who found in America the failure, rather than the fulfilment, of the promised freedom Southey and Coleridge imagined in their Pantisocratic scheme, this famished and bleeding labourer shows up at the very locus of the canal that, by the poem's end, will become (as in a related poem 'The Stoic') the site of failed, and female, reproductive labour: 'womb, For Hire' (Muldoon, 2002, p. 103).

Muldoon here, as elsewhere, represents formally the virtually unrepresentable impasse of our enthralment before this empty site where life, but also words, begin, and where they fail. This vacant source, as he writes in 'It Is What It Is', evokes in his art the void where a heart might be hoped for, a lack where all the ladders start, 'the foreshore / of a country toward which I've been rowing / for fifty years' (Muldoon, 2006, p. 49). In 'Yarrow' this source is a mother dying in a hospital of ovarian cancer. '*From* Last Poems' (*Quoof*) gives us the following: 'IV. Not that I care who's sleeping with whom / now she's had her womb / removed, now it lies in its own glar / like the last beetroot in the pickle jar' (Muldoon, 1983, p. 31). In 'At the Sign of the Black Horse' the St Louis Arch echoes that empty, or emptied, centre, and ominously echoes another arch that bears the inscription *Arbeit Macht Frei*. Indeed, in that dual image Muldoon reminds us that countries as well as individuals may suffer from the Pantisocratic delusions of the Enlightenment. At a climactic passage the speaker is on the banks of the Mississippi, beneath this monument to manifest destiny as westward expansion. The motherland, or fatherland, perhaps cannot be figured except as where 'every start was a bad start / since all conclusions were foregone' ('The Old Country', Muldoon, 2006, p. 38).

In considering the implications of Muldoon's cyclical forms – are they dead ends or second chances? – we might take into account the numerous examples of the self-inwoven, or self-reflexive, simile in his poetry, so many of which are bound up with maternal nurture and its failures (or its refusals). A notable example may be found in the opening lines of 'Gathering Mushrooms'. The *rain* that 'comes flapping through the yard' is likened to his mother's tablecloth left hanging on the line, itself 'sodden with *rain*' (Muldoon, 1983, p. 7). This self-reflexive simile remains trapped, one might say, like the small grey squirrel of 'Madoc' within a kind of perpetual-motion machine, the vehicle and tenor endlessly turning, and turning into, one another (rain:tablecloth, tablecloth:rain…). The mushrooms *grown in dung* which were ingested by the speaker deliver their words through the mouth of the animal (the poem's speaker has become a horse) in whose dung they were grown. Here 'voice', mediated by so many vehicles in 'Gathering Mushrooms', renders precisely the ethical impasse for which Romantic subjectivity has so often been blamed, including by that arch-critic of the Lakers, Lord Byron: solipsism. Yet passage from that state is at least implied in the poem's final stanza. The tablecloth, which in everyday life would be a vehicle for the serving of food, turns into a prison blanket that will one day, if left on the line, 'bleach itself white' (ibid., p. 9).

Associating the tablecloth in this second reference not with food but with its refusal (the H-block blanket protest followed by the hunger strikes), the poem leads us to look back at the first stanza, where we now see between the 'rain' and the 'tablecloth' that burdened word that denotes the historical and political dimension of hunger in Ireland: 'sod'. If we continue reading the first stanza of 'Gathering Mushrooms', we will encounter a subsequent image that evokes an image of food (cultivated mushrooms) but also of hunger, both in this 1983 volume and in the 2002 'At the Sign of the Black *Horse*'. The 'pile of horse keek / held to the rain' by the starving Irish labourer in the later poem is, in 'Gathering Mushrooms', a 'self-renewing gold-black dragon' from which will grow the interned mushrooms who plead 'if sing you must / let your song / tell of treading your own dung, // If we never live to see the day we leap / into our true domain, / lie down with us now and wrap / yourself in the soiled grey blanket of Irish rain / that will, one day, bleach itself white. / Lie down with us and wait' (Muldoon, 1983, p. 9).

Wills claims that Muldoon 'abhors' the rhetoric spoken through this horse's mouth, characterizing it as 'a rhetorical plea for conformity with the Republican ideals of suffering and sacrifice' that are 'fanatical, deluded, masochistic' in their 'fusion of religion and politics', in their 'coercive idea that the endurance of suffering may bring future benefit' (Wills, 1998, p. 99). To the contrary, I would argue that the poem asks us to imagine, through this voice, the possibility, promoted by Benjamin in 'Critique of Violence' (and, more recently, by Slavoj Žižek) that the body might yet find a cause beyond itself worthy of its sacrifice. Such sacrifice would defy the hegemony of a biopolitics that, in its insistence that the body be kept alive regardless of the subject's wishes, turns every subject into *homo sacer*.

In *homo sacer*, as Žižek writes in *Welcome to the Desert of the Real*, we encounter 'in Kantian terms, a short circuit between the noumenal and the phenomenal' where, in a 'desubjectivized subject, the noumenal dimension (of the free subject) appears in empirical reality itself' (Žižek, 2002, p. 139). We might perceive Muldoon's speaking mushroom, or his Irish labourer, as what Žižek (following Lacan) calls 'the noumenal Thing', the Neighbour, 'appearing in phenomenal reality; as such, it is the witness of what one cannot bear witness to' (ibid.), that is, the origins of the sovereign self, now situated in ex-timacy to himself, in that crisis termed individuation, the ideology of selfhood that claims to offer 'freedom'. Extending this observation to everyday political life, Žižek argues that what we prefer not to acknowledge when we accept 'crisis' as the price of 'freedom' is that in doing so we exempt ourselves, as privileged citizens of the global economy, from political responsibility within the state. To turn ethical principle into political engagement would require the citizen willingly to occupy the very place of lack that underwrites power, or sovereignty, in the everyday state of emergency, consciously acknowledging he is not sovereign but in fact *homo sacer*, exempted at the level of bare life from the law's protection. Such occupancy would undermine the comforting illusion that 'crisis' happens elsewhere, in Baghdad, Beirut or Belfast. Yet this leads to an uncomfortable thought: do we diminish the suffering engendered by states of emergency in those 'real' sites by making them commensurable with the democratic subject's individual crisis of 'subjection'? Further, in calling for an ethics that recognizes the necessity of sacrifice are we in fact simply subscribing, in a different form, to the mercenary's 'Prohibition', the grandfather or 'nonno' whose 'non' 'no' commands enjoyment, but on its terms, even as it demands that the body sacrifice the subject's own singular, and ethical, insight into what constitutes 'the good'? Without exploring further the role of sacrifice in whatever might constitute an alternative to the ethics of exception, we could be left with the suspicion that Žižek's call to find a cause worthy of self-sacrifice may not really differ from the nationalist figure of a female Sovereignty who rewards the political lover willing to die for her.

III

Keeping in mind these questions, let me first make more pointed my departure from Wills's reading of the final lines of 'Gathering Mushrooms': spoken through the mouth of the animal from whose dung they sprang, they declare that even the barest of bare life during a political crisis in the North of Ireland may declare itself not only worthy of sacrifice but also capable of speaking – through the creaturely life whose dung engendered them – a song that tells a truth that has meaning beyond its confinement. Between the tablecloth, in the first stanza, that is metonymically associated with plenty, and the blanket, in the final stanza, that is now not only the emblem of the dirty protest but also the sign of a refusal of oral sustenance that becomes itself symbolic – a form of speech – emerges the word for that future that would, as Wills rightly states in her reading of *Madoc*, suggest 'a forward movement of creation': 'white'. Jacques Lacan, the central figure in Žižek's writing, would call this ethical act *creatio ex nihilo*. As in Muldoon's stunning translation of Nuala Ní Dhomhnaill's '*Dubh*' ('Black'), itself a powerful poem on the state of emergency in Bosnia, the word embedded in 'blanket' – 'blank' – has the last word where it matters most: in the written poem, on the page. That same word, 'blank', appears where we would expect to find a final rhyme in 'Blenheim', the central poem of the sequence 'Horse Latitudes': 'that he might yet animadvert / the maiden name of that Iron Maiden / on which he was drawing a *blank*' (Muldoon, 2006, p. 12; emphasis added).

Because the Iron Maiden is one of the many versions of the matrix, or to use Muldoon's recurring words in 'Horse Latitudes', *grids, girdles* and *griddles* – including those that not just squeeze but impale the flesh – one might understandably but erroneously fill the blank with the female who haunts 'It Is What It Is'. 'Her voice at the gridiron coming and going // My mother' (Muldoon, 2006, p. 49). But the answer (if we consider which maiden name of a sovereign has the ending '–ert' to rhyme with 'alert') is in fact Maggie Thatcher née Roberts, who among other political acts showed an iron fist in the face of the H-Block strikes. One more brief example might be offered of the poetics, and ethics, of blankness that is also an incompletion. To the maternal raven in Muldoon's elegy for his mother who caws (a rhyme-word with 'cause')

'Nevermore' in 'Yarrow', Muldoon counters in his more recent elegy, written for the sister who died (like the mother) of ovarian cancer, the buzzard. In 'Turkey Buzzards', while the final phrase circles back, like the gyring vultures, to match the poem's first line ('They've been so long above it all'), the abab rhyme scheme falls, like the buzzard, into its own white poop, its lime that bleaches, its spoils mingling with its faltering body (ibid., pp. 78–81).

But is the alternative to a poetry that dwells so much on viscera that are barely contained by epidermal or prosodic structure simply the solving of all riddles with 'mother', substituting for the sovereign Iron Lady, or the victimized Kathleen, or the hypersarcomic 'Carlotta', the Iron Maiden of the maternal imaginary: a grid, a *form* that – like Carlotta's wetsuit, or her sarcoma – squeezes, or, like the Iron Maiden, riddles? Or might we find in Muldoon's poetry an alternative beyond that imaginary, which is to say, beyond either successful or failed identification with a national or ethnic idealized identity, beyond a fantasized union with the death-bearing female or revenge against her, beyond violence towards and of the Neighbour?

On initially considering this possibility, what comes to mind is yet another version of bleaching, or blankness, which Muldoon offers in the powerful closing pages of *The End of the Poem*: whitewash. In his final Oxford lecture, Muldoon comments not only on Heaney's 'Keeping Going' – in which the speaker's brother turns a whitewash brush into a tool for pantomime, parodying the Orange Order 'sporran' that whitewashes with 'culture' the uglier and daily truths of oppression – but also on another poem from *The Spirit Level*, 'A Brigid's Girdle'. If we put ourselves in Muldoon's personal 'trench' (his term) as a reader of this poem, we will recall that 'Brigid' is Muldoon's mother's name. When he praises 'Keeping Going', singling out the line 'But you cannot make the dead walk or right wrong', most Heaney readers may remember a quite different line in a Heaney poem that is based on a woven device not unlike the Brigid's girdle, the harvest bow, and that also concerns the end*s* of the poem: 'the end of art is peace' (Heaney, 1998, p. 175).

Muldoon's understanding of the ends of poetry during a state of public crisis, or as he more modestly keeps it, the end of 'a' poem, is more limited, closer to the despair of what art – whether it is Hugh Heaney calling a brush a sporran or Muldoon turning a tablecloth into a prison blanket, or historical hurt, personal or communal, into a 'blank' – cannot do: 'make the dead walk or right wrong' ('Keeping Going', Heaney, 1998, p. 400). The end of life, regardless of the ends that sustained that life, is final. Or, to use the operative word that haunts *Horse Latitudes*, finally any voice of truth will be 'cut'. While human hope transforms the griddle of suffering into the homeliest of girdles, into an emblem of hope that the *cailleach* will have a second birth as a bride, there remains, as Muldoon concludes in 'It Is What It Is', one missing piece, 'if not more' (Muldoon, 2006, p. 49). I will return to that word, 'cut', in just a moment.

If it seems impossible to establish a critical vantage point that, without succumbing to the state of exception, would allow the reader to see a work in its entirety, as unitary rather than incomplete, then it also seems, in Muldoon's way of reading, impossible to establish critical distance between writing and reading. There is an umbilicus between the two acts, and between writer and reader, that can't be cut. In his reading of Heaney's 'Widgeon', a poem Heaney dedicates to Muldoon, we have the uncanny experience that Muldoon, as though his critical voice occupies a state of ex-timacy to 'Muldoon' the poet, speaks simultaneously from within and beyond the poem. He uses this position (which obviates the possibility of excepting the shaping spirit of imagination from either the medium or the ends of speech) to suggest that what Heaney had in the back of his mind in writing 'Widgeon' was the Widgery 'whitewashing' (Muldoon's term) of Bloody Sunday. (*Nomen est omen* is, in *The End of the Poem*, Muldoon's frequent recourse during moments of critical impasse.) In making, if not complicit, then at least (to use a Muldoon term) *immarrhagic* the official, state error of judgement and the twice-thrown voice of Muldoon, *The End of the Poem* leaves us wondering where mimicry, or the pantomime horse, begins and the poor judgement being judged, ends.

This problem of 'voice' leads us to the problem of how to establish meaning, which is surely the first act of critical judgement, in Muldoon's recent poetry. Beyond this initial, and unavoidable, task, where do we find in *Horse Latitudes* the position of the *poet* who judges and, more particularly, the ethics implied by his judgement? The final line in the sequence 'Horse Latitudes' is a correction, offered by a grandfather for whom distinctions are literally critical, of Carlotta's syntax: '"And give *away* their *position*"' [Muldoon, 2006, p. 21]). If good judgement implies a careful consideration of the relationship between means and ends, however that relationship is construed, we face a related problem in assessing as a whole the collection *Horse Latitudes*: where do we find the meaning carried by the vehicle, or (to borrow from Muldoon the title of his published Oxford lectures) the end that drives, or the object *toward* which drive these poems at this point in the poet's life and its historical contexts? Is it a moment, indeed, when the poet is questioning that very drive? These questions are not unrelated to the question of poetic form and content: if syntax, like ethics, is a matter of position, so, in poetry, is meaning.

'Horse Latitudes' consists of a series of nesting, but inverted, rhyme schemes, the rhyme scheme in the penultimate poem inverting that of the second poem, the third of the seventeenth, and so forth. But when, after reading the final poem of the sequence, we retrospectively return to the first poem ('Beijing'), to the final poem's end words 'cut' (the first line) and 'position' (the final line) we encounter 'musicians' (so far, so good) and a word that does not, in fact, rhyme with 'cut': 'seize'. Denied a relationship of oral or aural contiguity, if we seek to establish the relation, in the state of emergency known simply as 'war', between seizing and cutting, we might acknowledge that the former, an act of aggression against the enemy, is made possible by censorship, the silencing of those who are declared, by the state of emergency, to be enemies within. Indeed, let us remember that Carlotta's grandfather, in order 'not to give away their position', 'cut / the vocal chords of each pack mule / with a single, swift incision'. We are thereby faced with the task of reconciling this reference to the larynx of the mule as a form of censorship – is it self-censorship, given Muldoon's career-long association of that animal with his own name? – with that of the widgeon, where the poet, through the voice of another poet (Heaney), takes as his vehicle the tenor, the high cries, of the larynx of a creature felled by the poet's own violent act, his shooting of the widgeon. While the word 'cut' indeed suggests censorship, it also suggests the severance of a relationship that, to use Agamben's term, 'captivates'. It is this release to which Muldoon's ethical art, his end of the poem, aspires.

Voice, writes Mladen Dolar in the chapter 'A Politics of the Voice' in his insightful book *A Voice and Nothing More*, '*is structurally in the same position as sovereignty*, which means that it can suspend the validity of the law and inaugurate the state of emergency' (Dolar, 2006, p. 121). That 'point of exception', he continues, is also the site of 'ex-timacy', the intersection of *zoe* (nature) and *bios* (culture) where Agamben locates both the sovereign and *homo sacer*. Dolar defines 'emergency' as the 'emergence of the voice in the commanding position, where its concealed existence suddenly becomes overwhelming and devastating. The voice is precisely the unlocatable spot in the interior and exterior of the law at the same time, and hence a state of emergency.' As such, the 'politics of the voice' can be used for authoritarian purposes, or more subtly for what Althusser theorized as the interpellation of the 'call' of the law as the subject's own voice *as* self-censorship. Yet within this voice, which Dolar calls the 'fat voice' of the superego's ideological prohibitions, there persists a starving Irish labourer, a hunger striker, a 'foreign kernel' that 'cannot be appropriated by the self' (ibid., p. 123). From this 'still small voice' may emerge, Dolar concludes, a will to act, to make 'the heteronomic break in which one cannot recognize oneself' in the imaginary dialectic of subject/other. Urging that we heed this ex-timate, or *object*, voice, he concludes that 'ideological interpellation can never quite silence this other voice, and the distance between the two voices opens the space of the political' (ibid., p. 123).

Muldoon's citation of Heaney as he brings to an end *The End of the Poem* may enlist future readers on that poet's – Heaney's – behalf, keeping the poem so titled going. One might say that Muldoon, in throwing Heaney's voice which had situated *Muldoon*'s voice in the larynx of the widgeon, recognizes, even as he assumes, the place of the Neighbour. But just as important is his extension of that place into the future. Agamben, whose own book *The End of the Poem* Muldoon favourably cites, may be right: the end of every poem may be a crisis comparable to the states of emergency under which, in 2010, we live our ordinary lives, where the poem's very reason for keeping going – the anticipation of a rhyme to come, the thrust of enjambment into the future – is the drive that leads, line by line, perhaps asymptotically, to something like truth, something like change, but which in any case wishes not to arrive at the end. That wish may precede, and exceed, even the Benjaminian temptation to believe as possible a better, rather than a bitter, end, a future and favourable judgement on behalf of history's losers. But is that simply a view that comforts those with everything to lose, those who are happy to make small sacrifices to a cause but not (in Žižek's words) willing to 'sacrifice' the half-measure of *particular* sacrifice when what is required is the repudiation of a utilitarianism in which sacrifice to the greater good is a matter of calculation? As Žižek argues in *Welcome to the Desert of the Real*, within the discourse of universal human rights there has always existed '*the Wall separating those covered by the umbrella of Human Rights and those excluded from its protective cover*', a partition that imprisons those who occupy the point of exception that sustains the very universality of that ethics. 'Any reference to universal rights as an "unfinished project" to be gradually extended to all people is here a vain ideological chimera' (Žižek, 2002, p. 150). Or as Muldoon leaves us, in the unresolved rhyme in 'Basra', the final poem of 'Horse Latitudes' – that unrhymed word 'cut' – judgement as a prerequisite to the ethical act may lead to violent ends, indeed is likely to do so if such judgement leads to change, but it may also lead into the new and unfamiliar, and perhaps welcome, release from the endless cycle of the crisis narrative. Again that question: what is the relation between 'cut' and the word to which it is paired, 'seize'?

'Cut', in the language of Lacanian psychoanalysis, means to staunch the flow of suffering from the ex-timate site of personal crisis by putting bodily affect into symbolic meaning. Such a ceasefire is what both Alain Badiou and Eric Santner have celebrated as an ethical 'event', or 'miracle'. One might say that the state of emergency, even the misery of what Muldoon in 'Incantata' calls a 'deep-seated hurt', may be required to lead the subject from crisis to his or her moment of judgement, an act that not only suspends the exceptional subject from a state of suspense but also allows for a historical, and personal, break with the repetitions driven by unresolved trauma. The ethical act does not so much redeem the past as revise the foretime of that past of which we are conscious, retroactively constructing it as a source for a different future. Kenneth Reinhard draws on the ethics of Alain Badiou to propose that it perhaps requires a figure of the feminine, captured in such names as 'Iron Maiden' and 'Sovereignty', to accomplish this difficult work of separation from a crisis that has spellbound the subject, enacting a 'violent cut that is *inhuman* precisely in getting at the dead heart of the human' (Reinhard, 2005, p. 62). Whereas the masculine subject seeks to renew a universal ethics by 'totalizing' through the work of 'metaphor', the feminine 'infinitizes', refusing the masculine urge to 'conclude'. Only through such absolute judgement as Muldoon – with Reinhard – proposes is it possible to sever the self-reflexive envy that sustains the illness into which Enlightenment hope has declined, its illusion that the divided community, no less than the divided self, may be made whole or washed clean, the illusion that gives rise to every state of emergency.

If we are to release the Neighbour held hostage to our impatient hope for wholeness (and who holds us hostage to his), we must, as Muldoon writes in 'Quoof', lay words between us like the sword in which 'word' is held, so that 'yet' – the word that at once means 'hope', the promise of the future, but also, of course, means 'however', the gesture to the other's hand in that future – may enter the language (Muldoon, 1983, p. 17). This may in fact be the fate of Sara Fricker, assimilated into Muldoon's re-invention of Southey's *Madoc* much as she was assimilated into Native American culture, and of South, whose brutal interrogation introduces the poem even as the eyeball from which the narrative has been read disintegrates. Dissemination on the one hand, and disintegration on the other; both are acts such that dispersal, or diaspora, presses forward.

References

Carey, John (1987) 'The Stain of Words', *Sunday Times* (21 June 1987), 56.

Dolar, Mladen (2006) *A Voice and Nothing More* (Cambridge, MA: MIT Press).

Heaney, Seamus (1998) *Opened Ground: Poems 1966–1996* (London: Faber and Faber).

Muldoon, Paul (1983) *Quoof* (London: Faber and Faber).

—— (1994) *Annals of Chile* (London: Faber and Faber).

—— (1987) *Meeting the British* (London: Faber and Faber.

—— (2001) *Poems 1968–1998* (London: Faber and Faber).

—— (2002) *Moy Sand and Gravel* (London: Faber and Faber).

—— (2006) *Horse Latitudes* (London: Faber and Faber).

Phillips, Ivan (2005) '"Madoc: A Mystery"', *The Literary Encyclopedia*, 29 August 2005, http://www.litencyc.com/php/sworks.php?rec=true&UID=3776 (accessed 26 September 2009).

Reinhard, Kenneth (ed.) (2005) with Slavoj Žižek and Erik L. Santner, *The Neighbor: Three Inquiries in Political Theology* (Chicago: University of Chicago Press).

Santner, Eric (2006) *On Creaturely Life* (Chicago: University of Chicago Press).

Wills, Clair (1998) *Reading Paul Muldoon* (Newcastle-on-Tyne: Bloodaxe Books).

Žižek, Slavoj (2008) *In Defense of Lost Causes* (London: Verso).

—— (2002) *Welcome to the Desert of the Real* (London: Verso).

13

Displacing the Crisis: New British Poetry, Cultural Memory and the Role of the Intellectual

Eva Mueller-Zettelmann

According to publisher Neil Astley, 'all the talk in poetry publishing is of crisis' (Astley 2006). Judging by the sheer number of articles, editorials and public lectures devoted to the subject, the crisis can be said to be severe. Hardly a prize-giving ceremony goes by without the jury voicing their view on the deplorable state of contemporary British poetry. Hardly a poetry festival passes without its guest of honour lamenting the low sales figures and poetry's marginalized position. In what has become something of a partisan war, contestants engage in the question of exactly where the blame lies for poetry's rapid demise.

What is striking to any outsider is the intense emotionality invested in defining British poetry and in determining just who is responsible for denying it the attention it deserves. Contestants in the poetry war certainly do not mince words when it comes to attacking members of the opposite camp: there is talk of 'challenged' academics, 'tone deaf Oxbridge admirers' (Astley, 2005), 'fundamentally talentless poet-commentators' (Paterson, 2004), 'Poetry's mere cheerleaders' (Schmidt, 2006) and of 'infantilising [the] art' (Paterson, 2004). More often than not, the conflict is kept on the boil by publishers and critics, many of whom are active poets themselves, making their interest in poetry's welfare a professional, commercial and keenly personal one.

The arguments brought forward to explain why poetry is losing readers and reputedly vanishing from bookshop shelves are interesting in both what they address and what they choose to ignore. This study seeks to explore the contending voices of the 'gamekeepers' (Schmidt, 2006) of contemporary British poetry, thus attempting to unearth the underlying issues. To narrow down the vast body of vindictive prose I shall restrict myself to a close reading of two key texts, one being a response to the other, which have the additional advantage of having been written by two of the foremost representatives in the field. Neil Astley is editor of Bloodaxe books which he founded in 1978. He has edited a number of poetry anthologies, two of which (*Staying Alive*, 2002, and *Being Alive*, 2004) are themed collections of mostly contemporary poetry which have been huge commercial successes. The second author, Michael Schmidt, is professor of poetry at the University of Glasgow, founder and managing director of Carcanet Press and founder and editor of *PN Review*. Schmidt has also edited a number of influential poetry anthologies and is a published poet himself.

When in 2005 the organisers of StAnza, the annual St Andrews poetry festival, invited Neil Astley to address the subject of Britain's divided poetry culture, Astley seized the opportunity to have his opponents 'named and shamed' (Astley, 2005) and made Michael Schmidt bear the brunt of his onslaught. In his own StAnza contribution a year later, Michael Schmidt responded with a lecture whose observations were less openly abusive, perhaps, but no less acidic.

One of the major principles underlying both Schmidt's and Astley's arguments is the construction of what could be called 'clear-cut binaries'. (The term is also fitting because images of war and conflict are frequently evoked by both speakers and indeed by virtually everyone dealing with the subject.)[1] While both sides repeatedly make a case for diversity and multiplicity, their discourse evolves in strictly antithetical terms. In fact, together, the 2005 and 2006 StAnza lectures could be taken as a perfect case study for ideological inflexibility and the incongruity between self-image and external perception. There is considerable personal involvement on both sides, and neither contestant is afraid to retaliate with a glancing blow. But between the two of them, and aside from emotional polemics, Astley and Schmidt manage to draw a comprehensive map of the (antithetical) lines of argument along which British poetry is constructed today.

At the beginning of his lecture, Neil Astley elaborates on his role as publisher and promoter of poetry, emphasizing the importance of staying in touch with the 'grassroots level' (Astley, 2005). Responding to being called a 'wind-sock' by Michael Schmidt in a 2004 issue of that editor's *PN Review*, Astley muses on what this epithet might mean:

> Being a wind-sock presumably means being listening to readers: being responsive to readers as well as to writers. If I pick up a growing interest amongst readers in a certain poet [...] that's me being a wind-sock. If I then decide to publish a poet admired by readers, that's me not having any ideas of my own. I prefer to think it's yet

> another case of Bloodaxe giving the readers a say in what's published. In the poetry world, readers are almost always ignored, and I think it's important that they should have a voice.
>
> (Astley, 2005)

Astley sees his role as mediator between the poet and his or her audience. He frequently alludes to Bloodaxe's 'postbag' and his regular visits to festivals and poetry venues strengthen his claim to know what the 'general reader' wants. Thus for Astley the poetry market is, or ought to be, a fundamentally democratic one: readers voice their thematic and stylistic preferences, and publishers (and presumably also poets) are expected to act accordingly. At present, though, Astley claims, what readers want has little influence on what gets published. In his view, a white, male, Oxbridge-educated, self-perpetuating Anglocentric academic elite is dominating the poetry market, jealously guarding what it perceives as the timeless standards of lyric quality – to the detriment and ultimate demise of the genre:

> In crude terms what this means is: 'We, the *cognoscenti*, the boys in the club, decide which poets and what kinds of poetry you lot should read, and since we do most of the reviewing and the publishing, we'll make sure that those poets and those books are the ones that get into the bookshops, and we'll ignore or castigate the rest'.
>
> (Astley, 2005)

In this situation, Astley deems it a publisher's most pressing task to promote new talent, providing a platform for those whose work is loved by the grassroots poetry readership. But because this work has a 'common touch', it tends not to appeal to what Astley acrimoniously calls the 'poetry police'.

Not surprisingly, Michael Schmidt sees the situation rather differently. When he surveys the poetry scene, he is struck by the failure of poetry promoters (that is, the editors and critics) to alert readers to precisely those characteristics that make poetry special. While its aesthetic texture, resistance to formulas and intrinsic otherness may make it a difficult object to consume, that is exactly the point for Schmidt: in many ways poetry can be contrary to the 'decorums' (Schmidt) of capitalist society. To ignore its disruptive potential, to gloss over its defamiliarizing quality in favour of texts which display a facile sentimentalism and banal sincerity amounts to a betrayal of the genre: 'Acquiescence is to be resisted, in particular acquiescence in the programme of market development pursued by those who believe poetry is a good, however good or bad the poems are' (Schmidt, 2006).

For Schmidt, reading is an acquired skill, and he calls for a 'culture of reception', a diverse and vigorous review culture where experts like himself (and, indeed, like his StAnza predecessor Astley, were he not of an antithetical persuasion), that is, people who work as critics and publishers of poetry, fulfil their function as educators – providing valuable feedback to the poet and an informed evaluative reading for the general reader:

> We are talking 'reader development' in an early sense, appraisal and judgment intended not to sell the idea of reading, and therefore always recommending, but to make sure that new works and editions are valued, that the factitious, meretricious and merely conventional are identified as such. That culture has value only if it is informed and sets out to inform; if it takes positive and negative risks, and if it is willing to risk giving offence in the interests of truth [...].
>
> (Schmidt, 2006)

Consequently what Astley calls 'reaching out', Schmidt would call a 'dumbing down'. What Astley sees as selling poetry, Schmidt sees as 'selling poetry out'. For Schmidt, editing a volume of poetry means painstakingly separating the seriously innovative from the tritely mediocre. In this respect, the editor's position is a highly responsible one, and editors must never be seen to tailor their decisions to market demands or demographics – an approach which Astley follows as a matter of course, and in which he firmly believes.

Obviously, what lies at the bottom of much of the dispute is a fundamental disagreement as to what constitutes 'good' poetry and what its concomitant social role should be. Michael Schmidt clearly takes a formalist-aestheticist stance, citing McLeish's 'A Poem should not mean / But be' (MacLeish, 1996, p. 1271) as one of his earliest formative influences. Poetry for him is explorative; it can develop new forms in order to afford the reader a glimpse at what might otherwise be barred from view; barred, that is, by ingrained convention. The lyric is anti-pragmatic; it has epistemological and social potential precisely because it runs counter to what is ideological and commercial, to the commonplace and the mundane. Poetry is impersonal; it evolves more 'out of an engagement with language, and with poetry, than with life' (Schmidt, 2006). The poem's voice, Schmidt insists, is not to be mistaken for that of the author; the potential for fraternization between the poet and the reader is merely fictional. It only arises through simplistic wishful thinking, and in turn that thinking is potentially detrimental to poetry since it narrows down its imaginative scope. Contrary to A.E. Housman's (1933) claim, poetry does not call for an instinctive, spontaneous and physical response. Schmidt cites Housman as an early representative of the readerly stance he would wish to negate. To appreciate a poem we need to follow our judgement rather than our taste, and if a work proves resistant to easy reading (as Schmidt concedes can be the case with much of the poetry of Geoffrey Hill, for instance), we are to resort to our knowledge of poetry theory and the lyric tradition rather than follow Housman and rely on physical reactions only.

To Neil Astley, anyone suggesting that poetry does not arise out of the concrete and the personal has fatally lost touch with poetry's quintessence: to talk from the heart to the heart, to express 'emotional truth' (Astley, 2005), to 'engage [...] with people and what people do and think and feel and fear in their lives' (ibid.) Interestingly, Astley is much less coherent than Schmidt when it comes to describing the kind of poetry of which he approves. He frequently invokes poetry's potential to 'offer people spiritual wisdom in a spiritually bankrupt age' (ibid.) Put in the language of literary theory, the poetry of his choice might display features such as lisibility, heteroreferentiality and teleology, thus suggesting its pragmatic relevance. A little further down the page, however, Astley's brief reference to poetry's reader-reception effect is faintly reminiscent of Shklovsky's concept of '*ostranenie*' (Shklovsky, 1988, p. 1917), which in essence is precisely the opposite of literature with a strongly utilitarian bias.[2]

What is conspicuously lacking in Astley's account is any reference to a poem's *discours*, as an independent aesthetic entity. According to Astley, the formal aspect is clearly subservient to the referential one and functions as a mere vehicle for the poem's content. If poems 'take the reader by surprise' (Astley, 2005), they usually do so not because of their innovative form but because the 'stance or angle of approach [is] different from what's expected' (Astley, 2005). It is obvious that, as far as Astley is concerned, a poem should not be, but mean. He certainly has no patience for poets whose work engages in formal experimentation for its own sake. Berating such 'obscure avantgardists' as a 'chorus of articulate but fundamentally talentless poet-commentators' (Paterson quoted in Astley, 2005), he sees their secret aim as being a self-promoting display of their cleverness, appealing to the 'egos of the *cognoscenti*' (Astley, 2005).

Both speakers use the words 'condescension' and 'conservatism' – they use them to refer to things that are, however, poles apart. But with these words they are both describing what they perceive as their opponent's principal shortcomings. Michael Schmidt regards the commercial publishers' refusal to draw a line at marketing openly commonplace and platitudinous poetry as condescending. For him their hostility towards lyrical experiments reveals a fundamentally anti-progressive and reactionary stance: 'Surely we can, without necessarily being academic, [...] demand a little less solidarity, a little less local backslapping, more debate and engagement, at the same time giving the reader less of a condescending embrace? Down with the poetry cheerleaders, I say!' (Schmidt, 2006).

By contrast, Neil Astley identifies Schmidt's conservatism in his adversary's partiality for modernist aesthetics. He berates the 'poetry police' for sweeping aside the general poetry readers' wishes and for setting themselves up as the nation's sole legitimate guardians of the lyric grail: 'Too often, poetry editors think of themselves and their poet friends as the only arbiters of taste, only publishing writers they think people *ought* to read and depriving readers of other kinds of poetry which many people would find more rewarding' (Astley, 2005).

'Condescension' and 'conservatism' can thus be considered two of the semantic focal points in a debate that may owe its existence as much to construction as to empirical fact. Indeed, leaving aside the regular publication of fresh polemics, the alleged 'crisis' of British poetry is hard to detect. On the contrary, for a continental observer used to modern poetry being an all but extinct genre precariously kept alive by a handful of aficionados (most of whom are poetry producers themselves), the British poetry scene appears to be a striking exception. A short look at Austria may suffice to outline what I take to be the average situation in many European countries.

In Austria, poetry is the novel's unimposing little sister. Not infrequently, new novels and their authors make it into quality paper review columns, literature programmes of the national radio broadcaster Oe1, bookstore display windows, and hence, into the public consciousness. Poetry books rarely do so.[3] Poetry readings are very small scale, within-the-group events which are largely ignored by the reading public, who prefer sleekly styled happenings such as the successful 'Rund um die Burg', a much publicized non-stop 24-hour event where novelists read from their latest works, perennially drawing large crowds. Contemporary Austrian poetry owes much of its shape to the radical experiments of the Wiener Gruppe (H.C. Artmann, Oswald Wiener, Konrad Bayer, Ernst Jandl, Gerhard Rühm) of the 1950s and 1960s; many texts are published privately and in very small quantities; the works and their authors remain largely unknown.[4]

If one takes the continental situation – where poetry is produced in obscurity and read far from the public eye – as a yardstick, Britain's diverse poetry scene seems to be a paradise by comparison. The very fact that so much media attention is given to what is in effect an in-house quarrel may be taken as a strong indicator that poetry in Britain leads anything but a marginalized existence. It would suffice to list a few of the large number of poetry organizations and events in order to identify Britain as a place offering poets and poetry lovers a range of opportunities for presenting and appreciating their art.

The prestigious T.S. Eliot prize has its more open, more democratic counterpart in the Poetry Society's National Poetry Competition. Both competitions, together with many lesser ones of a similar ilk, foster individual talent and develop and maintain a readership for poetry in the UK. The country also hosts an impressive number of annual festivals exclusively devoted to poetry, mostly offering poetry readings and poetry workshops. Some, like the Ledbury festival, include literature development events in their portfolio, with schools and community programmes, reaching out, for example, to day centres and old people's homes.

Londoners commuting on the underground have a daily opportunity to read poetry displayed in advertising spaces on the trains. This opportunity is provided by a programme that was thought up by American writer Judith Chernaik and launched in 1986, and which aims at bringing a wide range of (mostly British) poetry to an equally wide-ranging audience of chance readers. Poems selected for display are also available in book form, with the ninth edition of *Poems on the Underground* selling more than a quarter of a million copies since its first publication in 1999.[5] The format of 'Poetry Please', a weekly BBC Radio 4 programme where listeners request poems which are then read by a set cast of actors, may not have seen much modification since it was first broadcast in 1979, but its status as the world's longest running poetry programme[6] testifies both to the format's aptness and to poetry's undiminished relevance in private lives and in public discourse in Britain.

But British poetry organizers have also developed a range of novel formats, and indeed, if one takes innovative programming as a bill of health for an art form, the British poetry scene seems to be in fine fettle, as far away from a life-threatening crisis as it could possibly be.[7] In London, particularly, events like 'London Liming' or 'Shortfuse' now offer an intermedial combination of poetry readings, performance poetry, stand-up comedy and music to attract younger audiences. 'Speed Poetry' is another example of poetry organizers inventively taking over new formats from non-literary areas with which a young audience will be familiar. This is a quick-paced recital format designed analogously to speed dating, where poets move from table to table, spending only a limited time with each group to present their texts. Another, highly competitive scheme is 'Poetry Idol', which has been set up in imitation of the successful knock-out pop contest show on television.

Book groups, academic creative writing courses, poetry programmes specifically targeting schools, poetry societies, poetry laboratories, poetry archives, poetry cafés, poetry surgeries and, *pace* Astley, fairly substantial contemporary poetry sections in quality book shops – to an insider all this may still not seem nearly enough. For an outsider, though, whose own culture provides few if any of these formats, this is indeed profuse. Thus, on closer inspection, the alleged crisis that fuels the debate between 'popularizers' and 'elitists', a debate heightening the protagonists' relevance and lending their decrees immediacy, turns out to be something of a contorting fiction, a constructed decline in British poetry's public relevance which is simply not there.

Much of the discussion revolves around the – either too restrictive or too encompassing – choice of poetry deemed suitable to reach the stage of publication. Listening to Neil Astley and Michael Schmidt, the impression arises that due to their discrepant lyric credos, a poet favoured by one will surely be spurned by the other. But again, a closer look at their respective portfolios of published poets reveals that the situation is not quite as clear-cut as they would have us believe. Neil Astley's popular theme-based anthologies *Staying Alive* and *Being Alive* include poems by Ezra Pound, W.S. Graham, Geoffrey Hill, Basil Bunting and Roy Fisher, poets commonly regarded as belonging to the opposite camp. And indeed, for the continental poetry lover accustomed to works that routinely take the linguistic medium well beyond its communicative limits, there is often little enough difference between what is traded in Britain as 'serious' versus what is openly declared as 'light' poetry.[8]

Since neither the claim of a genre in crisis nor the contest between divided poetic camps can be seen to stand the test of reality, is the poetry debate perhaps only a skirmish within a larger literary battle? Is the poetry controversy – for reasons yet to be ascertained – acting by proxy for other art forms? Are we witnessing an all-embracing national battle between the *lisible* and the *scriptible* (Barthes, 1970, pp. 4f.), the accessible and the avant-garde? Surely, if this were the case, a brief look at other genres would soon reveal the existence of general hostilities, where poetry has been selected as the central battleground.

But neither in the media commentary on the contemporary British novel, nor in the published analyses of contemporary British theatre is there any indication that a discussion is raging in comparably pessimistic and confrontational terms. Because it 'privileges consciousness and interiority' (something that could equally be said of the lyric, by the way), the novel is described as being 'as vital now in this time of profound political crisis as it has ever been' (Cowley, 2005). British contemporary theatre is seen to be enjoying 'an amazing resurgence from about 1993 onwards [which] has more or less continued since then' (Billington, 2004). Poetry, then, stands alone. The remainder of this chapter is concerned with the elucidation of this curious fact.

To explain British poetry's special position both within the British literary system and in relation to the role modern poetry takes in other European countries, one needs to take a closer look at contemporary constructions of poetry's generic make-up, its ideal form and its social function. How is poetry perceived in generic terms in Britain today? Which of its historical realizations lie dormant in its modern conceptualization? And what are the underlying assumptions about its relation to the individual, language, history and the nation? It would be a gross simplification of the complexity of the phenomenon to perceive its genres as forming a timeless aesthetic system solely regulated by inner literary factors. Genres are social and thus historical phenomena and as such are deeply entrenched in the general cultural enterprise of producing meaning. Because of their historical dimension, genres can be seen to fall under the aegis of 'cultural memory', a notion first conceptualized by German Egyptologists Jan and Aleida Assmann.[9]

'Cultural memory' is a collective term for a body of culture-specific knowledge focused on the past, which, through its assessment of a community's shared history, governs the way a society perceives itself and the world. This collective memory can never be encountered in its entirety, nor does it ever occur in a 'pure', unmediated form. The non-material components of cultural memory, that is, its constitutive ideas, precepts, narratives and evaluative assessments, are always dependent on concrete material manifestations, on a culture- and epoch-specific corpus of canonized texts which a society ingests in acts of repeated consumption, in order to stabilize and mediate its collective self-image.

Collective retrieval of a shared past can take on two different forms: we may either perceive of the present as a state which has grown out of a unique national past and by recovering its buried origins seek to 'make sense' of the present – or we may insist on a contemporary phenomenon's timeless, universal character. In the case of the latter, we choose to ignore temporal distance, cultural otherness and the inherent historicity of culture and instead construct a text-borne national essence. Texts and groups of texts, that is, whole genre conceptions, are perceived not as testimonies of the otherness of past experience but as a superior corpus of cultural heritage expressive of 'what we acknowledge as our own' (Assmann and Assmann, 1987, p. 7; my translation). Documents of the 'canonical'[10] kind are exempt from the eroding forces of cultural evolution; in their role as providers of absolute meaning they are situated in a realm of the ever-valid and the nationally distinctive.

In its predilection for emotion, nature, sincerity, and the 'egotistical sublime' (Keats, 1958, p. 387), modern British poetry exhibits a curiously Romantic streak, something that is decidedly lacking in the modern poetry of other European literatures. It seems, then, that it is English Romanticism that has been chosen to serve as an underlying canonical model for the way poetry is conceived in Britain today. As with all dealings with history, however, whether they are focused on historical otherness or the timelessly universal, the retrieval of a past epoch will by necessity be a creative endeavour. In the case of the canonical resuscitation of Romanticism, the period's two most distinctive elements of nature and transcendence have been retained – with the important addition that nature has been furnished with a national marker – the attribute of 'Englishness'. Rather than centring on a universal, abstract, deified (and capitalized) 'Nature', the modern template of the British lyric ascribes transcendental significance to a specifically and emphatically English countryside (and by extension to any recognizably English setting). In its creative reconstruction of Romanticism, the canonical model of poetry has thus turned the Romantic lyric into poetry that celebrates the English countryside, and the lyric genre into a corpus, which, by definition, is devoted to providing a transcendental vision of nationhood.[11]

Once alerted to the intimate connection between poetry and national identity, it is easy to detect its manifold traces in poetry's evaluation within academia and the way it is treated by the British public. Since poetry provides textual focal points for the construction of a homogeneous tribal identity, people feel the need – and indeed the entitlement – to read, recite, revere and pass aesthetic judgement. This was particularly noticeable in 1999 and again in 2009, when the selection of a new poet laureate became a matter of national concern. Whatever literary critics, potential candidates and celebrity onlookers had to say on the subject was sure to make the headlines. To outsiders for whom the post of a state-paid national bard seems rather quaint and outdated, the media hype surrounding the quest was such that it could only have been evoked by a strong nationalist sub-current.

Equally unique to Britain[12] is the institution of National Poetry Day, which has been celebrated since 1994, when a nationwide day of poetry-centred festivities was first introduced by the Poetry Society. Since then, National Poetry Day, which every year is given a different lyric theme as its motto, 'has engaged millions of people with poetry, through a range of live events and web-based activities for people young and old throughout the country'.[13] In 1995, joining the festivities, the BBC asked its viewers to vote for the nation's favourite poem. They chose not 'Prufrock', nor 'The Waste Land', nor 'Goblin Market', nor 'The Good-Morrow' nor Shakespeare's sonnet 116, nor any of the vast number of frequently anthologized and, one would have thought, well-loved poems – but 'If' (1910), Rudyard Kipling's (in)famous poem, which sports a prescriptive listing of genuine British virtues. Taken together, the uniquely British institution of a National Poetry Day, the similarly patriotic endeavour of nationwide elections of Britain's most popular poem and the populace's choice of a text that culminates in a masculine imperialist vision of the role of the British race – all of these are singularly weighty instances of poetry's ascribed power to gratify the nation's need for a stable collective identity. In this respect, the genre of poetry is indeed unique; neither novel nor play are ever viewed in equally nationalistic terms, since because of their generic construction, neither is deemed to be a canonical tool for defining the soul of the nation.

Now that poetry's special position has been defined, let us return to the initial issue of the so-called poetry war and the critics' curious penchant for constructing British poetry as a genre in deep crisis. Quite a large part of the controversy, for which I have taken Neil Astley's and Michael Schmidt's consecutive lectures at the StAnza Festivals of 2005 and 2006 as representative case studies, is evidently due to personal animosity and differences in poetic taste, as well as to social background, education and personal allegiances. But while both contestants have their professional reputation, their publishing firms and their poet protégés to think of, much more than individual interest is at stake. It is primarily not the publishers' nor their favoured poets' image, it is the self-image of an entire nation that is being defined through the canonical genre of poetry.

The corpus of the 'canonical' in Assmann's sense of the term is an essential ideological device, which through its mechanisms of selection, preservation and exclusion becomes a means to pass on and process tribal experience; experience that may prove beneficial to a community by providing it with a sense of unity and identity which might otherwise be lacking. We would underestimate the kinetic impetus of cultural evolution, however, if we were to assume that an atemporal canonization of texts and genres could be sustained more or less 'naturally' and 'as a matter of course'. As with all other mechanisms of cultural memory, the canonical is heavily reliant on social structures for its preservation and circulation, and depends on the mechanisms and institutions of cultural transmission to ensure its unfaltering relevance. The dehistoricization of texts and genres requires a favourable contextual setting and strong institutional support. This institutional backing can only be judged to be in continuous supply when the so-called 'custodians of tradition'[14] ensure its prolongation – as official bodies and professional individuals geared towards stabilizing what would otherwise be prone to erosion and cultural change.

From a systemic point of view, then, this is what disputatious poetry editors are: they are custodians of something that has been canonized, guardians of a genre conception that elevates the historically specific to the timelessly universal and nationally distinctive. The contentious haggling about whether or not a poetry editor should have an Oxbridge background, and whether that background is a necessary prerequisite or a debilitating impediment, is less petty than it might seem when viewed from the angle of cultural memory. In this debate, contestants are vying for the post of 'custodian-in-chief of tradition' and as participants in the complex system of creating and mediating national identity, their every attribute takes on a wider, representative significance. What is being disputed, after all, is less the specific shape of poetry than the specific shape of the nation, with the all-pervading sense of crisis derived less from literary, than from social factors. At the end of the day, the United Kingdom has witnessed an unprecedented erosion of its time-honoured self-images, one brought about by the centrifugal tendencies of decolonization, immigration, devolution, European integration and globalization. What we hear when we listen to Neil Astley and Michael Schmidt arguing about the state of poetry, then, are the contending voices of custodians of the genre: their dissent over poetry has an unvoiced objective, namely to bring forth an elevating self-image for a nation in crisis.

Notes

1. Compare for instance Andrew Duncan, who in his book-length study on the failure of conservatism in modern British poetry talks of the 'Defence of Territory' (2003, p. 303) and of revanchist conservative groups fighting a 'ruthless war against innovation' (ibid., p. 324).
2. It may be no coincidence that when Astley undertakes this brief excursion into enemy territory he does not use his own words but quotes poet Paul

Muldoon: 'The point of poetry is to be acutely discomforting, to prod and provoke, to poke us in the eye, to punch us in the nose, to knock us off our feet, to take our breath away' (Muldoon, 1998, p. 516, quoted in Astley, 2005).

3. While it is true that with novelists like Peter Handke, Thomas Bernhard and Nobel Prize winning Elfriede Jelinek, Austria can boast of several novelists of international renown, contemporary Austrian poetry with its marked linguistic self-consciousness and penchant for experimentalism is a corpus which is no less innovative and would deserve equal attention.
4. For an introduction to contemporary Austrian poetry see Spiel (1980) and Zeman (1999).
5. 'Transport for London: Poetry on the Underground' (n.d.). See also, Benson (1999).
6. See Wikipedia, 'Poetry Please'.
7. Novel poetry formats described in this paragraph are taken from Novak (forthcoming).
8. Although there are indeed a great variety of groups, factions, fashions and styles, the difference between them has often more to do with personal allegiance than with poetic discourse. The populist, the confessional, the politically committed, the neo-pastoral and even the moderately 'modernist' all share the philosophical basis of a logocentric empiricism and a self-present Cartesian subject. Irrespective of which subgroup they represent many such poems are characterized by lisibility, 'authenticity', mimetic realism and a marked focus on the level of *histoire*. (See Schlaeger, 1993; Mueller-Zettelmann, 2003, 2004.)
9. For an introduction to the theory of cultural memory see Halbwach (1925), Assmann and Assmann (1987), Assmann (1992) and Bal (1999). For an in-depth analysis of the relationship between cultural memory, genre theory and British poetry see Mueller-Zettelmann (2005), on which the following discussion of the ideological implications of the lyric genre are based.
10. Rather than denoting an open collection of works set apart from other literature by virtue of their literary quality and historically representative character, 'canon' in the context of cultural memory designates a body of texts and genre conceptions which were made (or rather chosen) to defy time. See Assmann (1992, pp. 103–29) and Assmann and Assmann (1987).
11. Alice Oswald's *Dart*, which won the T.S. Eliot Prize in 2002, is a case in point. Written as a homage to the River Dart in Dorset, the poem retraces the stream from its source in Cranmere Pool all the way to the sea. Prior to the writing of the poem, Oswald had spent three years recording conversations with people living and working on the Dart. The text is made up of quotations from these voices, some authentic but some the product of her literary imagination, which are meant 'to be read as the river's mutterings' (Oswald, 2002, preface). If the reader disregards the clemently prosaic diction and the occasional inclusion of the mundane (the text makes mention of 'a sploosh of sewage' and a 'stinkmass of loopaper and whathaveyou', p. 30), there is not much in the underlying épistemè of the poem that would distinguish it from a Wordsworthian nature panegyric (compare, Riley, 2006). In strictly logocentric language, the text depicts a natural phenomenon and does so in terms of something non-problematic, something richly meaningful and

self-evident. Serving as the focal point of an organic existence, the River Dart's rural authenticity and associations with ancient lore become redolent of a unifying communal history. Its allusions to river-dwelling figures from Britain's mythic past provide a mythopoetic backdrop that lends the river poem a central function: that of a text which transports its readers to a place of proto-transcendental significance.

12. While there is World Poetry Day (21 March) which was declared by UNESCO in 1999, neither Austria, France, Germany, Italy nor the Netherlands have a day in their national calendar dedicated to the celebration of their national poetry (see Wikipedia, 'World Poetry Day').
13. 'National Poetry Day'.
14. For an extensive definition see Assmann and Assmann (1987).

References

Assmann, Aleida and Jan Assmann (1987) 'Kanon und Zensur', in A. Assmann and J. Assmann (eds) *Kanon und Zensur* (Munich: Fink).

Assmann, Jan (1992) *Das kulturelle Gedaechtnis. Schrift, Erinnerung und politische Identitaet in fruehen Hochkulturen* (Munich: Beck).

Astley, Neil (ed.) (2002) *Staying Alive* (Highgreen: Bloodaxe).

— (ed.) (2004) *Being Alive* (Highgreen: Bloodaxe).

— (2005) 'Bile, Guile and Dangerous to Poetry', StAnza Lecture 2005, http://www.st-andrews.ac.uk/standrews/stanza/lecture.htm (accessed 1 October 2009).

— (2006) 'Give Poetry Back to People', *New Statesman,* 23 October 2006, http://www.newstatesman.com/200610230043 (accessed 1 October 2009).

Bal, Mieke, Jonathan Crewe and Leo Spitzer (eds) (1999) *Acts of Memory: Cultural Recall in the Present* (Hanover: University Press of New England).

Barthes, Roland (1970) *S/Z: Essais* (Paris: Seuil).

Benson, Gerard (ed.) (1999) *Poems on the Underground: No. 9* (London: Weidenfeld & Nicolson).

Billington, Michael (2004) 'Interview with Mireia Aragay and Pilar Zozaya', *ATLANTIS,* 26 (1): 89–100.

Cowley, Jason (2005) 'A New Life for the Novel', *Observer,* 7 August, 2.

Duncan, Andrew (2003) *The Failure of Conservatism in Modern British Poetry* (Cambridge: Salt).

Halbwachs, Maurice (1925) *Les cadres sociaux de la mémoire* (Paris: Alcan).

Housman, Alfred E. (1933) *The Name and Nature of Poetry* (Cambridge: Cambridge University Press).

Keats, John (1958) '"Letter to Richard Woodhouse", 27 Oct. 1818', in H.E. Rollins (ed.) *The Letters of John Keats 1814–1821,* vol. 1 (Cambridge: Cambridge University Press).

Kipling, Rudyard (1910) 'If', in *Rewards and Fairies* (London: Macmillan).

MacLeish, Archibald (1996) 'Ars Poetica', in Margaret Ferguson (ed.) *The Norton Anthology of Poetry,* 4th edn (New York: Norton).

Mueller-Zettelmann, Eva (2005) 'Poetry, Cultural Memory and the English Lyric Tradition', in Eva Mueller-Zettelmann and Margarete Rubik (eds) *Theory into Poetry: New Approaches to the Lyric* (Amsterdam/New York: Rodopi).

—— (2004) '"The British Right to Ignorance": Metatextualitaet und Sprachkritik in der englischen Lyrik des zwanzigsten Jahrhunderts', in P.V. Zima (ed.) *Krise und Kritik der Sprache. Literatur zwischen Spaetmoderne und Postmoderne* (Tubingen: Francke).
—— (2003) 'Von der Rueckkehr des "Realen": Das lyrische Subjekt in der englischen Moderne und Postmoderne', in M. Fluderni and J. Alber (eds) *Das 20. Jahrhundert* (Trier: Wissenschaftlicher Verlag Trier).
Muldoon, Paul (1998) 'The Point of Poetry', *Princeton University Library Chronicle*, 59 (3): 503–16.
'National Poetry Day', http://www.poetrysoc.com/content/aboutus/npd/ (accessed 1 October 2009).
Novak, Julia (forthcoming) 'A Theory of Live Poetry – Analysing Poetry in Performance', dissertation, University of Vienna.
Oswald, Alice (2002) *Dart* (London: Faber and Faber).
Paterson, Don (2004) 'The Dark Art of Poetry', T.S. Eliot Lecture 2004, http://www.poetrylibrary.org.uk/news/poetryscene/?id=20 (accessed 1 October 2009).
Riley, Peter (2006) 'Review of Alice Oswald's *Woods etc.*', http://www.shearsman.com/pages/editorial/reviews2006/riley_oswald.html (accessed 1 October 2009).
Schlaeger, Juergen (1993) 'Postmodern British Poetry: Stalking a Phantom?' in H.U. Seeber and W. Groebel (eds) *Anglistentag 1992 Stuttgart: Proceedings* (Tubingen: Niemeyer).
Schmidt, Michael (2004) 'Editorial', *PN Review*, 31(2): 1.
—— (2006) 'What, How Well, Why?', StAnza Lecture 2006, http://www.stanzapoetry.org/stanza06_archive/lecture06.htm (accessed 1 October 2009).
Shklovsky, Viktor (1988) 'Art as Technique', in David Lodge (ed.) *Modern Criticism and Theory: A Reader* (London: Longmans).
Spiel, Hilde (ed.) (1980) *Die zeitgenoessische Literatur Oesterreichs* (Frankfurt/M: Fischer).
Transport for London: 'Poetry on the Underground', http://www.tfl.gov.uk/corporate/projectsandschemes/2437.aspx (accessed 1 October 2009).
Wikipedia contributors, 'Poetry Please', *Wikipedia, The Free Encyclopedia*, http://en.wikipedia.org/w/index.php?title=Poetry_Please&oldid=308962725 (accessed 1 October 2009).
Wikipedia contributors, 'World Poetry Day', *Wikipedia, The Free Encyclopedia*, http://en.wikipedia.org/w/index.php?title=World_Poetry_Day&oldid=298847008 (accessed 1 October 2009).
Zeman, Herbert (ed.) (1999) *Geschichte der Literatur in Oesterreich: von den Anfaengen bis zur Gegenwart. Das 20. Jahrhundert* (Graz: Akademische Druck- und Verlagsanstalt).

14
The Body of Text Meets the Body as Text: Staging (I)dentity in the Work of SuAndi and Lemn Sissay

Deirdre Osborne

The work of two of Britain's leading indigenous black poets and performers, SuAndi and Lemn Sissay reinforces the powerful, self-fashioning capabilities of the art of poetry as counterstance and counterbalance – both to prevailing social norms that devalue and oppress certain groups of people based upon race and sex-gender categories, and to prevailing aesthetic traditions which denote inclusion or exclusion within the British literary compass and its markers of artistic merit. This chapter explores the idea of 'poetry as its own vindicating force' (Heaney, 1988, p. 92) in SuAndi's and Sissay's creative aesthetics, while remaining mindful of the implications of contexts – explicit or implied – and their effect upon meaning. As black artists evolving in white-dominated creative contexts, their poetic voices interweave the dual legacies of being born in Britain (inheriting British literary and performance heritages) and yet also frequently identifying with African diasporic traditions as a resistance to their socio-political marginalization in national, racial and familial relations. Their work spans written and spoken-word genres (poetry, monodrama) and presents a challenge to existing critical methodologies.

Both writers position themselves unequivocally within the scope of Black British writing, a category which crystallized at the end of the twentieth century and towards which critical attention has been increasingly turned in the new millennium. It is understood as encompassing the writing of indigenous black Britons whose work speaks from a sensibility and standpoint quite distinct from the arriviste or migration narratives of previous generations in the UK, who termed themselves black writers. In asserting their indigenous and creatively represented identities, SuAndi and Sissay exemplify a generation whose work, Jackaman claims, subverts 'a reductive hard core notion of "Englishness" in poetry' as it is 'directed precisely towards the breaking of English as a monopoly concern', to assert 'a multiplicity of different but equally valid voices' (Jackaman, 2003, p. 12). Writing about Sissay, Padel notes how his poems 'speak of British supermarkets, dreams of Africa [...] they dance between different registers of English' (Padel, 2004, p. 33). This testifies to the formal and linguistic experimentation necessary to access and render experiences that produce '*other ways of knowing*' and function as 'a challenge to the taken-for-granted normative assumptions of prevailing discourse' (Mirza, 1997, p. 5).

Poetry as spoken-word has in particular been associated with black poets in Britain and is a means whereby many poets writing from marginality have found their most strident poetic voice. Spoken-word sharpens the divergences between poetry as written to be read on the page – as an act of introspection – and poetry written to be relayed as an extroverted utterance to an audience. SuAndi and Sissay have also penned and performed auto/bio/graphical monodramas, *The Story of M* (SuAndi, 2002) and *Something Dark* (Sissay, 2008). These auto/bio/graphical works can be termed in this way as they combine both aspects of autobiographical and biographical genres, intimately dramatizing odysseys to self-knowledge through retrieving and paying homage to their respective mothers' struggles in raising or rejecting them in a surrounding, hostile, white-dominated English society of the sixties and seventies. Traversing generic boundaries through cross-pollinating spoken-word poetry with confessional and dramatic monologue forms, they stage their monodramas in theatre and live art contexts, to produce a unique experiential aesthetics.[1]

The contexts which reverberate through their work encompass literary legacies, poetic traditions and socio-cultural factors that shape contemporary British culture. This might fulfil Heaney's vision in *The Government of the Tongue*:

> [...] this aspect of poetry as its own vindicating force. In this dispensation, the tongue (representing both a poet's personal gift of utterance and the common resources of language itself) has been granted the right to govern. The poetic art is credited with an authority of its own.
>
> (Heaney, 1988, p. 92)

However, in the history of writing by black people in the UK, the 'government of the tongue' is not necessarily a self-naming experience but one of being governed and named. It evokes the discrediting, silencing and disregarding inextricably laced to marginalization in a white-majority society and its imperial past.[2]

As with other contemporary black writers, SuAndi and Sissay's poetry was initially received in a politicized way, as is nearly inevitable since audience expectations (of all demographics) persist that being a black artist means making social or issues-based art rather than work with universal themes. In staging (I)dentity assertions, both writers/performers flex traditional parameters accorded to black-centred creativity and to some degree sidestep this representational pressure (Osborne, 2008a, pp. 7–11). Not wishing to collapse the poets' craft into some inevitable autobiographical realization (a familiar reflex of much white-led criticism), the fact that these monodramas articulate, inescapably, the poets' own experiences – as uttered by them alone – does require foregrounding. To date, they alone have performed the pieces. It is untested as to whether they could be performed plausibly by others or if, indeed, either writer would wish this to happen. This is not to interchange the poets' actual lives with their poeticized auto/biographical material, but to recognize how *self*-performed monodrama demands a particular version of the personal *and* personalized voice. The use of 'I' (within contexts of history and cultural practices), is also further shaped and constrained by the poetic systems to which the writers adhere as poets, first and foremost, rather than as dramatists.

Paterson identifies how pitching written language in a non-performative context demonstrates 'the hopelessly attenuated emotional palette of written speech; spoken, it's easy to draw out shades of meaning' (Paterson, 2007, p. 59). SuAndi and Sissay's speaking of their poetry is a vital constituent to its conception and reception but the written form is key. In claiming roots in many oral traditions, SuAndi confirms, 'I compose and write all my performance pieces in my head, complete', while Sissay begins by writing, *not* improvising or devising in front of a live audience (Osborne, 2008c). By frequently slipping between, and re-working, literary genres and performance traditions, their work raises questions about the need for critical languages which can meet the demands of the forms and experiential aesthetics they forge. Their work draws attention to the ways in which two distinct routes (literary criticism and performance analysis) offer an unsatisfactory separation of approaches. It ratifies the development of a lexicon and inter-referential analytical methodology that will service the critical requirements of generic and performance overlaps.

'Our mothers, ourselves'

The birth metaphor is well-established in relation to artistic production. To borrow Harrison's phrase, *Something Dark* and *The Story of M* are 'poetically conceived' (SuAndi, 2002, n.p) but theatrically delivered. As the sole performers of their monodramas, conduits for transmitting their self-penned texts, both writers literally and literarily perform themselves into being with each performance. Adopting certain techniques of delivery, their writing styles convey an (illusory) authenticity yet also signal the artifice of rendering auto/biographical material. Sissay dramatically poeticizes his life story of his quest to find his mother who gave him up at birth. In locating her, he fulfils a self-odyssey to securing the bloodlines of a biological family. Through his acting in the piece about himself and by himself (as a solo performer), a contrived act of theatrical (re)creation coexists with the stylized moment-by-moment unfolding of a life story – as if for the first time – which characterizes the acting of drama. The affinity Sissay feels for dramatized language – whether in terms of poetry spoken live, or as the staged idiom of theatrical performance – is demonstrated in *Something Dark*. He describes his methodology as 'a device to communicate the story' (Osborne 2008b), emphasizing how the relationship between audience and poet differs from that between audience and actor: 'whenever I wanted to change the lines as an actor in rehearsals, the director would say well no, "the writer wrote it that way and that's the way you do it"' (Osborne, 2008a, p. 323).

The Story of M is SuAndi's tribute to her white mother and the trials she faced when raising her mixed heritage children in 1960s Britain. As the primary caregiver in most children's early lives (whether as birth mothers or carers in foster homes), white womanhood was the first experience many mixed heritage British children had. When Tizard and Phoenix surveyed 'the racial identities of young people of mixed black and white parentage', they found that 'Defining oneself as "black" *was* associated with a more politicised set of attitudes towards racism' (Tizard and Phoenix, 1993, p. 161). As white society perceived mixedness as black, Tizard and Phoenix also found that their participants were not always accepted as black by black people:

> Thus, looking into society, they see no reflection or validation of themselves. [...] For those who regarded themselves as black this was a disturbing experience, [...] Further, opting for a black identity entails discounting the white part of one's inheritance. Most (but not all) of the young people's closest attachments were to their mothers, who were generally white.
>
> (Tizard and Phoenix, 1993, p. 164)

By writing and playing her mother, M, SuAndi's own life is ultimately just as vividly brought to life in a satisfying concordance. She herself notes the interplay of race and reception in an audience's possible framings of her monodrama – 'As a Black woman playing my white mother, I "colour" the audience's view of M [...] But M is not Black [...] In crossing racial lines M, a white working-class mother, is "writing" her children's future histories into Africa' (SuAndi, 2006, pp. 126–7). SuAndi is ultimately born through her articulation of the piece, as herself. She clearly separates her own theatricalized version of herself from the body of her dramatized text of her mother's story and from being the dramatic vehicle that transports her mother's story when she utters, 'For this was the story of M – / M for Margaret, / M for Mother, / And now M for Me. / And my name is SuAndi' (SuAndi, 2002, p. 18). This adroit birthing of herself in the final moments, by proclaiming herself M's daughter, not M, is a stepping-out-of-role that functions so as to invoke her actual birth from her mother's body. The *coup-de-théâtre* undermines audience assumptions about who is playing whom as SuAndi distinguishes herself from having been a bearer of her mother's experiences. Aston identifies this recognition as being premised upon racial stereotypes:

> It is not until the last slide is shown, and the audience sees a photograph of Margaret for the first time, that it is clear that Margaret was white. At this point, SuAndi steps out of character [...] For the spectator, especially the white spectator, what is demonstrated through the Gestus of the slide is an assumption that the victim of racial abuse must be black, not white.
>
> (Aston, 2003, p. 144)

However, Aston's account of the effects of the performance, synthesized with visual narrative-making, does not engage with the piece as published, where the visual text functions in a role akin to that of marginalia. In the typographical margins, the point at which a reader may see the photograph of M is unknown, dependent upon a chronological line-by-line privileging of the printed text over accompanying visuals and that there is no skipping ahead in reading it. Moreover, how might a black or mixed heritage spectator have responded – or, indeed, would a white spectator necessarily assume that SuAndi's mother was black, or perhaps mixed? Her Liverpudlian, working-class, single parent identities might have resonated more powerfully in such a context. Aston does not negotiate the conflating of SuAndi the performer and the characterization of M with the way in which she perceives that the audience (never a unified group) might read her. This imposes a white-assumptive perspective that ignores the possibility that M's skin colour might provoke a potential diversity of reactions and conclusions. Such responses are linked to assumptions that, arguably, have altered over recent decades in the face of the increasing heterogeneity of the British population.[3]

Ethnic identifications can be at odds with the racial identifications imposed by surrounding society and audiences. Regarding her own self-terming, SuAndi has written: 'It is the Black that I am most comfortable with which, well, seems ironic because my most successful writing has been based around my white mother and through her "voice" the exploration of racism on family life' (SuAndi, 2006, p. 123). This evokes the 'insider' information that writer and performer Mojisola Adebayo speaks of – growing up knowing how to be white in a world that perceives you as black and, therefore, being able to simultaneously objectify and inhabit whiteness (Osborne, 2009, p. 14). Similarly, Ali has explored 'the ways in which some kind of "colourism" can be a powerful force within identity acquisition'. She asks,

> Is blackness only *authenticated* through culture? A person may take on 'white' middle-class *culture* and it is that aspect that can cause rejection on the basis of 'authenticity' from black communities. Simultaneously, they may still suffer racism from whites, which cannot be based on cultural difference, but is about the colour of their skin.
>
> (Ali, 2003, p. 8)

In assumptions about audience perceptions (she underscores a white one), Aston unwittingly replicates the invisibilizing of *metis/isse* experience in cultural representation brought about by the inevitable black-white binary of prevailing social relations. SuAndi's monodrama restores an experience and perspective that has been too easily lost within this binaristic relentlessness. A matrilineal inheritance (the mother-daughter bond) allows a seamless transmuting from M to SuAndi as the final lines recognize and defy the oppressive constraints of value-laden categories of gender and race. The speaker weaves together political identity, nationality and personal experience to assert a self-naming clarity. She delivers this playfully, continuing the intimate register of the relationship established with the audience/reader throughout:

> I know exactly who I am –
> I am a Black Woman
> A mixed race woman.
> I am proud to be a Nigerian daughter

[...]
And I am equally proud to be the daughter
of a Liverpool woman of Irish descent.
Confused? Get out of here.
If you're loved you're...
hell I wish you'd known my mother.
Oh, I forgot, you do now.
(SuAndi, 2002, p. 18)

The affirmation of the first-person singular 'I am' throughout this closing section and the trajectory of social demographic identities (Black, mixed race, Nigerian, Liverpool, Irish) fuses a diasporic heritage (that is not fixed or reduced to race alone) with a proclaimed and confident individual (I)dentity. SuAndi renders one woman's private history as a celebrated herstory, rescued from oblivion. Audience members become the beneficiaries of this representation, occupying a key part in the retrieval/archival/revival process that creates artistic and cultural longevity.

Critical condition(ing)

In writing poetry, Sissay validated a sense of identity that countered the annihilation of self-worth he faced in his nightmarish upbringing as the only black child in care of the 1970s Wigan Social Services.[4] Through necessity, he forged a continuity of being, an exertion of his creative powers against all odds.[5] An early anthology which includes contributions by Sissay, *Black and Priceless*, is prefaced with a proclamation of this evolving sense of self (almost a self-charter). This is inextricable from his impulsion to write; something he returns to and augments throughout subsequent work:

I am a writer and it is my life
I would slit my wrist with a pen not a knife
I am a writer from now until then
My life is my paper, my knife is my pen.
(Artiste, 1988, p. 151)

While this might evoke the opening of Heaney's 'Digging' – 'Between my finger and my thumb / The squat pen rests; snug as a gun' – the equation of pen and weapon has completely different implications for conceptions of lineage and heritage in this context (Heaney, 1990, p. 1).

Heaney aligns the persona's father's physical digging of an ancient peat bog with the poetic voice's linguistic, ancestral and cultural excavation. For Sissay's persona, the act of writing (without known roots or any indication of where he can 'dig' for them) keeps at bay the ending of one's life, presumably by suicide. The desperation or knife-edge existence of Sissay's persona is more frantic and fraught than the reassuringly stolid, Larkinesque, 'squat' pen Heaney employs.[6] The latter's sense of being anchored enough in the first place (knowing your father, grandfather, Gaelic heritage) to begin purposefully digging for cultural origins through a sense of national history, pre-dates the destabilizing, sectarian rifts of Northern Ireland's Troubles. Heaney can recall his father's farming activities in the fields around Mossbawn. Sissay knew neither his father's identity nor his true name until at eighteen, no longer a ward of the state, he was given his birth certificate. He *only* had his writing as a means of self-affirmation.

Understandably, the symbol of the tree (recalling his own lack of a genealogical 'family tree' until adulthood) recurs in Sissay's work – as does his landmarking of his birth-date in relation to influential poets. Rooting himself in a literary family just as he sought his biological one, he notes how the year of his birth, 1967, coincided with the publication of the Mersey poets and 'Langston Hughes died the day after I was born' (Sissay, 2006). For not only was his biological family absent, and therefore unable to provide context and reference points for him, but as a poet, he initially experienced the lack of an accurate critical placement in prevailing literary circles. He recalls: 'when I came on the scene there was Benjamin Zephaniah and Linton Kwesi Johnson, that was it, and Grace Nichols was there, Jean Breeze, James Berry – Ameryl Johnson was sort of skirting around the circumference – John Agard'. He found himself (as a black British-born man of Ethiopian parentage) classified as a Caribbean poet rather than an African-British one – 'All the reference points up until that point concerning black British writers had been black British writers who'd come from outside Britain. I was not a patois poet' (Osborne, 2006).

Sissay's searing poem 'Mourning Breaks' offers a particular retreading of his literary routes to self-worth, as it represents an uncompromising evocation of the persona's self-awareness and faith in himself as an artist and a man, consolidated in the image of climbing (and hanging onto) the rungs of a ladder against the odds. It articulates the torment, rebirth and ecstasy of this renaissance through an array of images of supreme suffering. They range from Christ on the cross to the slave lashed to death; from allusions to Sissay's earlier poems to the tumultuous grief over his childhood, and, above all, include an iron-like determination expressed through the speaker's mantra. The mantra protects him against all seductions advocating his defeat and obliteration: 'I am hanging on. I am hanging on. I am hanging on' (Sissay, 1999, p. 62). Throughout the poem, voices of authority woo him to give in, give up, let go, as both poetic spectators and readers witness the speaker's physical and bloodied suffering.

Yet, a counterpoint of reassurance hums throughout – that the fingers will grasp, that faith in the gripping will be maintained against the odds, that the outside voices will be disregarded and the inner voice heeded, that these words will not prove his last. As such, the poem is a testimony to a life survived so far, represented as the self-gestation of identity from within: 'Because I was growing. I was growing wings all the time. And I can fly.' The persona achieves the transcendence of his surrounding circumstances, through the exertion of will – just as the poet Sissay achieved this in order to reach the position where he could create *any* poem at all.

SuAndi's work is also finely attuned to evoking a number of social and artistic contexts. Positioning SuAndi's published work in the spoken-word tradition – one which, she states, restores '[b]lack poetry to its roots of dialogue, commentary and intimate recordings of a people's story' (Collins, 1991 [1990], p. 4) – issues a challenge to those critics who seek to confine interpretation of this work to existing categories. Collins specifies that 'it presents a reality that is difficult to analyse within a tradition which has come to depend too exclusively on a disembodied written word which sometimes seeks to divorce itself from reality' (ibid., p. 4). That is, of course, the tradition of poetry as read and preserved by the white male (even more specifically Oxbridge-dominated) poetic canon and its self-affirming criteria of evaluation and admission.

In writing of the neglect of twentieth-century British women's poetry, Severin notes: '[w]ithout appropriate frameworks, twentieth-century British women's poetry has remained unreadable' (Severin, 2004, p. 1). To address this problem, she advocates Pearson's notion of intracompositional framing (Pearson, 1990, p. 16) to suggest multiple 'interartistic' frames (Severin, 2004, p. 4). For Severin, the legacy of the Victorian dramatic monologue is pronounced in the oeuvres of certain women poets known for their live performances. A seductive double disclaimer is fashioned, where the first-person pronoun and what *might* be the female poet's views (but not necessarily so) is created by the ambiguous conduit of the poetic voice performing the poem. This, she argues, is catalyzed by the poem's utterance (as the speaking of the poem frames the poet's voice through the enunciatory style it requires), which is then theatricalized through performance, where 'these women poets further extend the poetic border' as 'their life performances often become an integral part of their acts'.

In aesthetically asserting a customarily socially and culturally discounted voice, SuAndi's crafting of an (ambiguous) everywoman/particular woman/herself triad challenges a reductive engagement with her poetry. She observes that 'The life I put into my work only really matures in performance', and points out the limitations of the printed word. The latter is an unsatisfactory vehicle, unable to convey words sung, shouted or whispered. It is also unable to capture the quality of breath. Together, these attributes crucially distinguish spoken-word poetry from printed (read) poetry (SuAndi, 1991 [1990], p. 4). Her work often combines the extroversion of rebuttal and confrontation with the captured, private interiority of the confessional, producing an almost pedagogical poetics. As bell hooks points out, the confessional has long served black women writers – not simply traditions of European literature.[7]

In 'Playing for Life', SuAndi's conceit is identifiable in the parallel established between the legacy of slavery for black people ('For this play I am in is over / 400 years old') and acting in theatre 'The stage I play is all the world. / 'gainst backdrops painted shades of white' (SuAndi, 1991 [1990], pp.1–2). White male dominance of British theatre continues today, limiting the participation of black practitioners – and especially that of black women. SuAndi's persona is laced with self-irony, combining a confrontational challenge with a soothing, wooing tone: 'Am I an actress! You're fooling. / Ask me if I'm Black. / Ask me that go on ask me that'. The question initiated by the inversion 'Am' becomes a retort signalled by the exclamation mark (is the speaker affronted?) In contrast, 'You're fooling.' has no exclamation mark but an emphatic full-stop, as the speaker has no doubts on that score. Within two lines, a well-trodden subtext is uncovered. The implied (white) questioner is reprimanded for not articulating what they *really* want to know: that is, is the speaker (evoking SuAndi's own mixed heritage) black? The question's consequential racial chromatics are uncovered, shifting emphasis from her identity as an actor/artist, to a preoccupation with her perceived race which has nothing to do with her art – thereby revealing a traditional position in white reception of black people's culture.

Throughout the poem, the speaker acknowledges Euro-American performance traditions and their particular use for black people (moors, minstrelsy, negro stereotypes, blackface, dance): blackface ('In mime

I'm brilliant'), minstrelsy and black stereotypes ('Yes, yes, laugh at me. / Laugh on till your tears flow') and dancing ('There's that rhythm in my feet / Upon which you insist'). The conclusion the speaker offers is that the end of black people's cultural objectification by white-dominated society is white self-awareness: 'That the need for all my acting / Has been your oppression, / White man'. This anticipates bell hooks's call to debunk the normativity of invisible whiteness and expose it to the same scrutiny to which blackness has been subjected. Here, 'your oppression' works ambiguously, signalling both towards oppression as an agent of black people's denigration *and* that white people are themselves diminished morally in perpetuating the dynamic. This deconstruction of the category of whiteness is integral to the process of debunking and eradicating white supremacist attitudes.

SuAndi's implied addressees generally range from black women who share the speaker's viewpoints of being oppressed racially and sexually, to all women who exist in potential danger from male acts of violence, to a clarion call for white society to be held accountable for racism. This reveals the personae's multiple speaking positions and anticipated mixes of listeners and readers. In many ways, her work supports Severin's claim that women's poetry, 'as proponents of the multiple poem', is responsible for 'carrying forward Victorian traditions of social critique through a narrative poetry enhanced by performance' (Severin, 2004, p. 6). It also fulfils Tutu's account of contemporary UK performance poetry: 'the dissemination through art is comparable to the African oral tradition, where cultural and historical information would be passed on to younger generations through song and poetry by a griot' (Tutu, 2007, p. 162). SuAndi exploits her dual inheritance of African and European performance poetics.

Performance poetics

Performance features such as gesture, facial expression, the live relationship between the speaking poet and the listening, responding spectator are sufficient to indicate that critical examination of this work must at least partially move into the field of performance analysis. In using performance theory to account for the written word, vital tools of literary criticism are inevitably missing – one cannot fully address the effect of rhyme, rhythm, punctuation, diction, the work's form upon the page that suggests how it might be read and so on. Comparably, as with drama, the scope of poetry which has been written to be performed is reduced if one considers it without highlighting the factors of live reception, such as space, venue, visuals, sounds, audience, reviews and other indicators that characterize it as a live art. The way in which this form of expression starts its life as having been written down but is subsequently brought to life through being spoken aloud activates two systems of traditionally separate critique, confirming the need for an informed interplay between critical languages. Goddard's *Staging Black Feminisms* (2007) acknowledges (in her description of Patience Agbabi's work) the radical generic innovations of women spoken-word poets as they are written 'against canonical traditions of literary poetry, creating works that are framed in terms of an oral tradition and written with performance in mind' (Goddard, 2007, p. 168). She notes the often arresting typography in the printed-word versions, yet goes on to conclude that 'the text offers only the bare bones of the poems as performed live, where they are fully fleshed out with accents, gestures, tone, repetition and the performance of character'. Re-printing SuAndi's 'Playing for Life' complete (as it is the only piece in her book to have this treatment, this promises a significant close reading), Goddard positions her discussion of it in its multimedia performance context:

> a 'resistance to racism' slide show of images of black power, black heroes, musicians and actors [...] SuAndi directly addresses the audience with ad libbed ironic asides and self-reflective critiques that explain the direction of the piece, offer reassurance and tell stories of the personal experiences that inform the work.
>
> (Goddard, 2007, p. 155)

Close readings of literary texts are conducted in the present tense – the act of reading is forever in the present. However, Goddard's use of the present tense to describe the already permanently past and finished as an unfolding experience (a feature of performance analysis) underscores the problem of revisiting the ephemeral – live performance's unavoidable *raison d'être*. This can only produce recollection, a second-hand access where outlining the performance sign system involves a selective re-telling of the pieces and the supplying of descriptive interpretations. Claims made in Goddard's account are not connected in convincing detail to the aesthetic repertoire forged by SuAndi. Goddard notes that this performance 'epitomises how SuAndi's confrontational poetry style raises pertinent questions about race and representation [...] the poem sardonically recounts the various ways that acting is central to her survival as a black woman in a white-dominated society' (Goddard, 2007, p. 156). Yet the questions remain: how does the poem achieve this? What language in the poem, what rhythms, cadences, diction, rhymes, inversions, repetitions and wordplay for instance – cultivated by SuAndi in her design of this poem – create effects which are heightened by the live performance? It may well be that witnessing SuAndi's particular performance of the poem clarifies this, but the poem has a wider dissemination and longevity in its published form. In concentrating only upon the context of performance, the interpretative possibilities are reduced. Poetry, rather than drama, is the genre SuAndi has chosen. She thus joins a written poetic legacy – whether as re-writer, perpetuator or rejecter of its tenets.

Clearly, there *is* something about on-stage delivery that underscores the transitory nature of the spoken word. Dawes observes that '[a] poem's "performability" enhances its presence on the page and it is informed by features of poetry that all poets tend to value and celebrate'. For many poets, the poem is actually '"performing" on the page' (Dawes, 2005, p. 294). Performing poetics (on and off the page) problematizes, and even indirectly parodies, the guise of spontaneity that performance poets rely upon, revealing it as actually a calculated camaraderie with the audience. Grabner has drawn attention to Sissay's disingenuous (and perhaps even unintentional) questioning of audience expectations with regard to how poets should utter their poetry live, terming his approach as 'showing doing' as borrowed from Schechner's performance descriptors (Grabner, 2007, p. 81). The 'showing doing' is evident when Sissay breaks off in the middle of a poem, starts again if he does not like it or interjects with commentary on it, or makes asides. It might be ventured that Sissay is inclined to DJ his poetry. He establishes a persona, or dramatized self, by which he often appeals to an imagined (or sometimes assumed) listener through staged arguments and explanations, thus gesturing to a traditional route of rhetoric and the dramatic monologue. Grounded in measured rationality, his poems often address turbulent emotional states and frequently demonstrate connections to and influences from musical forms, such as hip-hop and jazz. Yet, Sissay is notorious for his rejection of the term 'performance poetry':

> If Lemn Sissay's live audience is moved by his work – and he loves reading live – this does not equate with his readings being a 'performance.' He believes the description (in its everyday usage) implies an act. And an act implies an untruth. Indeed it is often used as a disingenuous accolade, particularly in Britain. To truly see the misapplication of the term simply look at its supposed opposite (or supposed opponent) – 'Page Poetry'.
>
> (Sissay, 1999, p. 70)

His desire to characterize himself as *not* a performance poet emanates from his resistance to an establishment cultural elitism that tends to confine and consign the creative works of contemporary black British poets to an ephemeral rank. He subverts live-performance inevitability through typographically activating a page performativity of poetic strategies that cannot be achieved in live performance. Evoking influences ranging from George Herbert, to ee cummings to Patience Agbabi, words in 'Slipping' visually mimic the shape of stairs. In the alliterative 'Erratic Equipoise', letters in bold type spell out 'police' in a block of text that is overloaded with adjectives, thereby implying a challenge to the ability of any reader or speaker of the poem actually to articulate it (Sissay, 1999, pp. 22, 27). Thus the grapholectic point made by the poem's typographical construction (and its whole point) is lost if you cannot see it, for this cannot be conveyed by merely speaking the poem.[8]

'Slipping' gestures towards ekphrasis.[9] Sissay builds a literal, visual step of words to figuratively sculpt the poem. The right-angled, geometric layout of the words delineates the stairs, painting a one-way direction downwards as dictated by the order of reading. No climbing back up is possible. At the end of each step of words, 'you' forms the connection with the next step, simultaneously completing a thought and beginning a new one. This syntax evokes a precariousness of moving from one state of being into another, the teetering realization of vertiginous loss – all enhanced by the word's placement on the page, on the verge of the step. The sharp angularity of the edge-of-the-step shape contrasts with the smooth fluidity of the aspirated sibilance, 'slipping'. Simultaneously captured are the rupture of unlooked-for change (shock, separation and loss) and wistful recognition of a relationship's demise and dissolution into an ending. The placement of 'Don't' in each of the first four vertical sections of the step-stanzas connects the speaker's contradictory inner desires and external utterances. The speaker outwardly reacts to the addressee's leaving through a repeated, defiant imperative, yet also yearns for the relationship to continue: 'Don't / Go if you want to', 'Don't / Leave if you want to' 'Don't / Call if you want to' and 'Don't / Wave if you want to'. Sissay exploits the proximities of words, undermining their initial signification through sparse punctuation. The symbiosis of the words aurally and syntactically, which occurs in the reading process, suggests the slippery slope of human emotions and relationships. The structured shape of the step evokes the step-by-step movement to acceptance the speaker faces – an incremental process – poignantly approached in the ebbing repetition of the final lines, 'slipping / slipping / slipping / away' and Sissay's last change of word and shifting stress from first syllable ('slipping') to final ('away'). The wistfulness of this elongation of 'away' is notably onomatopoeic, the relationship ends as does the poem.

* * *

The risks and demands made by the live context emphasize how poets can function as vehicles for the articulation of their creations. SuAndi and Sissay's work demonstrates how key performance repertoires and techniques outlined above enable a fuller expression of the poet's experience and produce a polyaurality which undoes what Ward terms 'the monoglossic assumption that one only "speaks" if one writes, is published, distributed, and read' (Ward, 1997, p. 127).

In her introduction to Sissay's *Tender Fingers in a Clenched Fist,* Valerie Bloom observed that in the work of black poets in Britain from the 1980s onwards, there was 'a simultaneous evolution when black people decided that silence was not so golden' (Bloom, 1988, p. ix). As children growing up in Britain at a time when racism was politically, culturally, ideologically and institutionally entrenched, SuAndi and Sissay have, both in their lives and their poetry, carved out identities that name and defy the discrimination they faced. In doing so, they have foregrounded self-authenticating representations of black and mixed-heritage people's experiences. Nelson has identified the ways in which 'counterstories' operate to 'allow oppressed people to refuse the identities imposed upon them by their oppressors and to reidentify themselves in more respectworthy terms', an account which is clearly applicable to both writers (Nelson, 2001, p. 22). No generation has forced Britain to re-conceptualize and to realize a transformation of British culture more intensely or more effectively than the current crop of British-born black writers, including such figures as SuAndi and Sissay. The majority of their poetry and their monodramas employ neither patois nor vernacular. Written and spoken in standard English (inflected by tone and accent in performance), they could be perceived as succumbing to what Gilbert and Tompkins describe as 'the dominance of the imposed standard language' (1996, p. 16) and its accompanying encoding of a negative social identities for black and mixed origin people.

However, the narrating speakers of their monodramas, Lemn and M/SuAndi, resist and challenge the realities they are dealt, to carve paths of their own agency. In doing so, the writers assert their automatic place as British indigenes; as the heirs presumptive of British literary traditions and rightful contributors to British culture. Their work is not introspective but declamatory, having 'taken the contemporary style of self-disclosure and raised it to a roar…' (SuAndi, 2002, n.p).

Notes

1. Spoken-word poetry is performed to an audience rather than read aloud – which activates a reading voice rather than interactive engagement. Monodrama is solo performance of a drama rather than a poem or speech but is not a dramatic monologue which, while spoken by the poet, is spoken through a persona who is not the poet.
2. 'In Britain, the concept of blackness with which most of us are obliged to work [is] a notion which has been partly constructed in Britain, but not for Britain, and not solely or necessarily by black people' (Phillips and Phillips, 1998, p. 143).
3. In the 2001 census, '661,034 people chose "Mixed", of which the "Mixed: White and Black Caribbean" category was the biggest mixed race group, followed by "Mixed: White and Asian", "Mixed: Other" and "Mixed: White and Black African" [...] significant differences in age distribution are a clear indication that the mixed race group is a young phenomenon concerning children and young people' (Owens, 2008).
4. Key representations of the experiences of black and mixed race children trans-racially adopted or fostered in the care system between the 1960s and the 1980s include poet Jackie Kay's *The Adoption Papers* (1991), novels by Joanna Traynor, *Sister Josephine* (1997), Alex Wheatle, *Seven Sisters* (2002) and Valerie Mason-John, *Borrowed Body* (2006), Sissay's play *Storm* (2000), Winsome Pinnock's play *One Under* (2003), Mojisola Adebayo's play *Mohammad Ali and Me* (2008) and Lennie James's film, *Storm Damage* (2000).
5. D.W. Winnicott's emphasis on the *continuity of being* in the infant resonates poignantly with Sissay's early life (Osborne, 2008a, p. 318).
6. See Larkin's poem 'Toads' (Larkin, 2008, p. 62) .
7. 'More than any other genre of writing, the production of honest confessional narratives by black women who are struggling to be self-actualized and to become radical subjects are needed as guides, as texts which affirm our fellowship with one another' (hooks, 1992, p. 59).
8. Walter J. Ong observes that 'Writing gives a grapholect a power far exceeding that of any purely oral dialect' as it provides 'a recorded vocabulary of at least a million and a half words, of which not only the present meanings but also hundreds of thousands of past meanings are known' (Ong, 2002 [1982], p. 8).
9. Challenging 'the reification of media around a single sensory organ', Mitchell liberates literature's ekphrastic potential, 'literature insofar as it is written or printed, has an unavoidable visual component which bears significant relation to an auditory component, which is why it makes a difference whether a novel is read aloud or read silently' (Mitchell, 2005, p. 350).

References

Ali, Suki (2003) *Mixed-Race, Post-Race: Gender, New Ethnicities, and Cultural Practices* (Oxford: Berg).

Artiste, Cindy (ed.) (1988) *Black and Priceless: The Power of Black Ink* (Manchester: Crocus Books).

Aston, Elaine (2003) *Feminist Views on the English Stage: Women Playwrights, 1990–2000* (Cambridge: Cambridge University Press).
Bloom, Valerie (1988) 'Introduction', in Lemn Sissay, *Tender Fingers in a Clenched Fist* (London: Bogle-L'Ouverture Press).
Collins, Merle (1991 [1990]) 'Introduction', in SuAndi, *Style in Performance* (Manchester: Pink Heater Press).
Dawes, Kwame (2005) 'Black British Poetry: Some Considerations', in Kadija Sesay (ed.) *Write Black Write British: From Post Colonial to Black British Literature* (London: Hansib Publications Ltd).
Gilbert, Helen and Jane Tompkins (eds) (1996) *Post-Colonial Drama: Theatre, Practice, Politics* (London and New York: Routledge).
Goddard, Lynette (2007) *Staging Black Feminisms: Identity, Politics, Performance* (Basingstoke and New York: Palgrave Macmillan).
Grabner, Cornelia (2007) 'Is Performance Poetry Dead?', *Poetry Review*, 97(2) (Summer): 78–82.
Heaney, Seamus (1988) *The Government of the Tongue* (London and Boston: Faber and Faber).
— (1990) *New Selected Poems 1966–1987* (London: Faber and Faber).
hooks, bell (1992) *Black Looks: Race and Representation* (Boston, MA: South End Press).
Jackaman, Rob (2003) *Broken English/Breaking English: A Study of Contemporary Poetics in English* (Madison, NJ: Fairleigh Dickinson University Press; London: Associated University Presses).
Larkin, Philip (2008) *Collected Poems* (London: Marvell Press).
Mitchell, W.J.T. (2005) *What Do Pictures Want? The Lives and Loves of Images* (Chicago and London: University of Chicago Press).
Mirza, Heidi Safia (ed.) (1997) *Black British Feminism: A Reader* (London and New York: Routledge).
Nelson, Hilde Lindemann (2001) *Damaged Identities, Narrative Repair* (Ithaca and London: Cornell University Press).
Ong, Walter J. (2002 [1982]) *Orality and Literacy* (London and New York: Routledge).
Osborne, Deirdre (2006) Personal interview with Lemn Sissay, June 2006.
— (2008a) 'Lemn Sissay's Life's Source: an Interview and Commentary', in Deirdre Osborne (ed.) *Hidden Gems* (London: Oberon Books).
— (2008b) Conversation with Lemn Sissay, 27 June 2008.
— (2008c) Email exchange with SuAndi, July 2008.
— (2009) 'No Straight Answers: Writing on the Margins, Reclaiming Heroes', *New Theatre Quarterly,* XXV (Part 1) (February): 6–21.
Owens, Charlie (2008) in Marcia Lise (rapporteur) ESRC Series, Seminar 1: *Spaces and Places,* 12 December, London South Bank University.
Padel, Ruth (2004) *52 Ways of Looking at a Poem* (London: Vintage).
Paterson, Don (2007) 'The Lyric Principle, Part 2: The Sound of Sense', *Poetry Review* 97 (3) (Autumn): 54–70.
Pearson, John (1990) 'The Politics of Framing in the Late Nineteenth Century', *Mosaic* 23 (1): 15–30.
Phillips, Mike and Trevor Phillips (1998) *The Irresistible Rise of Multicultural Britain* (London: HarperCollins).
Severin, Laura (2004) *Poetry Off the Page* (Aldershot: Ashgate).

Sissay, Lemn (1999) *Morning Breaks in the Elevator* (Edinburgh: Payback Press).
— (2006) *Presiding Spirits* (Poetry International postcard).
— (2008) *Something Dark*, in Deirdre Osborne (ed.) *Hidden Gems* (London: Oberon Books, pp. 327–47.
SuAndi (1991 [1990]) *Style in Performance* (Manchester: Pink Heater Press).
— (2002) *The Story of M*, in SuAndi (ed.) *4 For More* (Manchester: Black Arts Alliance).
— (2006) 'Africa Lives on in We', in Elaine Aston and Geraldine Harris (eds) *Feminist Futures? Theatre, Performance, Theory* (New York: Palgrave Macmillan).
Tizard, Barbara and Ann Phoenix (1993) *Black, White or Mixed Race: Race and Racism in the Lives of Young People of Mixed Parentage* (London and New York: Routledge).
Tutu, Samera Owusu (2007) 'The Resounding Underground: Performance Poetry in the U.K. Today', in R. Victoria Arana (ed.) *'Black' British Aesthetics Today* (Newcastle-upon-Tyne: Cambridge Scholars Publishing).
Ward, Cynthia (1997) 'Bound to Matter: The Father's Pen and Mother Tongues', in Nnaemeka Obioma (ed.) *The Politics of (M)Othering: Womanhood, Identity and Resistance in African Literature* (London and New York: Routledge).

Selected Critical Bibliography

Adorno, Theodor W. and Max Horkheimer (2002) *Dialectic of Enlightenment*, trans. Edmund Jephcott (Stanford: Stanford University Press).

Bal, Mieke, Jonathan Crewe and Leo Spitzer (eds) (1999) *Acts of Memory: Cultural Recall in the Present* (Hanover, NH: University Press of New England).

Benjamin, Walter (1968) 'The Storyteller: Reflections on the Work of Nikolai Leskov', in Hannah Arendt (ed.) *Illuminations: Essays and Reflections* (New York: Schocken).

Blanchot, Maurice (1995) *The Writing of the Disaster* (Lincoln: University of Nebraska Press).

Buell, Lawrence (2005) *The Future of Environmental Criticism: Environmental Crisis and Literary Imagination* (Oxford: Blackwell).

Caruth, Cathy (1995) *Trauma: Explorations of Memory* (Baltimore: Johns Hopkins University Press).

Clark, Timothy (1997) *The Theory of Inspiration: Composition as a Crisis of Subjectivity in Romantic and Post-Romantic Writing* (Manchester: Manchester University Press).

Dawson, Graham (2007) *Making Peace with the Past? Memories, Traumas and the Irish Troubles* (Manchester: Manchester University Press).

Derrida, Jacques (1994) *Specters of Marx: The State of the Debt, the Work of Mourning & the New International,* trans. Peggy Kawuf (New York: Routledge).

—— (2003) 'Shibboleth', in Neil Levi and Michael Rothberg (eds) *The Holocaust: Theoretical Writings* (Edinburgh: Edinburgh University Press).

Farquharson, Danine and Sean Farrell (eds) (2008) *Shadows of the Gunmen: Violence and Culture in Modern Ireland* (Cork: Cork University Press).

Fitzpatrick, Lisa (ed.) (2010) *Performing Violence in Contemporary Ireland* (Dublin: Carysfort Press).

Fukuyama, Francis (1992) *The End of History and the Last Man* (Harmondsworth: Penguin).

Goddard, Lynette (2007) *Staging Black Feminisms: Identity, Politics, Performance* (Basingstoke and New York: Palgrave Macmillan).

Gubar, Susan (2003) *Poetry after Auschwitz: Remembering What One Never Knew* (Bloomington: Indiana University Press).

Harvey, David (1990) *The Condition of Postmodernity* (Cambridge, MA and Oxford: Blackwell Publishing).

Heaney, Seamus (1988) *The Government of the Tongue* (London and Boston: Faber and Faber).

—— (1995) *The Redress of Poetry* (London: Faber and Faber).

hooks, bell (1992) *Black Looks: Race and Representation* (Boston, MA: South End Press).

Jakobson, Roman (1987) 'Linguistics and Poetics', in Krystyna Pomorska and Stephen Rudy (eds) *Language in Literature* (Cambridge, MA and London: Belknap Press of the Harvard University Press).

Kirkland, Richard (1996) *Literature and Culture in Northern Ireland since 1965: Moments of Danger* (London and New York: Longman).

Kristeva, Julia (1980) *Desire in Language: A Semiotic Approach to Literature and Art* (New York: Columbia University Press).

Lefebvre, Henri (2000) *Everyday Life in the Modern World,* trans. Sacha Rabinovitch (London: Continuum).

Longley, Edna (1986) *Poetry in the Wars* (Newcastle-upon-Tyne: Bloodaxe).

Lyotard, Jean-François (1990) *Heidegger and the 'Jews'* (Minneapolis, MN: University of Minnesota Press).

Mallarmé, Stéphane: 'Crisis in Verse', in Thomas G. West (ed.) *Symbolism, an Anthology* (New York: Methuen).

McDonald, Peter (1997) *Mistaken Identities: Poetry and Northern Ireland* (Oxford: Clarendon Press).

Morris, Daniel (2006) *The Poetry of Louise Glück: A Thematic Introduction* (Columbia, MO: University of Missouri Press).

Murphy, Michael (2004) *Poetry in Exile: A Study of the Poetry of W.H. Auden, Joseph Brodsky and George Szirtes* (London: Greenwich Exchange Press).

Perloff, Marjorie (1996) *Wittgenstein's Ladder: Poetic Language and the Strangeness of the Ordinary* (Chicago: University of Chicago Press).

—— (2004) *Differentials: Poetry, Poetics, Pedagogy* (Tuscaloosa, AL: The University of Alabama Press).

Reinhard, Kenneth (ed.) (2005) with Slavoj Žižek and Erik L. Santner, *The Neighbor: Three Inquiries in Political Theology* (Chicago: University of Chicago Press).

Rowland, Antony (2005) *Holocaust Poetry: Awkward Poetics in the Work of Sylvia Plath, Geoffrey Hill, Tony Harrison and Ted Hughes* (Manchester: Manchester University Press).

Shklovsky, Victor (1965) 'Art as Technique', in L. Lemon and M. Reis (eds) *Russian Formalist Criticism: Four Essays* (Lincoln: University of Nebraska Press).

Wills, Clare (1993) *Improprieties: Politics and Sexuality in Northern Irish Poetry* (Oxford: Oxford University Press).

Žižek, Slavoj (2008) *In Defense of Lost Causes* (London: Verso).

—— (2002) *Welcome to the Desert of the Real* (London: Verso).

Index

Druck: KN Digital Printforce GmbH · Schockenriedstraße 37 · 70565 Stuttgart